Witness onstage

series editors
MARIA M. DELGADO
MAGGIE B. GALE
PETER LICHTENFELS

advisory board
Michael Billington, Sandra Hebron, Mark Ravenhill, Janelle Reinelt, Peter Sellars, Joanne Tompkins

This series will offer a space for those people who practise theatre to have a dialogue with those who think and write about it.

The series has a flexible format that refocuses the analysis and documentation of performance. It provides, presents and represents material which is written by those who make or create performance history, and offers access to theatre documents, different methodologies and approaches to the art of making theatre.

The books in the series are aimed at students, scholars, practitioners and theatre-visiting readers. They encourage reassessments of periods, companies and figures in twentieth-century and twenty-first-century theatre history, and provoke and take up discussions of cultural strategies and legacies that recognise the heterogeneity of performance studies.
also available

Directing scenes and senses: The thinking of Regie
PETER M. BOENISCH

The Paris Jigsaw: Internationalism and the city's stages
DAVID BRADBY AND MARIA M. DELGADO (EDS)

Street theatre and the production of postindustrial space: Working memories
DAVID CALDER

Death in modern theatre: Stages of mortality
ADRIAN CURTIN

Theatre in crisis? Performance manifestos for a new century
MARIA M. DELGADO AND CARIDAD SVICH (EDS)

World stages, local audiences: Essays on performance, place, and politics
PETER DICKINSON

Performing presence: Between the live and the simulated
GABRIELLA GIANNACHI AND NICK KAYE

Queer exceptions: Solo performance in neoliberal times
STEPHEN GREER

Performance in a time of terror: Critical mimesis and the age of uncertainty
JENNY HUGHES

South African performance and the archive of memory
YVETTE HUTCHISON

Unlimited action: The performance of extremity in the 1970s
DOMINIC JOHNSON

Jean Genet and the politics of theatre: Spaces of revolution
CARL LAVERY

After '89: Polish theatre and the political
BRYCE LEASE

Not magic but work: An ethnographic account of a rehearsal process
GAY MCAULEY

'Love me or kill me': Sarah Kane and the theatre of extremes
GRAHAM SAUNDERS

Trans-global readings: Crossing theatrical boundaries
CARIDAD SVICH

Negotiating cultures: Eugenio Barba and the intercultural debate
IAN WATSON (ED.)

Witness onstage
Documentary theatre in twenty-first-century Russia

MOLLY FLYNN

Manchester University Press

Copyright © Molly Flynn 2020

The right of Molly Flynn to be identified as the author of this work has been asserted by her in accordance with the Copyright, Designs and Patents Act 1988.

Published by Manchester University Press
Oxford Road, Manchester M13 9PL
www.manchesteruniversitypress.co.uk

British Library Cataloguing-in-Publication Data
A catalogue record for this book is available from the British Library

ISBN 978 1 5261 2619 1 hardback
ISBN 978 1 5261 6586 2 paperback

First published 2020
Paperback published 2022

The publisher has no responsibility for the persistence or accuracy of URLs for any external or third-party internet websites referred to in this book, and does not guarantee that any content on such websites is, or will remain, accurate or appropriate.

Typeset
by Toppan Best-set Premedia Limited

To my father, Dennis Flynn

CONTENTS

List of figures   *page* ix
Acknowledgements   xi
Note on the text   xiii

Introduction   1

1   *Called to the stand*
     The origins of Russian documentary theatre   26

2   *History on trial*
     Performing memory in twenty-first-century Russia   51

3   *Evidentiary hearing*
     The pursuit of justice in Russian documentary theatre   74

4   *Material witness*
     History, belief, and the theatre of enactment   97

5   *Burden of proof*
     New Sincerity and the performance of post-Soviet
     national identities   119

6 *A special verdict*
   Theatre and protest in Putin's Russia 141

Conclusion 164

Bibliography 169
Index 180

LIST OF FIGURES

1 *Akyn-opera 2* (2014), directed by Vsevolod Lisovskii. Featuring Adzham Chakoboev, Pokiza Kurbonasenova, and Abdulmamad Bekmamadov. Photo by Anastasiia Patlai   9
2 *Zazhgi moi ogon* (*Light my Fire*, 2015), directed by Yuri Muravitskii, featuring Talgat Batalov, Ilias Tameev, Arina Marakulina, and Anna Egorova. Photo by Oleg Karlson   10
3 The audience at the Liubimovka New Playwriting Festival (2016). Photo by Oleg Karlson   28
4 *Neiavnye vozdeistviia* (*Unapparent Influences,* 2016), directed by Vsevolod Lisovskii, featuring Vasia Berezin, Nikita Shchetinin, and Uliana Vaskovich. Photo courtesy of Transformator   46
5 *Demokratiia.doc* (*Democracy.doc*, 2012), featuring Georg Genoux, Elena Margo, and audience members from the project's tour to Chur, Switzerland. Photo courtesy of Democracy.doc   47
6 *Gruz molchaniia* (*Legacy of Silence*, 2010), directed by Mikhail Kaluzhskii, featuring Molly Flynn, Mikhail Kaluzhskii, Anastasiia Patlai, Georg Genoux, and (onscreen) Aleksei Devotchenko. Photo by Iakov Pechenin   56
7 *Vtoroi akt. Vnuki* (*Second Act. Grandchildren*, 2012), directed by Mikhail Kaluzhskii, featuring actor Svetlana

	Mikhalisheva, who performed in the play, as well as director Yurii Muravitskii and actor Ksenia Medveda in the audience. Photo by Vsevolod Luchanksii	65
8	*Dvoe v tvoem dome* (*Two in Your Home*, 2012), directed by Mikhail Ugarov, featuring Oleg Kamenshchikov, Maksym Kurochkin, Aleksei Maslodudov, Sergei Ovchinnikov, and Irina Savitskova. Photo by Oleg Karlson	75
9	*Chas vosemnadtsat* (*One Hour Eighteen Minutes*, 2010), directed by Mikhail Ugarov, featuring Anastasiia Patlai. Photo by Mikhail Guterman	78
10	*Chas vosemnadtsat* (*One Hour Eighteen Minutes*, 2010), directed by Mikhail Ugarov, featuring Aleksei Zhiriakov and Talgat Batalov. Photo by Mikhail Guterman	88
11	*Moskovskie protsessyi* (*Moscow Trials*, 2013), co-created by Mikhail Kaluzhskii and Milo Rau. Photo by Zoia Kuzikov. Courtesy of the Sakharov Center	92
12	*Pavlik – moi Bog* (*Pavlik – my God*, 2009), directed by Evgenii Grigoriev, featuring Donatas Grudovich and Maria Kostikova. Photo by Sergei Voronin	105
13	*Pavlik – moi Bog* (*Pavlik – my God*, 2009), directed by Evgenii Grigoriev, featuring Leonid Telzhenskii and Maragarita Kutovaia. Photo by Alkesei Lukianov	108
14	*Uzbek* (2012), created by Talgat Batalov. Photo by Anna Alferova	123
15	*Uzbek* (2012), created by Talgat Batalov. Photo by Oleg Karlson	125
16	*Uzbek* (2012), created by Talgat Batalov. Photo by Asia Karagodina	126
17	The original Teatr.doc on Trekhprudnyi Lane (2014). Photo by Oleg Karlson	148
18	Teatr.doc's second venue on Spartakovskaia Street (2014). Photo by Oleg Karlson	153
19	Portrait of Elena Gremina (2014). Photo by Oleg Karlson	160
20	Portrait of Mikhail Ugarov (2017). Photo by Aleksandr Chernykh	161

ACKNOWLEDGEMENTS

Witness onstage is the result of research conducted between 2010 and 2019 during which time I benefited from the input, assistance, and guidance of more people than I am able to thank here. Above all, I must express my gratitude to the artists whose work is at the centre of this book and, in particular, Elena Gremina and Mikhail Ugarov. Neither this research nor the community of artists at the heart of its analysis would have been possible without the commitment and brilliance of these two visionary artists. Thank you, Elena Anatolevna and Mikhail Iurevich, for your kindness, your courage, and your unimaginable devotion to the craft. You will be forever missed.

I would also like to thank the many scholars and academic colleagues who have helped me to develop this work. First and foremost Emma Widdis – to Emma, I offer my sincerest appreciation for your intellectual generosity throughout this process. I am additionally grateful to Nancy Condee, Julie Curtis, Julie Fedor, Alexander Etkind, Anna Hartnell, Olesya Khromeychuk, Susan Larsen, Mark Lipovetsky, Chris Megson, Helen Nicholson, Louise Owen, Rachel Polonsky, Rebecca Reich, Ellen Rutten, Raisa Sidenova, Laurence Senelick, and Boris Wolfson. Your insights and advice have played a crucial role in the development of this research.

Some sections of this book have been published before in earlier versions as articles. Parts of Chapter 3 were published as 'The Trial that Never Was: Russian documentary theatre and the pursuit of justice' in *New*

Theatre Quarterly, 30/4, 307–17 (2014); and segments of Chapter 5 were previously published as 'Show Us Your Papers: Performing post-Soviet national identity in Talgat Batalov's "Uzbek"' in *Problems of Post-Communism*, 63/1, 16–26 (2016). I thank these journals' editors for permission to include these materials here. Likewise I am grateful to the editors and reviewers of Manchester University Press for their support in the final stages of this project, in particular the book's commissioning editor Matthew Frost and copy-editor Juanita Bullough.

Special mention is due to the artists, critics, and theatre professionals who have kindly shared with me the archival material that informs every aspect of this book: Anna Banasiukevich, Talgat Batalov, Nina Belenitskaia, Ekaterina Bondarenko, Polina Borodina, John Freedman, Georg Genoux, Mikhail Kaluzhskii, Oleg Karlson, Viktoria Kholodova, Maksym Kurochkin, Maria Kroupnik, Elena Margo, Anastasiia Patlai, Pavel Rudnev, and Zarema Zaudinova.

Alongside those people who were essential to this research are my friends who encouraged, inspired, and challenged me throughout all the turns life has taken in these years: Hallimeda Allinson, Nicole Burgund, Michelle Carriger, Stephen Haley, Damon Jespersen, Inessa Keilbach, Maria Punina, Louise Robertson, John Sherry, Edward Speck, Lawrence Templeton, Paul Wann, Bonnie Jean Wilbur, and Alex Vukovitsch. Most of all, however, I must thank Tom Rowley, for his honest, critical, and insightful perspective on the work and its value from the start to the finish of this project.

Lastly, I would like to express my deepest gratitude to my sisters Anna and Mara for their love and inspiration, their children Aurora, Max, and Mae for the joy they bring to my life, and, finally my parents Judith Kamber and Dennis Flynn. I cannot thank you enough for your unerring faith in my ability to do this work and for helping me learn how to believe.

NOTE ON THE TEXT

This book employs a dual system of transliteration from the Cyrillic to the Latin alphabet. In the text I use the Library of Congress system without diacritics, an approach that facilitates greater access to an interdisciplinary readership. The bibliography adheres to the Library of Congress system, with diacritics, for the Russian language specialist. In some cases in the notes and references, publishers have employed different systems in rendering authors' names and titles of their work. When a Russian name has an accepted English spelling I have used the more familiar of the two (e.g. Stanislavsky instead of Stanislavskii and Meyerhold instead of Meierkhold). All Russian production titles are introduced together with an English translation and referred to by their translated titles thereafter. Unless otherwise indicated in the bibliography, translations are my own.

Introduction

In the decade following the dissolution of the Soviet Union, young Russian playwrights revived contemporary drama with their exploration and portrayal of everyday life in post-Soviet Russia. Their work has since come to be known as belonging to the genre *Novaia drama* (New Drama), a category that can be broadly understood to include plays that were written during or after the mid-1990s and express a clear interest in navigating the complexities of contemporary life and everyday language onstage. New Russian Drama put the playwright at its centre and eschewed traditional concepts of dramatic heroes. It was, in part, these playwrights' investment in the depiction of lived experience onstage that drew Russia's first generation of post-Soviet theatre artists to their exploration of documentary theatre forms, beginning in the late 1990s. In their pursuit of realistic dialogue, Russia's New Dramatists discovered a close affinity for 'verbatim' theatre as it was introduced to them through a series of masterclasses led by delegates of London's Royal Court Theatre in 1999 and 2000. Since that time, many of the country's most innovative theatre artists have taken to using material from real-life events to explore the intricacies of injustice in the civic sphere and to create a space for the collective renegotiation of cultural narratives in twenty-first-century Russia.

Verbatim is a playwriting technique theatre-makers use internationally to respond to current events, and to give voice to otherwise marginalized members of their societies. In its most orthodox form, verbatim involves identifying a topic or an event of social relevance and conducting interviews with those connected to the issue or event under discussion. The interviews are then transcribed, edited, and composed by the playwright into a documentary theatre text. In the UK, the term 'verbatim theatre' is often used to signify different types of plays that make an explicit claim to being rooted in real-life events, particularly those that draw on interviews, found texts, or other documentary materials for the basis of the play script. In Russia, the term 'dokumentalnyi teatr' (documentary theatre) is used to describe a category of work that includes but is not limited to forms such as verbatim, living newspaper, autobiographical works, interactive theatre, and so on. The term 'svidetelskii teatr' (witness theatre) is also used in Russia, and elsewhere in Eastern Europe, to describe documentary plays in which people tell their own stories onstage as well as performances in which individuals who are not actors join audiences in conversation about a particular event or topic.

This book traces the history of documentary theatre in twenty-first-century Russia. It contextualizes the form's rapid growth within the sociocultural setting of the Putin years (2000–) by conducting close analysis of specific plays from Moscow's documentary theatre repertoire in the first two decades of the twenty-first century. In doing so, *Witness onstage* argues that these years have proven a particularly generative time for the development of documentary theatre forms. It suggests that the remarkable potency of documentary theatre in Russia throughout the early 2000s developed as a result of the form's unique capacity to speak to a number of core cultural anxieties in contemporary Russia. These anxieties include questions about the evidentiary status of documents, the sincerity of testimony, and the performance of justice, as well as the country's fraught relationship to its Soviet past. In each of this book's chapters, I will demonstrate how, through its direct engagement with these four points of tension in contemporary culture, documentary theatre has come to constitute an important space for civic engagement in Russia since the turn of the twenty-first century.

The title of this book is drawn from a series of symposiums hosted by Moscow's leading documentary theatre venue, Teatr.doc. In 2012 and again in 2017, the artists at the heart of Russia's documentary theatre boom gathered in Moscow to discuss and explore the development of the form in its specifically contemporary Russian context. Both in the instance of these gatherings and in the case of this book, the title *Svidetel na tsene* (*Witness onstage*) serves to highlight the reciprocal act of speaking and listening that is key to documentary theatre practice. Use of the phrase for the title of this book is also meant to signal my involvement in Russia's documentary theatre scene, not only as a researcher, but also as a performer and a participant. As will be discussed in greater detail below, in addition to my work as an observer and a researcher of Russian documentary theatre, I also performed in one of the productions analysed in this study. In my year-and-a-half engagement performing the role of Gerda in the Russian documentary play *Gruz molchaniia* (*Legacy of Silence*, 2010) at Moscow's Sakharov Center, I had the opportunity to witness firsthand how the form was developed and deployed in Russia after the early 2000s. Since that time, I have collaborated on projects with several Teatr.doc artists as a performer, producer, and translator, experiences that have provided additional insight into how the form is distinguished from international documentary theatre practice. With this context in mind, I begin this introduction by reviewing the significance of documentary theatre as it has developed internationally in twenty-first-century culture, before situating the study within its specifically contemporary Russian context.

Materials and their properties

Russia's documentary theatre-makers are far from the only artists invested in the form's ability to address tensions in contemporary culture about truth, justice, history, and notions of identity. As Carol Martin observes, twenty-first-century theatre artists from across the globe deploy documentary theatre techniques in their efforts to challenge the dominance of media narratives and interrogate a 'global condition of troubled epistemologies about truth, authenticity and reality' (2010: 1). In her study *Theatre of the Real*, Martin offers an articulation of the parameters of the form and continues her inquiry into the nature and value of twenty-first-century documentary theatre practice. 'While there may be no universal agreement on individual terms,' Martin writes, 'there is an emerging consensus that theatre of the real includes documentary theatre, verbatim theatre, reality-based theatre, theatre of fact, theatre of witness, tribunal theatre, nonfiction theatre, restored village performances, war and battle reenactments, and autobiographical theatre' (2013: 1). By focusing on moments of rupture between theatre and 'the real' in productions from across the globe, Martin offers her readers insight into the cultural complexities of an art form that makes an overt claim to truth while simultaneously exposing its own artifice at every turn.

Beginning with Derek Paget in the 1980s, more and more scholars of theatre and performance have taken up the topic of documentary theatre, contributing seminal works such as Alan Filewood's *Collective Encounters: Documentary theatre in English Canada* (1987) and Attilio Favorini's *Voicings: Ten plays from the documentary theatre* (1995). In the introduction to their collection, *Get Real: Documentary theatre past and present*, Alison Forsyth and Chris Megson articulate how, in distinction to many late twentieth-century documentary theatre productions, twenty-first-century documentary theatre is 'often as much concerned with emphasizing its own discursive limitations, with interrogating the reification of material evidence in performance, as it is with the real-life story or events it is exploring' (2009: 3). That is to say that documentary theatre in the twenty-first century most often does not claim to represent an objective or an unbiased truth; it rather employs the form in order to confront the complexities of truth and bias in our increasingly mediated relationship to the world around us. In this sense, the resurgence of documentary theatre practice in twenty-first-century culture can be interpreted as a response to what Liz Tomlin calls the 'prevailing climate of scepticism in the final decade of the twentieth century' (2013: 114).

A desire for truth and authenticity and a kind of theatre one can believe in is also the topic of Daniel J. Schulze's 2016 study, *Authenticity in Contemporary Theatre and Performance: Make it real*. Drawing connections between documentary theatre, immersive theatre, and a genre of performance he calls 'intimate theatre', Schulze argues that together these forms are indicative of both a cultural and personal yearning for an elusive experience of authenticity in contemporary culture. Following on from the age of postmodernism, Shulze suggests, twenty-first-century artists and audiences are seeking out spaces in which an emphasis on interpersonal connection is heightened and, in a sense, unmediated. A cultural obsession with self-representation has collided with a growing distrust of mainstream media, leaving artists and audiences in search of an alternative form of interpersonal engagement. As debates about 'fake news' and 'alternative facts' fill the airwaves at the time of writing, documentary theatre artists are using the form to confront the complexities of truth, authenticity, and veracity onstage.

Consideration of this body of literature on global documentary theatre practice demonstrates how the form is deployed across cultures to facilitate meaningful conversations between artists and audiences and, in this way, enable the collective renegotiation of cultural narratives. As a live-oral practice, documentary theatre offers its participants a communal space in which the archive of the past is made mutable and accessible in the present. The actors onstage embody the documentary materials, and the pasts they represent are, in this sense, made manifest through performance.

In practice however, as Martin reminds her readers, 'much of contemporary documentary theatre is written contemporaneously with the events that are its subjects. It directly intervenes in the creation of history by unsettling the present' (2013: 5). Through its use of documentary materials – interviews, court transcripts, personal artifacts, found texts, etc. – documentary theatre declares openly its attachment to the events of the past and deals intimately in the interpretation of that past. Documentary theatre situates itself along the path between history and memory-making. Its performance in the present echoes the past, and its representation of that past resounds in the present. Martin describes precisely this dynamic when she writes that, 'More than enacting history, although it certainly does that, documentary theatre also has the capacity to stage historiography' (2010:1).

In Russia, where the country's history has for generations been largely a matter for dangerous, even lethal debate, documentary theatre's capacity both to enact history and to stage historiography is additionally complicated. From early Soviet efforts to shape pre-revolutionary history into a narrative of Socialist inevitability, to Putin's more recent rebranding of the Second World War as the foundation myth of modern Russia (see Wood, 2011), the country's official modern history has been continually and inconsistently revised. Access to historical documents and archives has become increasingly restricted since a brief moment of relative transparency in the mid-1990s. The blatant forgery of official documentation and revision of historical texts throughout the Soviet and post-Soviet years has, for many, coupled the public perception of official documentation with an instinctual distrust. The perceived instability of historical narratives in contemporary Russia in conjunction with an accepted scepticism about official documentation has created a cultural climate in which the events of the past are not always tied to their historical moment but rather maintain the ability to reappear as topics of debate in the present day, thereby transforming current public perception of the past. These are some of the factors that shape the culturally specific connotations of documentary theatre in twenty-first-century Russia and are among those I will return to in my consideration of particular performances in the chapters to follow.

The status of documents

Before reviewing the implications of documents and documentarism in their specifically Russian context, it is also worth pausing to reflect on how significantly our understanding of both the word and the concept of 'document' has shifted internationally since the turn of the twenty-first century. In 1996 a short article appeared in the magazine *Wired* entitled, 'What's a Document', written by former vice-president of the Open Text Corporation, David Weinberger. The article opens with the following question, 'Have you noticed that the word *document* doesn't mean much these days?' In the past, Weinberger contends, 'a document was a piece of paper – such as a will or a passport – with an official role in our legal system' (1996: 112). Ever since the advent of word processors and their appropriation of the word 'document' as the digital file extension for files of varied content, Weinberger suggests, the word has been stretched to the point of meaninglessness. 'The fact that we can't even say what a document is anymore', Weinberger writes, 'indicates the profundity of the change we are undergoing in how we interact with information and, ultimately, our world' (112).

When looking at the 'profundity of change' as it has unfolded across culture and technology since the 1990s, few can lay claim to a more drastic shift than modern-day Muscovites. With internet usage soaring across the country, Russia's social and cultural development since the early 2000s has inextricably coincided with its access to online media sources. The proliferation of Russian New Drama and documentary theatre has developed in parallel with online advancements, the centrality of which can be observed at first glance in the name of the movement's artistic home, Teatr.doc. By using the file extension '.doc' in its name, Teatr.doc founders tie their practice to online cultures such as blogs, Live Journal, and other modes of self-publishing. As Birgit Beumers and Mark Lipovetsky point out in their article 'Reality Performance: Documentary trends in post-Soviet Russian theatre', Teatr.doc's overt, self-identified link to modern technology connects their theatrical practice to the strengthening of an 'individual's contribution to the making of news, and taking over this function from the central media' (2008: 298, n. 14).

In her pioneering study *Losing Pravda: Ethics and the press in post-truth Russia* (2017), Natalia Roudakova discusses how the fall of the Soviet Union and the rise of capitalism in the 1990s came to shape the fate of Russian journalism in unexpected ways. While the collapse of Soviet censorship may have given way to certain types of freedom of expression, the lack of support from the state meant that individual journalists were largely left to their own devices in their search for a sustainable income within their field. These developments coincided with the introduction of electoral politics and resulted in an unfortunate association between politicians and the press. By the late 1990s, Roudakova argues, Russia's general population treated the field of journalism with an attitude of cynicism and suspicion, a trend that only really began to turn with the emergence of several independent media organizations in the years following the 2011–13 wave of protests in Moscow and around the country.

In the 2017 World Press Freedom Index, Russia ranked 148 out of 180 countries. That places the country well below Kyrgyzstan, Afghanistan, and South Sudan and only narrowly above the Democratic Republic of Congo, Iraq, and Libya. According to the US-based NGO the Committee to Protect Journalists, no fewer than 28 journalists have been murdered for proven political motives since Putin first came into the presidency in 2000. The independent watchdog organization Freedom House confirms that the Russian state or its proxies control the vast majority of the country's national television networks, newspapers, and news agencies and report that the restrictions on freedom of speech have increased significantly since 2012. Opposition journalists such as Sergei Reznik from Rostov-on-Don, for example, have been arrested and imprisoned on false charges, while individual bloggers such as Vadim Tiumentsev from Tomsk and Daria Poliudova from Krasnodar both faced substantial time in prison after writing online posts criticizing the Kremlin's role in the war in Eastern Ukraine, an issue that has been at the heart of much of the country's state-sponsored disinformation campaign since 2014 (*Reuters*, 2015; *Amnesty International*, 2016).

With these developments in mind, we might further our understanding of the complex role documents play in Russia's Kremlin-dominated media landscape, and the significance of alternative sources of information, by looking to cultural theorist David Levy's rebuttal to Weinberger's assertion discussed above. Levy contends that in fact we *can* say what a document is despite the notion's multifaceted forms in contemporary culture. 'What are documents?' Levy writes, 'They are, quite simply, talking things. They are bits of the material world – clay, stone, animal skin, plant fiber, sand – that we've imbued with the ability to speak ... Documents are exactly those things we create to speak *for us*, on our behalf and in our absence' (2003: 23). Conceiving of documents as stand-ins for ourselves and others, as things we create to speak 'on our behalf and in our absence', offers important insight into some of the paradoxes woven into the fabric of international documentary theatre practice.

To call a performance practice 'documentary' is to imbue it with a claim to truth and to the representation of reality. The categorization carries with it the connotation of authenticity, implying that what happens on the documentary stage is somehow more 'real' than what happens on the traditional theatre stage. Documentary theatre draws on archival resources (found texts, official records, artifacts, interviews, etc.), and in doing so creates the illusion of a traceable, if not reliable, past. As Janelle

Reinelt writes, 'Spectators come to a theatrical event believing that certain aspects of the performance are directly linked to the reality they are trying to experience or understand ... If we want to understand the minimal claim of the documentary, it is simple facticity: the indexical value of documents is the corroboration that something happened, that events took place' (2009: 9–10). Reinelt's description is a succinct articulation of the value and potential efficacy of documentary theatre in performance as it is practiced around the world. However, in Russia, a country where both historical and official documents are thought especially opaque and untrustworthy, the need for corroboration becomes slightly more complex. Moreover, to call one's work 'documentary' in a culture so coloured by the work of Kremlin spin-doctors carries an especially complicated connotation.

Birgit Beumers and Mark Lipovetsky have published several key studies interrogating these issues in connection with both Russian documentary theatre and New Russian Drama, including their 2009 book *Performing Violence: Literary and theatrical experiments in New Russian Drama* and their 2010 special edition of *Russian Review*, a collection of essays on the changing nature of documentarism in Russia. In their introduction to the 2010 edition, the authors point out that many artists across the literary and visual arts have revealed a keen interest in documentary forms since the early 2000s. They suggest that the current trend toward reality-based work in Russia is reflective of a shifting attitude toward questions of truth and authenticity and, in that sense, mirrors documentary movements of the country's past, including the 'literature of fact' of the avant-garde arts journal *LEF* (Left Front of the Arts) in the 1920s, and the intense interest in memoirs from former Gulag prisoners in the 1960s. In distinction to these twentieth-century documentary movements, however, Beumers and Lipovetsky argue that Russia's twenty-first-century documentary trend dismisses the notion of an absolute 'Truth' and favours instead 'the micronarratives of "truths" – generational, sub-cultural, personal' (2010: 561).

The prevalence of so-called 'micronarratives of truth' is apparent in numerous productions in Russia's documentary theatre repertoire. For example, this trend is especially evident in director Vsevolod Lisovskii's production *Akyn-opera* (2012) and its sequel *Akyn-opera 2* (2014), in which Central Asian migrant workers share their real-life immigration histories with audiences (see Aizman, 2015). The three performers sit onstage speaking in turns about how they first came to Moscow and how their lives have unfolded in the years since their arrival. They offer candid glimpses of the discrimination many Central Asian immigrants face in Moscow and provide details of daily life as an undocumented migrant worker. Another production that exemplifies an investment in subjectivity and personal narratives is the production *Obnimi menia* (*Hug Me*, 2014), in which actor-director Konstantin Kozhevnikov solicits input from the audience and from a professional therapist onstage in his repeated attempts to understand the intricacies of his real-life relationship history. A third example is one of Teatr.doc's most popular plays to date, the production *Zazhgi moi ogon* (*Light my Fire*, 2011). Written by Sasha Denisova and directed by Iurii Muravitskii, *Light my Fire* features six actors recounting the biographies of American rock legends Jim Morrison, Janis Joplin, and Jimi Hendrix while also sharing narratives from their own personal histories in such a way as to spin the stories together and create a musical tapestry of life, love, and loss in contemporary culture.

These are only a few productions that highlight how documentary theatre in Russia need not always be reliant on physical documents for its primary source material. As illustrations, they show how the hallmark of the genre is not an inherent investment in the staging of physical documents. The unifying feature of Russian documentary theatre productions is rather their dedication to the representation of lived experience and an attempt at an honest expression of that lived experience as articulated through spoken text onstage. If, as Levy argues, 'Documents are exactly those things we create to speak *for us*, on our behalf and in our absence' (2003: 23), then pinpointing the substance of the 'document' in Russian documentary theatre can prove a complicated task. Levy's conception of

Figure 1: *Akyn-opera 2*, directed by Vsevolod Lisovskii (2014)

Figure 2: *Zazhgi moi ogon*, directed by Yuri Muravitskii (2015)

documents as things we create to speak for us, as testimonial evidence of the past, is a notion woven throughout this book and one that highlights the intimate connection between Russian documentary theatre practice and an emphasis on everyday language as represented onstage.

Aside from Beumers' and Lipovetsky's groundbreaking studies, referenced above, extant scholarly material dedicated to twenty-first-century Russian documentary theatre is somewhat limited. Other book-length studies of New Russian Drama that incorporate discussion of documentary theatre practice include Marina Davydova's *Konets teatralnoy epokhi* (2005) and *Kultura zero* (2018), the French edition *Les nouvelles écritures russes* (2010) by Marie-Christine Autant-Mathieu, and Pavel Rudnev's *Drama pamiati: Ocherki istorii rossiiskoi dramaturgii 1950–2010-e* (2018). Each of these authors suggests, in one way or another, that the first decade of the twentieth century was the most productive and innovative period for documentary theatre and New Drama in Russia; they claim that by the late 2000s the form's vivacity was already beginning to diminish. My research suggests that 2008 was in fact the beginning of a new resurgence of Russian documentary theatre practice and that, since that time, the form has been refined and developed as an explicit path to promoting civic engagement.

Several articles on the topic have appeared in the intervening years illustrating the social relevance of Russia's documentary theatre repertoire, such as Maksim Hanukai's 'After the Riot: Teatr.doc and the performance of witness', which appeared in *The Drama Review* (*TDR*) in 2017. Moscow-based American critic John Freedman has been an assiduous chronicler of contemporary Russian theatre, and until recently his writing constituted much of the only English-language analysis of the New Drama movement in Russia. Most Russian-language analysis on the topic has been generated by Moscow's theatre critics, specifically Davydova and Rudnev as mentioned above as well as Anna Banasiukevich, Elena Kovalskaia, Kristina Matvienko, and others. These authors write primarily for periodicals and together their works are the most comprehensive analysis of the form to date. In April 2015 the Russian language journal *Teatr* published a special edition devoted to documentary forms that includes articles by many of the leading scholars, critics, and theatre historians in the field, including those mentioned above. And in June 2018, the same journal published a commemorative collection of writing by Mikhail Ugarov.

Witness onstage is therefore one of the first full-length studies dedicated to contextualizing the rapid growth of Russian documentary theatre within its national and international historical contexts and to analysing the cultural significance of the form. Its findings resonate not only in the context of twenty-first-century Russian art and culture, but within a wider study of the efficacy of theatre as a venue for civic engagement. Through close readings of specific plays, this book focuses on what transpires within the theatre space at the time of performance. It considers the cultural complexities of each play's narratives, and the significance of each production's staging; and it questions the mechanics of the relationship between audience and performance in every play under discussion. Through its investigation into the communicative method applied by Russia's documentary theatre artists, this book illustrates how, by playing the space between that which is real and that which is fabricated, Russia's documentary theatre artists point directly to the fungible nature of history and ideology as it has developed in the post-Soviet Russian context.

Staging historiography

The complexities of how Russia's Soviet past is or is not remembered in the present is a topic that has been taken up by many scholars in recent years, a trend that has corresponded to a growing international interest in the field of memory studies. Theories regarding Russia's 'memory disorder' (Ferretti, 2003) have proliferated, resulting in diagnoses ranging from nostalgic to ironic (Boym, 2002a; Yurchak, 2008), from compulsive to melancholic (Etkind, 2009, 2013). In this study, I do not pretend to diagnose the state of cultural memory in contemporary Russia, but I do rely on an assessment shared by the scholars referenced above, a belief that the issue of the past and how it ought to be handled in the present is a source of ongoing tension and underlying conflict in post-perestroika Russian culture. As discussed above, historical narratives in Russia are regularly unearthed and undone, revived and rewritten, all in service of the current political administration. The cultural traumas of Stalinism and the meaning of the Soviet past are two issues that remain unresolved for many people in twenty-first-century Russia, a fact that lends the narratives of the past particular power in the present.

In my consideration of Russia's twenty-first-century documentary theatre practice and its relationship to the Soviet past, I place the growing scholarly discourse on the country's contemporary memory culture into dialogue with notions of embodied memory as they have been developed in the works of performance studies scholars such as Joseph Roach, Rebecca Schneider, and Diana Taylor. These writers, among others, have looked to different national performance practices in order to examine how cultural perceptions of the past can be analysed not only in texts and material objects but also through what Taylor calls 'choreographies of meaning' (2003: 20). Taylor draws her readers' attention to the transmission and transformation of cultural memory via 'gestures, orality, movement, dance, singing – in short, all those acts usually thought of as ephemeral, nonreproducible knowledge' (2003:19). She thereby argues that performance can function as an embodied archive through which historical narratives are communicated via physical practice and co-presence. Her study demonstrates how physical performance practices have the capacity to, in a sense, *enact* the narratives of the past that they seek to represent.

Rebecca Schneider also considers important points of connection between performance and cultural memory through analysis of historical reenactment in her book *Performing Remains: Art and war in times of theatrical reenactment* (2011). In doing so she seeks to investigate the 'possibility of temporal recurrence and explore the claim lodged in the logic of reenactment that the past is not (entirely) dead, that it can be accessed *live*' (11; original emphasis). In these works, Taylor and Schneider employ theories of enactment, in part, to argue against the notion that performance is ephemeral, and to demonstrate how the influence of embodied creative acts such as theatre, dance, and performance art linger in the public consciousness (and unconsciousness) long after their moments of exchange between artists and audiences. Moreover, both Schneider and Taylor enlist the writings of linguist J.L. Austin and his speech act theory to illustrate the nuances of the acts of transference they seek to describe.

In his well-known publication, *How to Do Things with Words* (1975), Austin differentiates between a *constative* speech act, an utterance used to describe or indicate, and a *performative* speech act, an utterance that performs an action through the process of being spoken. His examples include: "'I do (sc. take this woman to be my lawful wedded wife)' – as uttered in the course of the marriage ceremony'" and "'I name this ship the *Queen Elizabeth*" – as uttered when smashing the bottle against the stem' (5). In both of Austin's examples the speaking of words performs a transformation. These distinctions are also embedded in my investigation into the active and transformative nature of Russian documentary theatre. Like Austin's notion of performative speech acts, the plays analysed in this study are instances in which the act of speaking not only indicates or describes various aspects of life in contemporary Russia, but they also exemplify how the act of speaking can in itself constitute an instance of enactment.

My use of the word enactment is therefore drawn from the work of the authors discussed above in that I use it to indicate the transformative capacity of theatre as a verbal and physical practice. It is a notion at the heart of my analysis of Russian documentary theatre and one I will return to in the chapters to follow. I use the word enactment to refer to established notions of performance as an act of social engagement and also to highlight important similarities between Russian documentary theatre and acts of commemoration. Like all documentary theatre-makers, Russia's theatre artists recall narratives of the past through their recitation of documentary texts in the present. In many productions, actors stand in as surrogates for historical figures or real-life witnesses, a practice that is also commonly employed in commemoration rituals. Like commemoration, documentary theatre often serves to recollect historical narratives and to mark the passage of time since the event being remembered. These are a few of the key commonalities between Russian documentary theatre and commemorative practices that will be discussed at greater length in Chapter 2. In order to lay bare my methodological approach to this material, however, I ought to draw the readers' attention to a central point of dissonance in my comparison of Russian documentary theatre to rituals of commemoration.

To commemorate someone or something is to remember that person or that event and to remember is to mark a person or an event as absent. In the case of Russian documentary theatre, conversely, performances serve as the vehicle through which the narratives of the past are not merely remembered but are in fact made present and accessible to the participants of the production in the present moment. That is to say that one primary difference between the performance of documentary theatre in Russia and the practice of commemorative rituals internationally is located in the role the past plays in each of these two collective processes. With this distinction in mind, I propose that the vital link between commemoration and enactment in Russian documentary theatre can be best characterized by the word anamnesis.

A multivalent term derived from the ancient Greek word ἀνάμνησις, anamnesis is commonly translated as 'remembrance'. In contemporary parlance, the word anamnesis appears primarily in three contexts; medicine, philosophy, and liturgical studies. When used by medical professionals, the word anamnesis refers to a patient's recounting of personal medical history. In order to assign a diagnosis, doctors elicit relevant information not only from their patients' written medical records but also from an oral narration sometimes called a clinical interview. According to a 2016 article in the *European Journal of Internal Medicine* entitled 'The Secret of the Questions: Medical interview in the 21st century' (Zuin et al., 2016), the rise of electronic filing of patients' medical records has resulted in a decreased emphasis on the in-person clinical interview for many medical professionals, a development that can lead to a decrease in accurate diagnoses. In order to obtain a patient's anamnesis, doctors traditionally ask their patients to narrate the details of their symptoms, the timing of their onset, and any external factors patients feel could be contributing to their condition. In the context of this study, I argue that the practice of speaking and listening to the narratives shared in Russia's documentary theatre productions can also be interpreted as a type of communal anamnesis. Artists and audiences speak their stories to one another and, through the shared practice of performance, seek to gain a greater understanding of their cultural condition.

The second meaning of anamnesis relevant to a study of twenty-first-century Russian documentary theatre practice is drawn from Plato's use of the word in his two Socratic dialogues, *Meno* (81df-5) and *Phaedo* (74e ff). In the first of the dialogues, Socrates demonstrates to Meno his doctrine of recollection (anamnesis) by arguing that people do not gain knowledge through a process of learning but rather through the act of remembering. For Socrates, the acquisition of this remembered body of knowledge serves as proof of the existence of an immortal soul which has developed ways of knowing before becoming attached to a human body. For the purposes of this study, I suggest that the notion of a body of knowledge accessed exclusively through remembrance is akin to Diana Taylor's argument that cultural memory can be transmitted across generations through gesture, movement, and other non-verbal strips of behaviour. For Russia's documentary theatre artists and audiences, the practice of remembering through performance offers participants access to a body of knowledge they may not previously have realized they had. As becomes particularly apparent in my analysis of the plays *Second Act. Grandchildren* in Chapter 2 and *Pavlik – my God* in Chapter 4, the anamnetic practice of documentary theatre in performance provides a space for participants to develop alternative ways of knowing directly through the process of remembering.

The third and final use of anamnesis which comes to bear on this study derives from the word's use in the Eucharist. Appearing in both Luke 22:29 and in I Corinthians 11:24–5, the term is used in the Greek scriptures as a command for remembrance: 'Do this in memory (anamnesis) of me.' Liturgical scholars debate the scriptural connotations of the word (see Gittoes, 2008) but are in agreement that the original term incorporates certain intricacies not immediately apparent in its English translation. As Gregory Dix argued in his influential 1945 study *The Shape of the Liturgy*, words like remembrance and memorial have the 'connotation of something itself absent, which is only mentally recollected' (161). In the context of the Liturgy however, anamnesis has the sense of '"recalling" or "representing" before God an event in the past, so that it becomes here and now operative by its effects' (Dix, 1945: 161). As we will observe in the chapters to follow, Russian documentary plays also have the capacity to call up an event in the past in such a way as to make it unusually operable in the present. This, I will argue, is partly a result of the sensitive role the past plays in the present in twenty-first-century Russian culture, and partly in connection to the uniquely non-illusory performance style Russian documentary theatre artists have developed.

By incorporating the notion of anamnesis in my analysis of the Russian documentary theatre repertoire, I ask readers to consider to what degree a reenactment of documents from the past can come to constitute an actual enactment of the historic moment represented, simply in the new context of the present tense. In each of the three instances described here, the term anamnesis, which underlies my vision of Russian documentary theatre as a unique space for civic engagement, provides important insight into how the process of recalling the past in the present has proven an active and transformative practice for artists and their audiences. By giving voice to documents and narratives of the past in the live space of the theatre, Russia's documentary theatre-makers offer audiences exclusive access to the past in the present. This is not to say that documentary theatre practice, or indeed any genre of theatre practice outside Russia, cannot take on anamnetic qualities; they can. However, from my experience the confluence of cultural and aesthetic particularities of the practice as it has developed in its contemporary Russian context makes documentary theatre an especially evocative form of theatrical recollection. In other words, this book suggests that the practice of theatrical reenactment has, in fact, become an important mode for the enactment of new cultural narratives in twenty-first-century Russian culture.

Practice research

The transformative capacity of Russian documentary theatre was one element of the practice I observed closely during my time performing in the Joseph Beuys Theatre/Sakharov Center co-production *Legacy of Silence* between 2010 and 2011. My work in the show gave me a chance to witness the production process, to participate in discussions about the significance of the play, and to see both artists and audiences sort through their complex relationships to the events of the past. I was asked by director Mikhail Kaluzhskii to participate in the production in autumn 2009. At that time he shared with me the two interviews he had excerpted and translated from the collection *Legacy of Silence*, conducted, collected, and published by the Israeli psychologist Dan Bar-On. Rehearsals began the following winter and several staged readings preceded the official opening in 2010. Performing in *Legacy of Silence* offered me an opportunity to experience the unique performance methods of Russia's documentary theatre artists via my own embodied practice, a process I will describe in detail here as it comes to bear on my overall analysis of Russia's documentary theatre repertoire.

As a performer in *Legacy of Silence* I was given very little direction. I found it challenging to gauge the efficacy of my own performance, particularly as it was the first time I had ever performed in Russian. Though I was no stranger to non-illusory performance methods, given my previous work as a writer, director, and performer with the experimental theatre collective the New York Neo-Futurists, I found it disorienting how little attention was paid to notions of character or any portrayal of emotions in rehearsals. The process was a collaborative one, and though Kaluzhskii was the director, everyone involved in the project, including performers and production staff, participated in lengthy discussions about the staging of the show, the editing of the texts, and most other aesthetic choices regarding the overall production. As for direction, I was asked to speak the text and to be present as I did so. There were occasional directives to pause, for example, to look up or to look away. These were generally drawn from gestures or impulses that arose during our rehearsed readings and constituted the extent of the explicit direction of my performance.

In 2014, three years after starting my academic research on the topic of Russian documentary theatre, I began work on a subsequent documentary theatre project, *Lynndie Sings the Blues*. The project was a collaboration between myself and the German director Georg Genoux. Originally from Hamburg, Genoux studied directing at the Russian Academy of Theatre Arts (GITIS) under the direction of Mark Zakharov from 1999 to 2003. In 2002 he became a co-founder of Teatr.doc in Moscow. In 2008 Genoux founded the Moscow-based documentary theatre company the Joseph Beuys Theatre and has since gone on to curate and direct documentary theatre productions throughout Russia and Europe. Our production *Lynndie Sings the Blues* staged an interview with the former American soldier Lynndie England, commonly recognized as the face of the 2004 Abu Ghraib prisoner-abuse scandal. Again, I experienced the lack of direction in rehearsals to be uncomfortable. As an actor I often felt uncared for and sometimes unprotected. I was offered no opportunity to explore any 'character' motivation. There was no direction relating to the speaker's emotional journey. There was never any discussion about how the mechanics of my performance were or were not effectively communicating any message the play was intended to relay to its audiences. Genoux and I performed *Lynndie Sings the Blues* for a short run in Cambridge, UK in February 2014 and again in Sofia, Bulgaria the following spring.

In many ways, it was my experience as a performer and co-creator of *Lynndie Sings the Blues*, after two years of academic research on Russian documentary theatre practice, that gave me the chance to reflect upon my work as an actor in *Legacy of Silence* years earlier. What I came to understand at that time, through a combination of practical and theoretical research practices, is that the lack of character building in Russian documentary theatre is completely intentional. In both productions, I spoke documentary texts that were originally spoken by someone other than myself. My task was never to imitate the original speakers or to create the illusion that the words I spoke were being articulated for the first time. My responsibility as an actor in these two productions was rather to embody the texts and thereby make them physically present through the live practice of performance.

This is the dynamic I am referring to when I use the term 'non-illusory' to describe Russian documentary theatre in performance.[1] It is a quality of the theatrical practice that can be observed by any audience member and is one of the elements that distinguishes how documentary theatre is commonly practised in Russia from how it is often presented in the UK and in the US. Many foundational verbatim and documentary productions with clear social themes, such as the works of Anna Deavere Smith in the US or Alecky Blythe in the UK for example, rely heavily on the characterization of the original speakers. A play's political message is communicated not only through a composition of the documentary texts, but also through the choices an actor and director make about how best to portray a 'character'. In most Russian documentary theatre productions, conversely, there are no characters, only people. Audiences and artists choose to come together to speak and to hear the texts presented onstage. They do not attempt to mimic the original speakers or generate imagined motivations for their actions or words.

As Liz Tomlin discusses in her 2013 study *Acts and apparitions: Discourses on the real in performance practice and theory, 1990–2010*, to apply traditional approaches to characterization in the context of documentary theatre runs the risk of perpetuating precisely the stereotypes a production may seek to challenge. By employing the kind of psychological characterization often seen in more representational performance practices, many documentary theatre artists end up reducing the reality of the testimonies to something more familiar and comprehensible than the complex and sometimes illogical patterns of everyday speech and thought. For example, the original speakers I represented in both *Legacy of Silence* and *Lynndie Sings the Blues* expressed views and perspectives very different from my own. In retrospect, I recognize that my desire to 'play' the roles in a more traditional sense came largely from my own aversion to accepting these figures' experiences. I had the impulse to fictionalize their texts as though they were characters that could be imagined and reimagined in such a way as to explain or justify why they made the choices they made. What I have since come to understand is that to imagine motivation would be to try to make sense of these events from the past, to explain them away into convenient logical categories, when in fact the events under discussion in these two plays are in many ways inscrutable.

Such a stripped-down style of performance, I came to understand, is what Teatr.doc's founders were referring to in the company's motto 'Teatr, v kotorom ne igraiut', a multivalent phrase in the original that can be translated as both 'theatre without the acting' and 'theatre that's not a game'. These are among the insights that my practical research working with members of the Russian documentary theatre community lends my academic research on the topic. Though I may have recognized the unique qualities of this style of performance as an audience member and as a researcher, my work as a performer in these productions offers additional depth to my interpretation of the plays and the community of artists and audiences in which they were created. My interest in the complexities of this performance style was further sparked in 2015 in my role as a curator and producer of a Ukrainian documentary theatre event hosted by the Gallery of Russian Art and Design (GRAD) in London. The programme included works by Genoux as well as Ukrainian playwright Natalia Vorozhbyt, who studied in Moscow and has worked closely with artists from Teatr.doc for much of her career. Vorozhbyt's contribution to the event was a work-in-progress autobiographical monologue that was, at the time, in development for a planned premiere at the Royal Court.[2] For this reason, the staged reading was performed and directed by Royal Court artists who rehearsed with Vorozhbyt the afternoon before the performance.

Observing the rehearsal, I was struck by the conversation between performer and director in which they imagined what the speaker of the monologue might have felt at certain moments in the story and discussed how best to portray the character. This conversation appeared to me particularly paradoxical in part because I had become so accustomed to the non-illusory approaches used at Teatr.doc and other Russian documentary theatre venues, but also because the original speaker who in this case happened to be the playwright was also seated in the rehearsal room. This experience in particular, made clear to me the centrality of a non-illusory performance style to Russia's documentary theatre repertoire. The power of the performances discussed in this book can therefore be located not only in the type of texts performed but, also, and perhaps primarily, in the style of performance the artists employ as they inhabit the theatre space together with their audiences.

Generation Doc

In 2014, Teatr.doc was evicted from their home of twelve years, a small black-box basement theatre in the centre of Moscow that the artists at the heart of the collective had essentially built with their own hands before the theatre opened in 2002. Teatr.doc's eviction was neither the first nor the last indication of the crackdown on arts and culture in Russia since Putin retook his position as President in 2012. The 2011–13 wave of protests in Moscow and around the country played an important role in the development of Russian documentary theatre and will be discussed throughout this book and in particular in Chapter 6. Since that time,

Teatr.doc and documentary theatre practice more broadly have become strongly identified as part of and as supporting the country's anti-Putin opposition movement. This element of Russian documentary theatre, which has come to the fore particularly since 2012, is an important factor that reflects the generative nature of the form as a venue for social change. However, this book's focus is not how Russia's documentary theatre artists have stood up against an oppressive regime (although they have) nor is it a study of documentary theatre as an explicit form of political resistance (although in some cases it is). *Witness onstage* is rather a study of how particular approaches to performance in specific historical circumstances can facilitate a confluence of meaning that offers important insight into the cultural anxieties of that moment.

This is one reason that this book focuses on plays that were produced between 2008 and 2012, a period of time I believe to have been an especially evocative moment for the development of documentary theatre forms in twenty-first-century Russia. According to my 2012 interview with Pavel Rudnev, prior to 2008 documentary theatre in Russia was viewed by many as a fringe activity and something with little relevance to daily life. 'It's just barely in the last three to four years that [Russian documentary theatre] has become any kind of major, top establishment', Rudnev claims. 'Before that everybody thought we were some kind of underground experiment that nobody needs' (Rudnev, 2013). The year 2008 marked a turning point for Russia's documentary theatre artists. Many of the plays to come out of Russia's documentary theatre repertoire at this time took on a newly political tone and yet were not so swiftly identified as a form of protest, since Putin's renewed attack on freedom of expression had not yet come into full effect.

Another reason for the relative success of documentary theatre in contemporary Russia specifically since 2008 is connected to a generational shift of both artists and audiences around that time. One of the most common early critiques of Russian documentary theatre was the assertion that it did not qualify as theatre. According to Rudnev in my 2013 interview with the critic cited above, this popular opinion grew out of a pervasive Soviet notion that art ought to present life as it 'should be', a sentiment introduced and enforced under the Socialist Realist diktat of the Stalin era. This view on what function art was meant to play in society introduced strict guidelines as to what did or did not qualify as art, in the traditional sense. In Rudnev's assessment, the greater the percentage of artists and audience members who enter the theatre without this Soviet-influenced preconception of what art or theatre 'should be', the greater the possibility for experimentation. Of course this generational shift does not apply to all theatre artists and audiences but, as subsequent post-Soviet generations come of theatre-going age, notions of what does or does not qualify as 'theatre' or 'art' are changing.

Rudnev's hypothesis was certainly proven accurate in my interview with playwright Nina Belenitskaia, one of the youngest writers to have joined the Teatr.doc collective in its early days. Belenitskaia first came to Teatr.doc at the age of 20, when the theatre was in its second season. When I asked her whether or not she considered the work she saw at Teatr.doc to be 'theatre', Belenitskaia responded by saying that at the time Teatr.doc was, to her mind, the *only* theatre and that in her opinion, any productions lacking Teatr.doc's signature, stripped-down style qualified as something other than theatre. 'For me the question wasn't whether or not it was theatre', Belenitskaia explains. 'In fact for me it was quite the opposite I had a whole other experience. Teatr.doc became, to my mind, the main theatre and for me anything that didn't resemble Teatr.doc wasn't theatre' (Belenitskaia, 2013).

Here Belenitskaia is primarily referring to the visual aesthetics of Teatr.doc productions which generally have no sets or costumes or, occasionally, a very sparse stage design, a design choice that follows the non-representational style of performance described above. The visual appeal of Teatr.doc's bare-bones, 'poor theatre' aesthetic is closely connected to the ethos of Russian documentary theatre as a space for the construction of community. Russia's documentary theatre artists eschew the use of footlights or other stage devices that purposefully separate the audience from the performance space. They do not attempt to suspend their audiences' disbelief but rather acknowledge the constructed nature of their theatrical practice. In doing so, Russia's documentary theatre artists manage to mirror and thereby reveal the seams of key constructions in contemporary Russian culture.

In his 2005 study, *Virtual Politics: Faking democracy in the post-Soviet world*, Andrew Wilson discusses how the legacy of Soviet political practice has continued to shape Russia's cultural policy into the twenty-first century. He illustrates the manufactured nature of the Kremlin's 'political technology' and shows how Russia's political elite dominate the country's media platforms and consciously use their supremacy in the press to construct the public they require to remain in power. Wilson writes that in Russia, 'Politics is "virtual" or "theatrical" in the sense that so many aspects of public performance are purely epiphenomenal or instrumental, existing only for effect or to disguise the real substance of "inner politics"' (2005: 47). The country's statecraft is closely tied to its promotion of Putin as a powerful leader, characterized by the staging of his regular media appearances in which he displays both his physical prowess and his deep commitment to traditional values. As the president of the country appears in magazines and on television rerouting the migration patterns of endangered Siberian cranes (*Reuters*, 2012), for example, or recovering ancient Greek vases from the floor of the Black Sea (Goscilo, 2013: 201), Russia's theatre artists conversely have sought new ways to root their work in the reality of their actual experiences.

Each of these aesthetic, political, and generational shifts has informed the selection of material I included in this book. The productions discussed in the following chapters have been chosen for their capacity to illustrate variations in the form as well as commonalities within the genre. Their content and styles vary, and yet they all address the four core cultural tensions that I set out at the beginning of this introduction: questions about the evidentiary status of documents, the performance of justice, the sincerity of testimony, and the complexities of Russia's difficult relationship to its twentieth-century past.

Though the emergence of Russian documentary theatre is traditionally traced back to the introduction of verbatim as initiated by the series of Royal Court workshops in 1999–2000, this book's first chapter seeks to refocus the form's own particular heritage, considering how the work of Russia's twenty-first-century documentary theatre artists draws on the example of the country's twentieth century theatre artists and their distinct investment in blurring the boundaries between lived experience and its theatrical representation. Situating Russia's contemporary documentary theatre practice within its national and international historical context, Chapter 1 presents a framework within which to consider why the form has come to prominence in the first two decades of the new millennium in Russia and explores how it operates in its particular cultural and temporal space.

Each of the following chapters conducts close analysis of one or two specific productions from the country's twenty-first-century documentary theatre repertoire. Chapter 2 considers the consequences of Russia's complex memory culture as depicted in the two productions *Legacy of Silence* (2010) and *Vtoroi akt. Vnuki* (*Second Act. Grandchildren*, 2012). Both productions were created and directed by Mikhail Kaluzhskii in collaboration with director Georg Genoux in the first instance and writer and curator Aleksandra Polivanova in the second. Produced by Moscow's Sakharov Center, these two plays were the first documentary productions to draw audiences into explicit dialogue about the Gulag and Stalinism. By placing the growing scholarly discourse on Russian cultural memory into dialogue with notions of embodied memory developed in performance studies, Chapter 2 illustrates how, through the presentation of historical narratives, Russia's documentary theatre artists offer audiences renewed access to the past via their performance in the present.

Chapter 3 investigates how the notions of justice and testimony come to bear on Russian documentary theatre practice through analysis of a series of productions that use either real or imagined trial transcripts as the basis for their performance texts. This chapter focuses in particular on the 2010 and 2012 versions of the play *Chas vosemnadtsat* (*One Hour Eighteen Minutes*) in which playwright Elena Gremina and director Mikhail Ugarov incorporate elements of Russia's suspect judicial history in order to implicate their audiences in an active process of witnessing and judging. The play uses verbatim and constructed texts to stage an imagined trial of the prison and medical staff involved in the final days of Russian attorney Sergei Magnitsky, who was arrested on false charges in 2008. Magnitsky was held in pre-trial detention for close to a year. While imprisoned he was denied critical medical treatment, and, as was later revealed, was brutally beaten in the hour preceding his death. With consideration of *One Hour Eighteen Minutes* at its centre, Chapter 3 investigates the interdependent nature of reenacting the past and the performance of justice in the Russian documentary theatre repertoire.

Chapter 4 extends this exploration of the relationship between memory, justice, and belief in Russia's documentary theatre repertoire through analysis of a 2008 production of the autobiographical play *Pavlik – moi Bog* (*Pavlik – my God*). In her play, Nina Belenitskaia uses the legend of the all-Soviet pioneer hero Pavlik Morozov as a vehicle through which to explore the resonance of history and mythology in one's experience of everyday life. This chapter proposes that, by utilizing a familiar literary trope and playing on the culture's history of temporal and spatial mutability, *Pavlik – my God* applies the practice of reenacting narratives of the past in order to stage the enactment of historical narratives in the present. It illustrates how the play instigates a process of exposure through which the intimate interlacing of past and present, mythology and reality, is brought to the fore. In its attempt to untangle the threads of national and personal histories, *Pavlik – my God* exemplifies how Russian documentary theatre encourages audience members to question their own presumptions about the past and, in doing so, the nature of belief in the present.

Chapter 5 follows the threads connecting the book's previous chapters by demonstrating how practices of everyday corruption in post-Soviet Russia undermine the notion of belief in contemporary culture. It analyses Talgat Batalov's play *Uzbek* (2012), an autobiographical solo-show about Batalov's experience as an Uzbek migrant at the age of 19. Untangling the themes of the play, Chapter 5 illustrates how, by artfully playing the space between sincerity and irony, *Uzbek* draws out the paradoxical nature of official documents in contemporary Russian culture and, in this way, addresses the precise complexities of the form in which it is performed. Chapter 5 suggests that *Uzbek* is, in part, a staging of inquiries into the nature of documentation in contemporary Russian culture. In this way, the chapter demonstrates how Russian documentary theatre artists ask their audiences to consider the contradictory status of documents as material testimonies that represent the untrustworthy aspects of official discourse in post-Soviet culture and, simultaneously, as influential arbiters of individual experience. Memory, justice, and belief are the threads that make up the material of Batalov's play, while humour, satire, and sarcasm are alternately woven throughout its performance. Through detailed discussion of Batalov's play, this chapter observes a convergence of each of the principal topics at the centre of this study.

Chapter 6 analyses the series of events that have taken place since Teatr.doc was first evicted from their original performance space in 2014. A twisted narrative that includes a falsified bomb-scare, multiple investigations by the Ministry of Culture, several more evictions, and numerous other instances of bureaucratic bullying by Moscow city officials, the history of Russian documentary theatre took a distinctly political turn after Putin's return to the presidency in 2012. Partly as a result of these proceedings, Teatr.doc has gained national and international notoriety as 'Russia's most daring theatre company' (Ash, 2015), a reputation that has influenced the atmosphere in which the work is created. This chapter not only recounts the trials Teatr.doc has faced since the company's initial eviction, it also explores how these events relate to the emergence of certain structures of feeling in Russia in the early 2000s.

As these chapter summaries indicate, the plays analysed in this study are not presented in chronological order. Instead, the chapters are organized in such a way as to allow the themes and styles of each production to speak to the readers and to one another most effectively. The structure of this book and the order of its chapters are presented in this manner to draw clear parallels between the productions discussed, and to gain greater understanding of the way individual productions relate to one another and the sociocultural circumstances in which they were produced.

Despite the variations in subjects and styles within Russia's twenty-first-century documentary theatre practice, *Witness onstage* argues that documentary theatre as a genre necessitates a direct engagement with the events of the past. By inquiring into the communicative method of select performances, I explore how the individual productions discussed operate within their specific cultural and historical contexts. I show how, by performing the events and texts of the past, the theatre artists at the centre of this study offer their audiences the opportunity to engage historical narratives anew and reconsider how such narratives of the past come to bear on their experiences in the present.

Through in-depth consideration of Russia's documentary theatre repertoire, this book inquires into the nature of the exchange between audience and performance. In it, I ask what it is about documentary theatre that so captured the imaginations of Russia's first post-Soviet generation of theatre-makers and what is at stake in the form's performance of the past in the present. I investigate how the form speaks to the nature of Russia's developing memory culture and, lastly, I ask, what can the practice be said to perform within the context of contemporary Russian culture? It is with these questions in mind that this book begins its investigation of Russia's documentary theatre repertoire and the insight it offers into the interdependent relationships between memory, justice, belief, and sincerity in twenty-first-century culture.

Notes

1 The term 'non-illusory' is borrowed from the rhetoric of the American experimental theatre ensemble the Neo-Futurists, a group with which I worked as a performer, writer, and director in New York from 2004 to 2006.
2 The monologue was later staged as the first part of the full-length play *Bad Roads* at the Royal Court Theatre, directed by Vicky Featherstone and premiered at the Jerwood Upstairs in November 2017.

1

Called to the stand
The origins of Russian documentary theatre

The emergence of New Drama in the 1990s and the development of documentary theatre methods in the early 2000s marked a vital shift in the development of Russian dramatic practice. It was, in part, the rapid changes to all spheres of cultural production following the dissolution of the Soviet Union that created the space for a new mode of theatre making. However, while the appearance of verbatim playwriting and the advent of New Drama at the end of the twentieth-century is often thought of as a total departure from Russia's dramatic past, this chapter explains how the development of Russian documentary theatre along with its related genre, New Drama, were both rooted in Russian and international theatre history.

Beginning with an overview of New Russian Drama primarily as a literary genre, Chapter 1 describes how documentary theatre came to the forefront of the theatrical avant-garde in Russia during the Putin years. After setting the scene for the founding of Teatr.doc in 2002, the chapter looks to certain twentieth-century performance practices both in Russia and abroad in an effort to parse particular threads of influence integral to Russia's twenty-first-century documentary theatre practice. By weaving between key moments in Russia's twentieth-century theatre history and important developments in the realm of documentary theatre internationally, this chapter places twenty-first-century Russian documentary theatre within its artistic and historic context and narrates the form's two interdependent origin stories.

We don't have contemporary drama

The years directly following perestroika and the end of the Soviet Union were, for Russian theatre, as for the rest of the region, a time of transition. 'The old theatre had died' writes historian A.V. Vislova, 'but the new theatre had not yet appeared' (2009: 11). Critics and artists have since recalled that Russian theatre in the early 1990s was often mistakenly characterized as completely lacking in new writing. In retrospect, crucial developments in contemporary drama are apparent throughout this so-called 'time of decay' (2009:11); however, the lack of publication options for playwrights, in conjunction with a dearth of directors and theatres willing to stage the new works, gave way to what John Freedman has called 'the myth of the collapse of modern dramatic writing' (1997: xiv). Many late-Soviet playwrights never overcame the obstacles to becoming post-Soviet playwrights. Those who did successfully navigate the transition, such as Liudmila Petrushevskaia and Vladimir Sorokin, gained the freedom to print their previously unpublishable work, often turning their attention away from the stage and more exclusively to novels, stories, and film.

As Beumers and Lipovetsky describe in detail in *Performing Violence*, the origins of New Russian Drama can be traced directly to the efforts of a select group of playwrights and teachers who, precisely during this transitional time, initiated events to support new theatre-making with the direct intention of developing a community of young post-Soviet playwrights. Nikolai Koliada's work at the Ekaterinburg Theatre Institute beginning in 1994 was an invaluable influence, as was his Eurasia Playwriting Competition which began in 2003. In 1998 Alexei Kazantsev and Mikhail Roshchin founded their Centre for Playwriting and Directing (*Tsentr dramaturgii i rezhissury*) in Moscow, a venue created for the explicit purpose of promoting new playwriting. In 1999 Vadim Levanov founded the May Readings in Togliatti thereby forming another hub of new playwriting which cultivated the early careers of renowned writers like Mikhail and Viacheslav Durnenkov as well as Iurii Klavdiev. In 2002, Eduard Boiakov launched the New Drama festival at the Moscow Art Theatre, an initiative that began as part of the Golden Mask Festival and continued to run in various venues and under different leadership until 2008.

Perhaps most influential was the revival of the Liubimovka New Playwriting Festival in 1990 by playwrights Elena Gremina, Alexei Kazantsev, Mikhail Roshchin, Viktor Slavkin, and Mikhail Ugarov. The Liubimovka New Playwriting Festival has since become one of the most

Figure 3: The audience at the Liubimovka New Playwriting Festival (2016)

important annual events for both new and not-so-new Russian language playwrights. The festival is named after Konstantin Stanislavsky's summer estate, thus recalling the event's twentieth-century roots. During the early years of Stanislavsky's and Vladimir Nemirovich-Danchenko's work at the Moscow Art Theatre, writers, actors, and directors gathered annually at Liubimovka, not far from Moscow, to share and discuss their most recent works. The Liubimovka Festival, held in recent years each September at Teatr.doc, retains not only its original name but also its purpose as a space for discovery and innovation in Russian theatre research.

With these support structures in place, Russia's first generation of post-Soviet theatre artists began to write and produce plays that portrayed the instability they experienced in their everyday lives. The plays of this period varied in style and content but were unified in their efforts to explore and expose the paradoxes of the post-Soviet experience. The immediacy and intimacy of theatre as an artistic medium made it an ideal genre in which writers could portray the new sociopolitical culture. It was also during these years that staged readings became particularly popular in Russia as a way for authors to share their play texts with audiences even before a full production could be mounted. Playwrights like those mentioned above, together with Maksym Kurochkin, Nina Sadur, Vasilii Sigarev, and Oleg and Vladimir Presniakov, were among those who led a generation of both artists and audiences into nuanced investigation of the shifting cultural environment in Russia in the late 1990s and early 2000s.

Among the first new Russian playwrights to break out of the relative anonymity of the nation's festival circuit and onto the Moscow mainstage was Olga Mukhina with her play *Tania-Tania*, which premiered at the Fomenko theatre in 1996. An exuberant narrative of friends who fall in and out of love with one another, Mukhina's play is credited by Freedman with breathing new life into Moscow's theatre scene (1998: xi). The text includes no reference to the political crises that dominated the social sphere outside the theatre at that time and yet, as Freedman argues, it was precisely its seeming lack of political engagement that made *Tania-Tania* as socially relevant as it was. By focusing exclusively on the individual subjective experiences of her characters, Mukhina's play testified to the fact that life and love continued even in the midst of Russia's unruly 1990s. Mukhina and her New Dramatist colleagues rejected the Soviet notion that theatre and art ought to reflect life exclusively 'as it should be', and rather aimed to portray life as it was. Though the plays of this period could not be broadly categorized as 'realist' per se, they shared a common trait in their use of quotidian language in performance as an important medium through which to interpret and reflect the sociocultural circumstances of their time.

Another influential work from the early days of New Russian Drama was Oleg Bogaev's play *Russkaia narodnaia pochta* (*Russian National Post*, 1997). An implicitly political satire, *Russian National Post* depicts an aging pensioner who spends his days alone in his room of a communal apartment writing letters to old friends and historical figures including Lenin, Stalin, and the celebrated Red Army commander Vasilii Ivanovich Chapaev. As it happens, the elderly Ivan Sidorovich also receives letters from his correspondents, or rather discovers letters that he has written himself and hidden away only moments before he finds them. As the play continues, the interlocutors of Sidorovich's imagination (including the Queen of England) begin to appear onstage and the audience learns that they have each been promised his room in the communal flat after the occupant's death. As the figures of Soviet dictatorship go head to head with Elizabeth II on the issue of who will be the heir to Sidorovich's meagre belongings, the audience is confronted with the lack of support for pensioners amid Russia's looming financial crisis. Moreover, the play captures the complexities of how numerous generations raised on Soviet propaganda were, after perestroika, confronted with seemingly sudden and undeniably extreme shifts in cultural values and societal structures. *Russian National Post* premiered with a reading at Liubimovka in 1997 and was awarded the Anti-Booker prize in the drama category in the following year. In 1998 the play was given a full production at the Tabakov Theatre Studio in Moscow, directed by the Lithuanian-Russian director Kama Ginkas, with the studio's namesake Oleg Tabakov in the leading role.

By the late 1990s, Mukhina, Bogaev, and their New Dramatist colleagues had revolutionized Russian theatre. They re-established the theatre as an important place for the discussion and representation of cultural narratives in contemporary Russian culture. Additionally, they appropriated everyday language set within the context of theatrical performance in an effort to understand and interpret the world around them. As Susanna Weygandt aptly articulates, the 'hollow' heroes of New Russian Drama represented a departure from their Soviet predecessors (2016: 118). Whereas Soviet trends dictated that plays celebrate the (primarily virtuous) deeds of dramatic heroes, many of the characters in New Russian Drama were riddled with inaction, indecision, and a lack of engagement with the world around them. In this way, the dominance of Russia's state theatres was tested by the emergence of small studios created for the explicit purpose of experimentation. Alternative theatre collectives across the country were, at this time, gaining notoriety for productions that challenged the theatre status quo in both form and content.

As described by theatre critic Elena Kovalskaia, the 'fourth wall' in Russian theatre collapsed at approximately the same time as the Berlin Wall.[1] Of course, the fourth wall had been dismantled many times in Russian theatre history before 1989; however, what Kovalskaia refers to is a notable and significant shift away from psychological realism towards the end of the Soviet Union and a marked increase in formal experimentation throughout the 1990s. In other words, extreme changes to all phases of the social sphere were, unsurprisingly, reflected in Russia's post-perestroika theatre practice. Though the new drama of the 1990s may have been slow to gain recognition amongst the country's most renowned theatre institutions, it is clear that the decade following the collapse of the Soviet Union was in fact an exceptionally generative time for new playwriting in Russia. Through the support of new drama festivals and the emergence of journals dedicated to the publication of new plays, Russia's first generation of post-perestroika playwrights transformed modern Russian drama and paved the way for further dramatic experimentation in the 2000s. As critic Daniil Dondurei observed in 2006,

> 'New Drama' is a major source of hope for our culture. Specifically 'new drama' and not new Russian theatre. That is to say drama as texts, as new kinds of meaning, a new philosophy, a new understanding of freedom, and as a path to an alternative understanding of morality.[2]

Dondurei's notion that New Drama offered a path to an 'alternative understanding of morality' is a testament to the performative nature of dramatic writing in Russia in the late 1990s and early 2000s. His statement explicitly emphasizes the role of text and the playwright's use of language as the leading forces behind this cultural and creative movement.

New Russian Drama, according to Beumers and Lipovetsky, 'undoubtedly represents the most distinct reaction to the identity crisis that characterizes the post-Soviet era' (2009: 34). After the collapse of the Soviet Union, notions of both personal and national identity came into question. New Drama arose as a creative practice through which artists and audiences could express and explore 'such diverse phenomena as the reassessment of history and the intensive production of historical myths, the increase of social apathy and a growing religiousness, nostalgia for the great empire and xenophobia' (Beumers and Lipovetsky, 2009: 34).

It was also during these years that many Russian theatre artists developed an interest in the work of British playwrights like Sarah Kane and Mark Ravenhill who were, at that time, gaining international recognition as the leaders of 'In-Yer-Face-Theatre', a genre of dramatic writing known for using violence, vulgarity, and confrontation to shock its audiences into direct engagement with the work and its subject matter (see Sierz, 2001). In the 1990s British playwrights were also leading the world stage in political and documentary theatre innovation, as the verbatim plays of the Royal Court and the tribunal plays at London's Tricycle Theatre were developing new ways to work with factual material onstage. It was in this capacity that the first representative from the Royal Court was invited to Moscow to give a public lecture in February 1999.

Graham Whybrow, the Royal Court's literary director, was commissioned to deliver a talk on the primacy of the playwright in the creative process of new drama in the UK. In his Moscow lecture, Whybrow informed his audience of primarily Russian theatre professionals that, in British new drama, the playwright is an essential part in the full rehearsal and production process of new plays. For Russian theatre artists the suggestion that a playwright could play as significant a role as the director in the creative process was a controversial notion. As Yana Ross describes in her article on the development of New Russian Drama, the country's theatre history is internationally renowned for its director-auteurs, and the system of theatre education had long relegated the role of the playwright to a period of pre-production, leaving directors the liberty to adjust the text at will and exclude the author from the play's rehearsal process (2006: 31).

The next event to follow Whybrow's controversial lecture was the first of the playwriting masterclasses that constituted the initial encounter between modern Russian dramatists and the verbatim playwriting technique. Sponsored by the British Council and produced by the Golden Mask Festival, the classes were conducted by a group of Royal Court artists including Stephen Daldry, Elyse Dodgson, Ramin Gray, and James Macdonald. Also instrumental to this process was the poet and translator Sasha Dugdale, who served at that time as a cultural liaison for the British Council in Russia, and translator and producer Tatiana Oskolkova from the international branch of the Golden Mask Festival. These workshops were intended to share a variety of playwriting techniques with Moscow's prolific community of young playwrights. The British artists conducting the classes considered verbatim to be one of the established writing techniques they had found especially generative in their efforts to capture everyday language onstage and to tell the stories of people who were not often given a voice in public media. Though the series of seminars was initially meant to include a variety of writing techniques, it was the introduction of verbatim that had the biggest impact on the playwrights in attendance. At the behest of Elena Gremina and Mikhail Ugarov, verbatim became the primary focus of the remaining seminars, leading to the staging of short plays at the Centre for Playwriting and Directing under the title *Moskva – otkrytii gorod* (*Moscow – Open City*, 2000).

The following year Gremina and Ugarov produced Russia's first documentary theatre festival, and in February 2002, along with a collection of other theatre artists from Russia and Ukraine, as well as Georg Genoux from Germany, they opened the doors to Teatr.doc, Moscow's first theatre venue dedicated solely to the production of new and primarily documentary plays.[3] Teatr.doc opened its first season with three plays in repertoire. One staged interviews with women serving time in the Shakhovsky maximum-security prison, Galina Sinkina's *Prestuplenniia strasti* (*Crimes of Passion*, 2002). The second play included in Teatr.doc's opening season was *Tseitnot* (*Time's Up*, 2002), written by Nina Sadur and directed by Genoux, which used interviews with soldiers who had fought in the Chechen war, and the third play produced that first year was a collaboration between Aleksander Rodionov and Maksym Kurochkin entitled *Bezdomnye* (*Homeless*, 2002). Ivan Vyrypaev's breakout hit *Kislorod* (*Oxygen*, 2002) soon joined the repertoire. The venue opened with support from the city's Committee of Culture, Open Society Institute (Soros Foundation), and a select group of dedicated theatre artists.

At the start, many artists and critics found the work at Teatr.doc controversial. As Sasha Dugdale describes in her preface to *Performing Violence*, some even blamed the foreign influence of the Royal Court for bringing everyday vulgarity to what they perceived to be the previously dignified realm of Russian theatre (2009: 18). As a whole, however, the project found immense support among a small but active community of artists and audiences. As Gremina wrote in her introduction to the first published book of Teatr.doc plays,

> In two years we've had eighteen premieres, five happenings and countless staged readings, and occasionally, very rarely, but no less than it happens in the very best theatre, on our own makeshift stage are magical moments of true art, which, as is well known, comes and goes as it pleases (2004: 4).

Since the first full season in 2002, Teatr.doc's artists have continued to experiment in new forms beyond verbatim including interactive and improvisational theatre as well as more traditional forms of dramatic writing. Their work has not only inspired and influenced theatre artists throughout the country, but their small 'makeshift stage' has also gained international recognition as the heart of new drama and experimental theatre in contemporary Russia.

In addition to their work in the theatre, Russia's documentary theatre artists have also initiated numerous outreach programmes volunteering in schools, hospitals, and prisons. Such programmes fall under the heading 'Teatr plius obshchestvo' (Theatre Plus Society), a series that began with partial government funding in 2010. Although the state funding for Theatre Plus Society has since dried up, Teatr.doc's artists continue their volunteer work and, in the words of Elena Kovalskaia, 'do the kind of work in society that no one but artists can do: offer hope to people in prison, to the disadvantaged, to parentless children, by showing them that the world is full of possibilities' (2015: 21).

The introduction of the verbatim technique to Moscow playwrights via the Royal Court workshops in 1999 and 2000 links the genre's history to European documentary theatre traditions as they have developed primarily in Germany and the UK since the interwar period. German directors Erwin Piscator and Bertolt Brecht in the 1920s, as well as Peter Weiss and Heinard Kipphardt in the 1960s, made invaluable contributions to the development of documentary theatre forms. Their works laid the foundation for further innovation in the genre by British artists Alecky Blythe, Peter Cheeseman, David Hare, Nicolas Kent, Richard Norton Taylor, Robin Soans, and others in the 1980s, 1990s, and early 2000s. While the connection between European documentary theatre in the late-twentieth century and Russian documentary theatre in the early twenty-first is an important lineage to consider, an over-emphasis on the Royal Court workshops as the defining moment in the development of Russian documentary theatre fails to take into account the significant ways in which Russian culture and Russian theatre history have also shaped the form as practiced in the country today.

Another approach to tracing the origins of Russian documentary theatre would be to set the practice within a tradition of documentarism in Russia as it has developed since the early twentieth century. To this end one might highlight the legacy of such fact-based performance practices as the so-called 'zhivaia gazeta' (living newspaper) plays of the 1920s or Sergei Tretiakov's subsequent development of 'Faktografik' theatre in the 1930s, an approach to documentary scriptwriting devised for explicitly political purposes. As Elizabeth A. Papazian describes in her book *Manufacturing Truth: The documentary moment in early Soviet culture* (2009), these early Bolshevik documentary works made a significant contribution to the redefinition of art and its role in society in Soviet Russia. Theatre artists and filmmakers of the era sought out new ways to use their creative practices as a method with which to respond and react to current events, a movement that anticipates the twenty-first-century work under discussion in this book. However, in the following historical overview I not only look to Russia's reality-based theatre traditions in my survey of the country's contemporary documentary theatre predecessors. I rather take a broader vantage point and investigate how shifting relationships to historical narratives and the staging of quotidian language have also played key roles in the development of twenty-first-century Russian dramatic practice.

The word made flesh

From the founding of the Moscow Art Theatre in 1897 to the present day, Russia's theatre artists have shown an historic interest in the active and transformative qualities of theatrical performance. In the years preceding what is commonly called Russia's 'failed revolution' in 1905, Konstantin Stanislavsky began experimenting in new approaches to psychological realism. The director's innovations in this area are still a primary point of reference for international theatre artists working today. It was also in these transitional years between the late nineteenth and early twentieth centuries that a group of writers and performance artists known as the Russian Symbolists began exploring pathways between theatre practice and spiritual transformation. While distinctive in many ways, both the work of the Russian Symbolists and the experiments at the Moscow Art Theatre during these years expressed a clear desire to create collisions between the experience of everyday life and its theatrical representation. By taking these two performance practices as its starting point, the next section of this chapter explores how a dedicated interest in reducing the space between lived experience and its theatrical representation is a pattern that can be traced throughout twentieth-century Russian theatre history. Moreover, I suggest that this blurring of boundaries between theatre and 'the real' in Russia's twentieth-century theatre history, has played an important role in the shaping of documentary theatre practice as it has developed in the country's twenty-first-century context.

By the time Stanislavsky and Moscow Art Theatre co-founder Vladimir Nemirovich-Danchenko met for their famed Slavianskii Bazaar summit on 22 June 1897, Realism had already arrived as the dominant artistic genre in Russia not only in the theatre but across all creative forms. Russians were far from the only theatre artists to have turned their attention exclusively to Realism at that time. In fact, the early Russian interest in theatrical Realism can, in part, be attributed to the influence of European developments like the writings of Émile Zola and the German Meiningen Company's first Russian tour in 1885. However, by the late nineteenth century, Russian artists had developed a culturally specific incarnation of theatrical Realism directly linked to notions of national identity. This connection is described in detail in the writings of critic Vissarion Grigorievich Belinskii, who vehemently advocated the importance of the individual ('lichnost') and insisted on realism as the ideal artistic genre through which to promote both the intellectual and emotional development of the Russian people. As Laurence Senelick writes, '[t]hroughout the nineteenth-century close observation of life and the reproduction of its details were taken to be preliminaries to reform a society', so much so that Belinskii was inclined to interpret 'even the fantastic grotesque of Gogol as "realism" in order to enlist the writer in his political cause' (1996: 193).

In their efforts to represent the truth and authenticity of individuals, Moscow Art Theatre artists employed new staging techniques which surprised theatre audiences with their unprecedented verisimilitude. Perhaps most famously, the theatre's first box-office hit, Chekhov's *Chaika* (*The Seagull*, 1898) created a stir with some of its outlandish staging choices; for example in Act 1 when the actors sat with their backs to the audience as they watched Treplev's play within a play. The company's innovative approach to recreating realistic material settings on stage spoke to the advancement of visual culture in Russia at that time and demonstrated a concerted interest in representing the experience of the individual with the most authentic means available. The radical nature and social significance of Stanislavsky's work at the Moscow Art Theatre can be observed in, if nothing else, the lively and vitriolic backlash against it.

Almost as soon as Stanislavsky and Nemirovich-Danchenko presented their vision of a new theatre to the public in the late-nineteenth century, they met stark opposition in the work and rhetoric of the Russian Symbolists. Early twentieth-century writers such as Viacheslav Ivanov, Andrei Bely, and Aleksandr Blok accused the Moscow Art Theatre directors of promoting a deceptive theatrical aesthetic and condemned their interpretation of Realism. Only three years after the founding of the Moscow Art Theatre, Russian Symbolist Valerii Briusov published his article 'Nenuzhnaia pravda' ('The Unnecessary Truth', 1902), in which he argued that all art is a mechanism of convention and that attempting to disguise a work's creative devices by imitating the details of daily life is futile. He describes the verisimilitude as seen on the Art Theatre's stage, the 'crickets' chirping, the curtains fluttering in the 'wind', and urges his readers to reject such deceptive theatrical practices in favour of embracing what he describes as the 'more holistic stylization' of the theatre of Ancient Greece and the Italian Renaissance.

In their efforts to blur the boundaries between art and the experience of everyday life, the Russian Symbolists embraced the conventions of theatrical traditions like Ancient drama, commedia dell'arte, and medieval morality plays. They interpreted these forms to be the type of non-illusory practices that held the potential to provoke audiences and inspire spiritual unity through provocation. As Viacheslav Ivanov, one of the most prolific theorists of the Russian Symbolist movement, wrote in his essay 'The Need for a Dionysian Theatre',[4] 'Not only does [drama] seek to enrich our consciousness by implanting within it a new image of beauty as an object of passive contemplation, but it also seeks to become an active factor in our spiritual life' (Ivanov, 1986: 113). Ivanov and his colleagues set out to discover creative forms that gave participants access to a spiritual synthesis in which art and life would become one. 'The stage must step across the footlights', he wrote, 'and draw the community into itself, or the community must absorb the stage' (116).

One example of the Symbolists' effort to reduce the distance between art and life in the pre-Revolutionary period can be observed in Aleksandr Blok's play *Balaganchik* (*The Little Showbooth*), written in 1906 and staged by celebrated director Vsevolod Meyerhold later that year. With its semi-autobiographical lyrical text, *The Little Showbooth* used irony to poke fun at the theatrical establishment, the growing popularity of mysticism, and, perhaps most resonantly, the author himself. In his two theatrical treatises following the success of the play, Blok describes his vision of the theatre as a creative form that holds the potential to unite its practitioners in a spiritual practice that moves beyond the simple representation of everyday life. He portrays theatre as a transformative practice that necessitates the active engagement of all its participants. 'More than any other art form,' writes Blok, 'theatre points to the blasphemous futility of the formula "art for art's sake" ... For the theatre is the very flesh of art, the exalted region where "the word becomes flesh"' (1986: 39).

As Blok clearly articulates here, the theatre of Russia's Silver Age, a term commonly used to describe the art and literature of Russia's late nineteenth and early twentieth centuries, was for the Symbolists a practice of enactment. The Symbolists believed that theatre had the capacity to provide vital insight into one's experience of life. They sought to provide audiences and artists access to a mystical realm in which art and life were no longer distinct from one another. These are among the elements of the Symbolist philosophy, I suggest, that maintain resonance in the context of Russia's contemporary documentary theatre practice. The twenty-first-century artists at the centre of this study may reject the tradition of a 'theatre-church' and seek to create work that reflects the harsh realities of everyday life; however, their commitment to the truths of their everyday experiences and honest observations arguably enacts its own type of ritual space, one that is rooted in the country's history and its continued resonance in the present.

In their investigation into the nature of language and violence in New Russian Drama, Beumers and Lipovetsky argue that New Drama 'directly continues [a] tradition begun by Anton Chekhov and radicalized by Artaud and Genet' (2009: 41). As this chapter seeks to illustrate, the roots of this tradition are also apparent in the works of Stanislavsky and the Russian Symbolists. These performance practices are, in the words of Beumers and Lipovetsky, 'united by a general aspiration to transform the play into a script for a ritual: not an ancient ritual, but a modern one designed to restore and recreate sacral meanings and corresponding psychological conditions in concrete social and cultural circumstances' (41). In the end, Beumers and Lipovetsky determined that New Russian Drama was largely unsuccessful in its attempt to establish such a repertoire of modern rituals as a result of the form's limited public outreach and what they observe to be the form's perpetuation of simplistic cultural narratives about an imagined 'Other'. I argue however, that Russian *documentary* theatre, as it has developed since 2008 specifically, has in fact achieved precisely this goal. By challenging the authenticity of documentation and questioning the sincerity of spoken testimony onstage, Russia's twenty-first-century documentary theatre artists invite both artists and audiences into a liminal space in which the past is recalled and embodied in such a way as to make the narratives represented onstage, in the words of liturgical scholar Gregory Dix, 'here and now operative' in the present (1945:161).

A hammer with which to shape it

Theatre in Russia had thus been established as an important venue for the negotiation of cultural narratives well before the Bolshevik revolution in 1917. Following the Revolution, theatre, like all art forms, was mobilized by the Bolsheviks as an effective instrument with which to re-shape the behaviour of the new Soviet public. Directors like Meyerhold and Nikolai Evreinov broke new ground in both their aesthetic and their political approaches to theatre practice. The Russian Futurists (in particular David Burliuk, Vladimir Mayakovsky, Vasilii Kamenskii and Velimir Khlebnikov) challenged the role of art and society. The group of writers and artists argued that such classic authors as 'Pushkin, Dostoevsky, Tolstoy, etc.' ought to be 'thrown overboard the Ship of Modernity' (see 'A Slap in the Face of Public Taste', 1917). Additionally, the period from 1910 to the early 1920s in Russia saw a significant rise in the formation of amateur theatre groups throughout the country. Agit-prop companies like the Blue Blouse troupes and organizations such as TRAM (Theatre of Young Workers) were deployed to the regions with performances meant to educate the public about the success of various Revolutionary activities around the country. Their performances were not focused on aesthetic or artistic goals as much as they were designed for the explicit purpose of propagandizing the Soviet public about the Bolshevik cause.

Many of these popular early Soviet agit-prop troupes rejected Realism and the search for emotional truths which they associated with Stanislavsky's work and what they identified as the bourgeois practices of Moscow Art Theatre. The explicitly political purpose of their performances also stood in direct contrast to the metaphysical aspirations of the Russian Symbolists given the strictly atheistic nature of the Soviet endeavour. However, these early-Soviet amateur theatrics did share one important trait with their pre-Revolutionary predecessors. In the polarized cultural climate of collectivization, when the Bolshevik party worked meticulously to re-shape the mentality of Russia's citizens across age, class, and geographic location, participation in theatre as either an actor or an audience member was widely believed to be a valid and effective vehicle for social transformation. The proliferation of amateur agit-prop theatre troupes and, as will be discussed in detail in Chapter 3, the staging of Soviet mock trials, created spaces for Russia's new Soviet citizens to rehearse and perform Bolshevik ideals. Artists reinterpreted real-life stories and events onstage in order to 'inform' the new Soviet public of the social progress underway in early Soviet Russia. Their performances purportedly played the stories of real Soviet citizens and aimed to exemplify the virtuous and heroic nature of life in these Revolutionary times. The dominant genre became known as 'living newspaper', a performance practice that was explicitly designed to educate audiences about the positive changes to both the public and the soon-to-be obsolete private sphere in early Soviet Russia.

Meanwhile, in the Weimar Republic, director Erwin Piscator was also beginning to incorporate newspaper stories and other documentary materials into his theatre performances. In fact, according to John Willett, it was in a description of Piscator's production *Trotz Alledem!* (*In Spite of Everything!*, 1925) that Bertolt Brecht first coined the term 'documentary theatre' (1978: 186). The production staged the history of the German Communist party and integrated preexisting documents such as newspaper stories and Communist party meeting minutes as the basis for the play's script. Though the early Soviet agit-prop troupes may have been at the forefront of the movement, documentary theatre and living newspaper performances were on the rise throughout Europe and the US in the 1920s and 1930s. Other examples include Hallie Flannigan's work with the Federal Theatre Project, founded in the US in 1935, as well as Joan Littlewood and Jimmie Miller's Theatre Union, founded in the UK in 1936. In each of these examples, the form was used to both entertain and educate audiences while simultaneously creating the space for a shift in public perceptions about society and citizenship. That is to say that Russia's theatre artists were not alone in their development of the form in these years as artists internationally were showing new interest in the use of found texts and factual material onstage. However, in the early-1930s when European and American theatre artists were only beginning their experimentation in the form, Russia's theatre artists were soon confronted with Stalin's system of censorship.

As the Soviet leader continued to consolidate his power, theatre became one of many weapons integrated into the state-wide arsenal of propaganda methods. Formal experimentation became restricted by the top-down imposition of a single aesthetic approach. Socialist Realism – first introduced by Maksim Gorky in 1932, became state policy with Andrei Zhdanov's speech to the All-Soviet Writers' Union Congress in 1934. From that date on, theatre as well as all other creative arts was restricted to depicting life exclusively in its imaginary and idealized Socialist form. As Zhdanov described the role of the artist in society, 'To be an engineer of the human soul ... means knowing life so as to be able to depict it truthfully in works of art, not to depict it in a dead, scholastic way, not simply as "objective reality", but to depict reality in its revolutionary development' (Zhdanov, 1934). To depict life 'truthfully' in Socialist Realist works of art was not to reflect the realities of people's day-to-day experiences but rather to imagine and portray the idealized revolutionary reality that was thought, at the time, to be the inevitable future outcome of the Soviet project. In other words, with their perpetually positive heroes and predictable stock storylines, Socialist Realist artworks presented fictions that were intended to take the place of reality in the imagination of the public.

This doctrine of an imagined utopia developed in parallel with the increasingly lethal authoritarian rule of the Soviet elites in the 1930s. As the heroic deeds of small-town tractor drivers, wheat farmers, and industrial engineers dominated both stage and screen, Stalin's murderous repressions transported millions of Soviet citizens to the expansive network of labour camps located across the nation's eleven time zones. Artists, intellectuals, and politicians were regularly arrested on suspicion of dissent as the state's terrorizing of its own citizens reached new heights in the late 1930s. The sinister incongruity between actual life in its so-called 'revolutionary development' and that which was represented in art and literature during these years resulted in an alarming dissonance between reality and representation that continued to haunt Russia's creative sector for decades, even after Stalin's death in 1953.

The Socialist Realist relativistic reinterpretation of what constitutes reality led directly to a unique set of cultural anxieties about the relationship between authenticity and creative representation in late Soviet culture. These anxieties were first addressed in print by literary critic Vladimir Pomerantsev in his essay, 'Ob iskrennosti v literature' ('On sincerity in literature', 1953). In this groundbreaking essay, the Soviet literary critic implores his fellow writers to abandon the formulaic literary patterns of the Stalin years and move toward a more genuine expression of individual experience. Without mentioning Stalin or his associated aesthetic by name, the connotations of Pomerantsev's essay were more than clear to his Soviet readers as he acknowledged Socialist Realism's 'fabrication of complete and total prosperity' and chastised writers of the era for 'varnishing reality'. The publication of 'On sincerity in literature' began a new era for Soviet theatre artists who, in the aftermath of the Stalin years, sought to reunite their actual experiences of everyday life and its creative representation onstage.

Pomerantsev's essay inspired an important shift in the artistic rhetoric of Soviet Russia. The early 1950s to the early 1960s were a period of relative freedom for Russian artists and writers as the rehabilitation of political prisoners, the loosening of literary censorship, influx of foreign films, and the burgeoning of alternative youth cultures in these years all contributed to a greater sense of freedom among Russia's creative class. The concerns expressed in Pomerantsev's essay were reflected in the artistic and literary trends of the era and, moreover, underpin two thematic strands that extend throughout works of late Soviet theatre artists and into the present day. The first of these threads is drawn from a longstanding investment among Russia's artists in articulating the paradoxes of everyday life and the integral role language plays in the construction of cultural narratives. The second thematic thread that can be traced back to the publication of 'On sincerity in literature' is how the essay encouraged artists to think critically about the past and to understand its continued resonance in the country's present. These are among the trends and interests that proved integral to the development of late Soviet playwriting as it came into full expression in the 1970s and 1980s.

Language and the 'post-Vampilov' generation

In his book, *Everything Was Forever, Until It Was No More: The last Soviet generation* (2006), Alexei Yurchak contends that it was, in part, the paradoxical nature of language and symbolic discourse in the late Soviet Union that led to the gradual but consistent leakage of significance in the average Soviet citizen's conception of the state. Yurchak's study dispels traditional notions of socialist history which rely heavily on the binary formulation of official versus unofficial, and the state versus the public, by suggesting that there were certain 'internal displacements at the level of discourse, knowledge, ideology, meaning, space and time' on which the inherent paradoxes of late Soviet life were predicated (2006: 35). In this Yurchak refers, in part, to the obligatory performance of Soviet rituals which had, by the late 1960s, become little more than pro forma for many Soviet citizens. As Helen Goscilo writes, 'Public life under Soviet rule required theatrical skills and participation in pompous, hollow rituals divorced from genuine experience and calculated to promulgate the state's chief product – ideology' (2013: 1).

The day-to-day performance of such paradoxical practices led to precisely the type of tensions that are apparent in the dramatic literature of Russia's 1970s and 1980s, a time when many playwrights sought new ways to craft honest expressions of the absurdities and paradoxes of late Soviet life. In the aftermath of Stalinism, Soviet theatre artists began a process of interrogation, in which the Stalinist perceptions of 'truth' and 'reality' came under explicit scrutiny. As Anatolii Smelianskii writes, '[Stalin's] shadow continued to strike fear into the country for many years, even after his death' (1999: 1). Nonetheless, by the 1970s select playwrights such as Aleksandr Galin, Grigorii Gorin, Eduard Radzinskii, and Liudmila Razumovskaia were already looking for new ways to express their experiences of late Soviet life in performance.

Among the first playwrights of the post-Stalin era to harness the language of the everyday into sincere expression of the disillusionment and contradictions of life in the late Soviet Union was Aleksandr Vampilov. Vampilov's plays began appearing on Soviet stages in the early 1970s and initiated a major departure from much of what had come before them. According to Smelianskii, Vampilov's text *Utinaia okhota* (*Duck Hunting*, 1970) 'was the first in a totally different dramaturgy that stood in opposition to Soviet official drama, its heroes and anti-heroes, its plots, its language, and its conception of human beings' (1999: 83). *Duck Hunting* tells the story of Viktor Zilov, a Soviet engineer who has become disillusioned with his work, his marriage, and his life. Zilov begins the play with a debilitating hangover and continues to stumble through the non-sequential flashbacks that make up the temporally scattered structure of the play. At one point he concludes his only way out of unhappiness is suicide. Failing even in this endeavour, Zilov does finally depart for his long-anticipated hunting trip, an effort which implies that even in his bleak state Zilov retains at least some modicum of hope. Vampilov's articulation of life's beauty and banality in the play spoke to his late Soviet audiences. His character's existential crisis was portrayed as simultaneously comically mundane and genuinely tragic and, in that sense, characterizes some of the paradoxes that Yurchak argues were embedded in the everyday practices of life in the late Soviet Union.

Plays like *Duck Hunting* inspired a new generation of writers who have since come to be known as the 'post-Vampilov generation'. The post-Vampilov writers used quotidian language to narrow the gulf between life and its theatrical representation, a gap that had grown significantly during the Stalin era. Their plays regularly depicted such national crises as the housing shortage, financial instability, and political uncertainty through more or less realistic depictions of everyday life. Their use of colloquial language and portrayal of average citizens represented an important shift in Russian drama, one that was perhaps developed most famously in the work of playwright Liudmila Petrushevskaia.

Though Petrushevskaia surely did not have the technologies of the verbatim playwriting technique in mind, the detailed quality of her characters' dialogue is so natural one might wonder if she had in fact transcribed the text from actual conversations. Petrushevskaia's work does not express an overt political position, but the everyday injustices her characters confront collect to form a portrait of late Soviet Russia as riddled with spiritual poverty and financial destitution, a country steeped in disappointment, alcoholism, and failed attempts at interpersonal connection. Despite the significant struggles so many of her characters face, however, Petrushevskaia's work is quite comical in its depiction of the absurdities embedded in daily life in the late Soviet Union. What truly distinguishes Petrushevskaia's plays is not only the naturalism of the dialogue but also the irony with which she portrays these absurdities. Her characters personified the paradoxical combination of irony and sincerity that Yurchak claims to have characterized the era, and the lineage of her pioneering synthesis of realism and absurdism is plainly apparent in plays of writers like Mukhina and Bogaev, as well as many of the early works of New Russian Drama.

In fact, the subsequent development of New Russian Drama in the 1990s and the proliferation of Russian documentary playwriting in the 2000s suggests that the post-Vampilov writers are among the most obvious and direct predecessors. These were the playwrights who set the precedent for using conversational language performed in a theatrical context to explore the complexities of modern life in the Soviet Union. Their works expressed a simultaneous acceptance of irony and a commitment to sincerity. Though most of their plays did not express any explicit or active dissident sentiments, their performance of disillusionment made an important contribution to their generation's critical dialogue about the Stalinist era. The works of the post-Vampilov generation of Russian playwrights expressed distrust in Socialist slogans and a lack of investment in the Soviet system. They used the language of the everyday and realistic depictions of ordinary life to express the paradoxes of their experiences. In this way the values of Stalinism and the aesthetic of Socialist Realism were judged and rejected by both artists and audiences of the era.

Another late Soviet theatre artist whose work might be said to presage contemporary Russian documentary theatre is that of writer-director Mikhail Shatrov. Throughout the 1980s, Shatrov staged pivotal moments in the nation's history. Though he wrote the texts himself, Shatrov's performances were based on interviews and minutes of party meetings, as well as published and unpublished memoirs of members of the Communist party. For example, in Shatrov's production *Diktatura sovesti* (*Dictatorship of Conscience*, 1986), a group of journalists decide to stage a trial of Lenin. The actors portray various historical figures as they condemn the tyranny of Stalinism in an attempt to revive investment in what Shatrov depicts as the 'real' Soviet values, i.e., Leninism. At one point in the play one of the actors steps off the stage and enters the audience with a microphone. They ask individual spectators about their impressions of the play, their nation's history, and its role in the country's present.

By putting the past on trial, Shatrov sought to renegotiate cultural values collectively and incorporated both artists and audiences in his effort to do so. His historical-judicial performances are important predecessors to contemporary Russian documentary theatre and, like the playwrights in Russia today, he drew on the tradition of living newspaper and *Faktografik* theatre in his portrayal of historical and current events by embodying documentary materials onstage. Though Shatrov did not employ the term 'documentary' to describe his plays, his works applied similar techniques to those of his German counterparts in their efforts to confront the complexities of their national pasts in the present.

Shatrov was likely unaware of such developments abroad, but his plays bear a notable resemblance to the judicial performances European documentary theatre artists had been developing throughout the 1960s and 1970s. The use of actual courtroom documents in documentary plays was a practice most famously developed by German writer and director Peter Weiss. In the 1960s Weiss, along with contemporaries, directors Heinar Kipphardt and Rolf Hochhuth, produced documentary plays utilizing material from such historic courtroom events as the Frankfurt Auschwitz trials (Weiss) and the J. Robert Oppenheimer inquiry (Kipphardt). Weiss's work and that of his colleagues presented the country's history for judgement and invited the public to participate in the process.

Like Weiss and Kipphardt before him, Shatrov employed the theatricality of the courtroom setting and invited his audiences to participate in an active reinterpretation of the past. The post-Vampilov writers, conversely, utilized the language of the everyday and realistic depictions of life's absurdities to expose the paradoxical seams of late Soviet discourse. Both developments revealed a desire to use theatre as a way to understand and interpret the events of the past in the present. Here again, one observes how the emergence of documentary theatre in Russia in the early 2000s is closely connected to the theatrical developments already apparent in Russia's late Soviet years. Though it is true that the late 1990s and early 2000s saw an important revival and reconstruction of New Russian Drama, it is also true that the artists of the twenty-first century have drawn on the innovations of their predecessors in their continued efforts to use their theatrical practice as a path toward a greater understanding and more precise articulation of their experiences of everyday life.

Our makeshift stage

In the years since the founding of Teatr.doc in 2002, documentary theatre has formed one of the most important artistic responses to contemporary Russian culture and politics. In 2008 Ugarov, together with award-winning filmmaker Marina Razbezhkina, opened their School of Documentary Film and Theatre, an educational programme that has since turned out many of the country's most innovative documentary filmmakers and theatre directors. Many of the artists who have graduated from the programme continue to work across disciplinary boundaries in theatre and cinema, and the energy and enthusiasm around Razbezhkina's work, as well as that of her students, has made a major contribution to the vibrant culture of documentarism in twenty-first-century Russia. The vivacity of documentary cinema in Russia continues to inform the work of the country's documentary theatre artists and vice versa.

In 2016, after facing multiple evictions and relocations, Teatr.doc opened a second venue called 'Transformater.doc' (Transformer.doc), under the directorship of Vsevolod Lisovskii. Originally housed in a former power station, Transformer.doc has since relocated to a gallery space just west of the city centre and dropped the '.doc' from its name. As a loosely connected group of artists, Transformer is dedicated to formal experimentation in performance art and has produced a number of groundbreaking events, including Lisovskii's ever-changing, roaming performance piece *Neiavnye vozdeistviia* (*Unapparent Influences*, 2016). Named 'the most radical theatre project of the year' by the newspaper *Vedomosti*, *Unapparent Influences* leads audience members on an improvisational and interactive journey through the city that recalls the work of Swiss-German performance art group Rimini Protokol and represents a first for performance art in twenty-first-century Russia.

The history of documentary theatre in twenty-first-century Russia as described in this chapter is focused on the founding of Teatr.doc and the radical influence the group has had across the country. However, it is also essential to note the essential developments in documentary theatre forms that have emerged in other Russian cities outside the capital. In particular, Theatre Lozha in Kemerova became one of the most significant regional theatre institutions in Russia in the early 2000s. Founded by writer/performer Evegenii Grishkovets before he gained fame with his autobiographical one-man-show *Kak ia sel sobaku* (*How I ate a Dog*, 1998), Theatre Lozha produced several historic documentary productions including *Ugolnyi bassein* (*Coal Basin*, 2003), a verbatim play about coal

Figure 4: *Neiavnye vozdeistviia*, directed by Vsevolod Lisovskii (2016)

mining in the Kemerova region that blended documentary materials and improvisation.

Other notable documentary theatre projects produced outside Moscow include the St Petersburg-based initiatives Baltiskii dom, Teatr na vynos, and Kult-proekt. Each of these loosely affiliated collectives of theatre-makers have made important contributions to the development of documentary and socially engaged theatre forms across the country. Director Boris Pavlovich in Kirov has produced several influential productions, in particular his work with local students in which teenagers speak their own stories onstage. In Glazov, director Damir Salimzia has staged several significant documentary projects at the Paraphrase Theatre. And, finally, it is worth noting the many regional documentary projects which have been directed and/or produced by Moscow-based artists, for example *Motovilikhinskii rabochii* (*Motovilikhinsk workers*, 2009) created in collaboration with playwrights Mikhail and Viacheslav Durnenkov in Perm and *Shkaf* (*Wardrobe*, 2014) by Talgat Batalov in Krasnoiarsk (see Banasiukevich, 2015). These are only a selection of examples of how the verbatim playwriting technique and documentary theatre forms have proven especially relevant and engaging to both audiences and artists across the country throughout the first two decades of Russia's twenty-first century.

Figure 5: *Demokratiia.doc*, on tour in Switzerland (2012)

Finally, it is important to consider the immense influence of the founding of Georg Genoux's Joseph Beuys Theatre in 2008 in Moscow. Beginning with the company's inaugural project *Democracy.doc* (*Demokratia.doc*, 2008), the Joseph Beuys Theatre generated several seasons of visionary and innovative documentary performance that challenged the boundaries of the genre and brought the Teatr.doc aesthetic into an increasingly socially engaged context. The company's mission was inspired by German artist Joseph Beuys and his notion that everyone is an artist. This concept was borne out in several forms, including a unique approach to interactive theatre that the director developed together with professional psychologists Elena Margo and Arman Bekenov.

By combining documentary theatre approaches and a method of group psychology known as 'World Work', the three collaborators staged a series of projects in which audience members were invited to speak their own stories onstage. The Joseph Beuys Theatre performed their works at several venues in Moscow (including Teatr.doc) and toured throughout Russia and Eastern Europe before Genoux left Moscow in 2012.

The zero position

In the early years of Teatr.doc, Russia's documentary theatre artists adopted an aesthetic approach they called 'nol pozitsiia' (zero position). The idea behind this method was that a playwright ought to do everything possible to refrain from expressing an opinion or bias about the subject matter represented in the play. Perhaps the most famous example of this approach can be observed in the play *Sentiabr.doc* (*September.doc*, 2003), written by Gremina and directed by Ugarov. The play staged found texts from online sources in which individuals expressed their reactions to the 2004 Beslan school siege. On 1 September 2004, a group of Islamic extremists from Chechnya and Ingushetia took hostage over one thousand people (most of whom were children) at a primary school in the North Caucusus. After a three day stand-off, Russian security forces stormed the building with tanks and heavy weaponry, resulting in the deaths of 330 hostages, many under the age of 18.

In their production about this attack, Gremina and Ugarov gave voice to individuals with diverse interpretations of what took place during those three days in September 2004. Some of the monologues included in the play express racist and xenophobic sentiments against Chechens. Other texts admonish the government's use of violence and highlight the plight of Islamic citizens in Russia's North Caucusus. All of the texts are subjective and in that sense come together to represent a polyphonic perspective on the political origins and implications of Islamic extremism and xenophobia in twenty-first-century Russia. In their application of the zero-position approach, artists do not intend to express their personal opinion on the matter but rather seek to make visible the diversity of perspectives that were circulating in the public sphere at the time. In this way, audience members were left to draw their own conclusions about what was discussed onstage as they gained the opportunity to hear a variety of different perspectives on what was unarguably a tragic sequence of events.

According to Ugarov, the 2010 production *One Hour Eighteen Minutes* was the first production in which the artists at Teatr.doc consciously abandoned their attempts at a zero position. The horror of the Magnitsky case and corruption of its subsequent cover-up was too great and close to home for Teatr.doc's artists not to express a clear position about it. Since that time, many productions at Teatr.doc and other Russian documentary theatre venues have included explicit expressions of political views, a shift Ugarov attributed to the worsening conditions of human rights and freedom of speech in the 2010s. My research suggests that the shift away from attempts at a zero position has, in part, allowed Russia's documentary theatre artists to interrogate the limitations of their own artistic practice. By releasing themselves from an unattainable goal of objectivity, Russia's documentary theatre artists have employed narratives of their own subjective experiences to great effect. Since 2008 in particular, many Russian documentary theatre artists have taken to drawing on their own pasts and those of other individuals close to them in order to question the reliability of memory and the authenticity of documentary evidence.

As this chapter illustrates, the popular notion that contemporary Russian documentary theatre marks a total departure from previous Russian theatre tradition falls into question, as the form can also be seen as a culmination of the historical and cultural circumstances which preceded its appearance. The Realism of the Moscow Art Theatre, the transcendentalism of the Russian Symbolists, the slippage between theatre and reality under Socialist Realism, and the exploration of irony and sincerity in late-Soviet theatre have all set the stage for a uniquely Russian variety of documentary theatre practice. In the chapters to follow, this study will continue to trace essential threads of influence from the country's twentieth-century theatre history. It will explore how the tensions between irony and sincerity, as observed in the language of the post-Vampilov generation, have persevered and become transformed in twenty-first-century performances, and show how the unnervingly intimate association between lived experience and theatrical representation as it developed under Socialist Realism has continued resonance in contemporary theatre practice. Lastly, the following chapters will illustrate how, like the Symbolists, Russia's documentary theatre artists do not merely seek to reflect their experiences of contemporary Russian culture. They rather use their artistic practice to engage those in attendance in an active process of transformation.

By incorporating core elements from the country's twentieth-century theatre history, the artists at Teatr.doc and other documentary theatre venues around the country create the space for a unique mode of theatrical practice in which artists and audiences come together to reconsider their relationships to their own national history. The artists whose works are at the centre of this study consistently root their performance of the present in the troubled legacies of the past. In doing so, Russian documentary theatre artists create a uniquely generative space for the negotiation and interpretation of cultural narratives, in addition to staging some of the most innovative and engaging approaches to documentary theatre-making on the world stage.

Notes

1 A claim included in Kovalskaia's presentation 'The New Drama: Plays for a Non-Existent Theatre', delivered at the conference *Literary Theatricality: Theatrical Text*, an interdisciplinary event held at Princeton University in Princeton, NJ on 27 October 2012.

2 As spoken by *Iskusstvo kino* editor Daniil Dondurei and quoted in segment on the online theatre news site *Teatralnaia Moskva* in September 2006 as promotion for that year's New Drama Festival, available at http://subscribe.ru/archive/culture.theatre.yan/200609/21175426.html (accessed 24 August 2018).
3 The founders included many of Russia's most accomplished young theatre artists with writers and directors from cities across Russia and Eastern Europe; Elena Gremina and Mikhail Ugarov (Moscow), Maksym Kurochkin and Natalia Vorozhbyt (Kyiv), Viacheslav and Mikhail Durnenkov as well as Iuri Klavdiev (Togliatti), German director Georg Genoux, and others. For a more comprehensive list see Beumers and Lipovetsky, 2008.
4 Quoted here from Green, 1986: 113–21, this essay appeared originally in Ivanov's collection of essays 'Presentiments and portents', first published in *Zolotoe runo* (1906).

2
History on trial
Performing memory in twenty-first-century Russia

As the fault lines of Eastern European cultural memory continue to lead to violence and conflict in Russia and other former Soviet countries it has become increasingly vital for artists and academics to do the difficult work of reprocessing the Socialist past in the present. The significance of Soviet history remains of crucial consequence throughout the region, a fact evidenced most starkly by the military conflict in Eastern Ukraine, a war that has claimed close to 13,000 lives since fighting began in 2014. In Russia, narratives about the country's Soviet past are used for explicitly political purposes by the Putin administration, a strategy that has played an important role in the rise of Russian nationalism in the twenty-first century. The cornerstone of the Putin administration's approach to memory politics is the glorification of Russia's role in the Second World War or, as it is known throughout the post-Soviet space, 'The Great Patriotic War'. As numerous scholars of the region have shown, Putin and his administration have purposefully reinscribed public perceptions of the Second World War in order to establish a new mythology of the Soviet past in the present (see among others Wood, 2011; Khapaeva, 2016; Kuzio, 2016; Sherlock, 2016). Commemorations of the war have been elevated to a pseudo-sacred status in contemporary Russia. 'Under Putin', as Dina Khapaeva writes, 'this Stalinist myth which glorifies the Great Victory over fascism as a major event in world history, was reanimated as the fundamental myth of post-Soviet Russian society (2016: 65).

By staging elaborate commemorative events, carefully revising historical narratives, and promoting his own family history as exemplative of Soviet sacrifice, Russia's long-time president managed to link his own biography to the creation of the country's modern foundation myth. In doing so he has also tied his administration's policies to the legacy of one of the twentieth century's most murderous dictators, Josef Stalin. Dozens of monuments to Stalin have been erected throughout Russia since Putin came into office in 2000. In 2009 Moscow's Kurskaia Metro Station underwent major renovation to restore the gilding of the entranceway's rotunda. Below the domed ceiling and above the regal-looking columns the entranceway has now been readorned with the Soviet-era slogan in golden text, 'Stalin reared us – on loyalty to the people. He inspired us to labour and to heroism'. In February 2013, to commemorate the seventieth anniversary of the battle of Stalingrad, multiple cities across Russia introduced a fleet of so-called 'victory buses' adorned with portraits of Stalin next to patriotic slogans and quotes from war veterans. These are but a few examples of how Soviet symbols and the veneration of Stalin have been purposefully reintegrated into public spaces in Russia in the twenty-first century.

This chapter explores the role of memory and commemoration in twenty-first-century Russian documentary theatre. It focuses on two documentary plays that were the first to draw their audiences into explicit conversation about how people do or do not remember both the victims and the perpetrators of Soviet totalitarianism. The first production, *Legacy of Silence* (2010), staged two interviews excerpted and translated from the book of the same title. First published in English in 1989 the book, *Legacy of Silence: Encounters with children of the Third Reich*, is a collection of conversations between Israeli psychologist Dan Bar-On and middle-aged children of Nazis. The second production analysed in this chapter, *Second Act. Grandchildren* (2012), recounts the personal histories of children and grandchildren of former members of the NKVD, the Stalin-era precursor to the KGB. Both productions premiered at Moscow's Sakharov Center and were staged under the direction of Mikhail Kaluzhskii and his collaborators, Georg Genoux in the case of *Legacy of Silence* and Aleksandra Polivanova in the case of *Second Act. Grandchildren*. The two productions were originally conceived as the first installments in an ongoing cycle of plays, hence the designation 'second act' in one of the titles. A third part in the cycle has yet to materialize, although Kaluzhskii, Polivanova, and Genoux have all continued to grapple with the topic of cultural memory in many of their subsequent works.

In order to appreciate the impact of these two plays, it is essential to set them within the context of Russia's fraught relationship to its Soviet past. As the examples above indicate, the pendulum of popularity has swung in favour of Stalin and the Soviet system for many people since the early 2000s. In fact, according to a February 2017 survey published by the independent Russian research organization the Levada Center, Stalin's approval ratings were higher in 2017 than they have been at any other point since Putin began his presidency in 2000, with approximately 46 per cent of respondents reporting that they view Stalin positively. The survey also shows that 21 per cent of respondents claim to hate and/or fear the leader who died in 1953, while 22 per cent of respondents described themselves as 'indifferent'. With these results in mind, one cannot help but ask: how can we account for the paradox apparent in Russia's active rehabilitation of an authoritarian leader who oversaw the systematic imprisonment and murder of millions of his own people, and the corrupt governmental system that facilitated it? At the heart of this chapter's investigation into Russian documentary theatre and its ties to commemorative practice is an interest in and an exploration of precisely this question.

This chapter begins with analysis of the first production in the series, *Legacy of Silence*, and considers why a play about German cultural memory claimed particular resonance for contemporary Russian audiences. Next, I will consider the activities of the international NGO, Memorial, Russia's primary organization for the preservation of historical memory of the Soviet repressions. Through discussion of Memorial I seek to demonstrate how the organization's multifaceted approach to the preservation of historical narratives has been of particular import in the post-Soviet Russian context. Lastly, through a close reading of the second play in the series, *Second Act. Grandchildren*, I consider how the practice of embodied memory as performed in the Russian documentary theatre repertoire gives its participants unparalleled access to the past in the present.

Breaking the silence

Legacy of Silence premiered at the Sakharov Center in May 2010. It was co-produced by the Sakharov Center and the Joseph Beuys Theatre with additional support from the Moscow Goethe-Institut. For his directorial debut, Mikhail Kaluzhskii staged two interviews with the middle-aged children of members of the Third Reich conducted by the Israeli psychologist Dan Bar-On. As discussed in the introduction to this book, I performed the role of Gerda in *Legacy of Silence* from 2010 to 2011. The part was subsequently taken up by the French-Russian actress Cécile Plaige from

2011 to 2012. The real Gerda, as the audience learns, lives under a pseudonym. She is convinced her father was never fully aware of the Nazis' persecution of the Jews, despite his high-ranking position in the Nazi hierarchy. The second interview in the production was performed by Georg Genoux, who portrayed Rudolph, the son of a former member of the National Socialist Party who was driven mad by the horrors he witnessed during the war. Kaluzhskii read the text of the interviewer, Dan Bar-On.

As they enter the space for a performance of *Legacy of Silence*, audience members see two actors onstage sitting on chairs with their backs to the audience. Once the audience is seated, Kaluzhskii steps onto the stage to introduce himself as director of the production. After a few words about the play, Kaluzhskii takes a seat centre stage and begins to speak the text in his role as Bar-On. Though his tone inevitably shifts slightly in the transition from speaking his directorial introduction to reciting the words of Bar-On, Kaluzhskii does not play a character. He rather delivers the text clearly and articulately as himself onstage. Behind Kaluzhskii sits a camera operator whose live video feed will be projected onto a screen upstage centre. After a brief introduction describing the parameters of his initial interview project, Bar-On begins his first interview with Gerda, a professor at a German university who has agreed to the interview on the condition that Bar-On does not try to uncover the identity of her father. As the interview begins, the camera operator sitting onstage behind Kaluzhskii turns on the camera and a close-up image of Gerda's face is projected onto the screen upstage.

Gerda's text includes descriptions of her childhood and fond recollections about her father. As a psychologist, Bar-On explains, he understands Gerda's need to preserve certain memories about her father and to block out others in order to, as he writes, 'sustain her favorable childhood image of her father' (Bar-On, 1989: 123). And yet, he does push his interlocutor, enquiring as to her father's specific involvement in the murder of millions under the Nazi regime. 'Do you think he knew and didn't tell you? Or do you believe he knew nothing?', Bar-On asks. Gerda struggles to respond, 'I just can't say. I don't think – and I was never told – that he was personally involved in the killing of Jews' (Bar-On, 1989: 123). The tone of the conversation is solemn, but far from tragic. As Bar-On notes in one of his asides spoken directly to the audience, Gerda appears sincere and open despite her seeming inability to confront the truth about her father's awareness of the Nazi's persecution of the Jews.

Within two hours of the end of their first meeting Bar-On has determined who Gerda's father was: Robert Ley, head of the German Labour Front from 1933 to 1945. He realizes he has 'unwittingly interviewed the child of one of Hitler's closest associates', and wonders, 'Did Gerda try to fool me, or does she really believe that her father did not know about the extermination of the Jews before the winter of 1944–45?' (128). After their following two interviews, each a year apart, Bar-On deduces that Gerda had never tried to deceive him but had set up a 'protective boundary … around her feelings for her father [that] allowed her to go on loving him and, perhaps, loving other people' (134). Gerda's experience depicts a relationship to the past that is heavy with denial. Despite the fact that her father's antisemitism is famously documented, she is unable to accept it as fact and chooses instead to portray him as the loving father she remembers him to have been. The live interview between Gerda and Bar-On is followed by a video projection of a third actor who reads out loud a letter. The letter was written by Gerda's father after his arrest but before his suicide and makes explicit his knowledge of the atrocities committed by the Nazi regime.

Gerda's face is seen only via the live-video feed projected on the screen. Neither she, nor the second interviewee, Rudolph, ever turn to face the audience during the course of the play, and in this way their identities can be said to remain hidden. On the other hand, the close camera angle allows the audience to observe the smallest shift in the actors' expressions as the faces of the interviewees are projected, larger than life, onto the screen above Bar-On. This staging physicalizes some of the contradictions played out in the course of the interviews. The audience shares the physical space of the theatre with the actors, and yet they encounter the actors' images only as mediated by the live-video projection.

For example, Gerda agrees to her interview on the sole condition that Bar-On does not try to ascertain her father's identity, and yet, as mentioned above, that is the first thing Bar-On does following their first meeting. Putting ethical issues of therapeutic confidentiality aside, one observes how the staging of the production physicalizes these tensions between private and public memory. Gerda shares her personal history with the understanding that it will be preserved as a private narrative. By uncovering her father's identity and publishing his name for the benefit of his readers, Bar-On draws Gerda's memories into place within her nation's history. In Kaluzhskii's production, the choice to have the interviewees sit with their backs to the audience is an embodied interpretation of anonymity. The actors do not see the spectators and focus solely on their conversations with Bar-On. Meanwhile, their every word, expression, and gesture is projected onto the screen for the audience's benefit. This staging draws attention to the relationship between intimacy and anonymity and thereby mirrors the tensions between private and public memory as portrayed in the text.

Figure 6: *Gruz molchaniia*, directed by Mikhail Kaluzhskii (2010)

The second interview in the play features Rudolph, the son of an unemployed textile worker who joined the Nazi party late in hopes that it might allow him to protect his Protestant church's congregation from persecution. During the war Rudolph's father was sent to Parafianovo in Belarus to work on the railroad where he became friends with a number of Jews living in the town. Rudolph, in distinction to his father, was seduced by the companionship and sense of superiority that came from his activity in the Hitler youth. He describes his evenings in a dimly lit room with black wallpaper, red benches, and the portrait of a famous Germanic king. Rudolph willingly admits that he was indoctrinated into the extreme antisemitic worldview and that he was ready to commit unjust acts of violence in support of the 'superior race'. '[W]e told stories about the ancient Germans, our Germanic forefathers. The Aryan race, which has the sole right to lead', Rudolph describes. 'We would sing songs in a minor key. It penetrated very deeply into our souls' (202). Rudolph's commitment to the Nazi party and to Hitler was a source of great tension between him and his father. 'It went without question', Rudolph recalls, 'in my eyes that what the Führer said and did was the truth. He was almost more of a God for me than the real God …' (202).

Rudolph tells Bar-On of how his father continued to visit the Jews in the ghetto of Parifianovo, to pray and to sing with them, until one morning when he woke to find that the SS had arrived and was marching the entire community out into an open field to be shot. Rudolph's father never recovered from having witnessed this massacre and was literally driven out of his mind by the memory of it. A few weeks after the shooting he was sent to an army hospital in Poland to be treated for hypertension, where his condition gradually worsened as he knew that he could not speak the truth of his experience to anyone around him. Eventually he was sent home, where his condition worsened further. Rudolph marks his father's history as the most influential element of his own identity formation,

> The thing that shaped and molded *me*, what influenced me, was that I was unable to comprehend what my father was talking about. I had been so fanatic about this idea of National Socialism ... But when he returned from Poland and told me these things – I was unable to understand various things by this time – I was unable to go on believing in it. (209; original emphasis)

At the end of his interview with Bar-On, Rudolph admits that this is the first time he has ever told his father's story. After seeing Bar-On's newspaper advertisement calling for interviews with children of the Third Reich, he understood that he needed to begin to tell his father's story in order fully to understand his own.

While the experiences of Rudolph's and Gerda's generation in Germany are vastly different from those of their generational counterparts in the Soviet Union, many audience members and critics were quick to identify central points of comparison. Every performance of *Legacy of Silence* was immediately followed by a discussion with the audience, the artists, and a rotating collection of moderators. Even though the production exclusively portrayed individuals who had struggled to come to terms with their own family's involvement in Germany's twentieth-century history, every post-show discussion came to revolve around the struggles Russian people face in *their* efforts to confront the complexities of Soviet history. By inviting audience members into dialogue about the culture of memory in contemporary Germany, the artists of *Legacy of Silence* created the space to address what Russian playwright Sasha Denisova called at the time 'one of the most contentious topics in contemporary theatre': the Soviet past (Denisova, 2011).

After the performance on 5 November 2011, human rights activist and director of Moscow's Sakharov Center, Sergei Lukashevskii, took to the stage to lead the conversation.[1] He gently acknowledged the heaviness of 'reprocessing the past' and invited audience members to share any feelings or impressions they might have had during the course of the show. 'It made me wonder', said the first speaker from the audience, 'if this really isn't enough for Russian people. Because even though we may not have had Fascism, a lot of terrifying things happened in the Soviet labour camps.'[2]

This audience member's comment may not appear especially remarkable at first reading. However, given the contested nature of Soviet history in contemporary Russia, opportunities to speak publicly and critically about the country's past are limited. What is further notable about this audience member's expression of concern is that she drew an immediate connection between the memories of one's personal past, as the people onstage had described them, and their historical significance on a national scale. Despite the apparent differences between the stories Gerda and Rudolph recount onstage and those of their primarily Russian audience members, *Legacy of Silence* audiences were quick to draw connections. Though the specifics of the discussions would vary depending on the audiences and the moderators, eventually the question always arose as to why such a project had never been undertaken to record people's memories of the Stalinist repressions. 'Where', an audience member would inevitably ask in one form or another, 'is the Russian *Legacy of Silence*?'

In the limited scope of production history, the answer to the question of why there was no 'Russian *Legacy of Silence*' was relatively straightforward. In 2007, writer and journalist Aleksandra Polivanova had begun work on a documentary project intended to stage a series of interviews with the children and grandchildren of men and women who had served under Stalin in the NKVD.[3] At the time, Polivanova was met with silence, as many of her targeted interviewees refused to share their family narratives in formal interviews. In the broader context of Russia's culture of commemorative practice, however, the precision and consistency of the audiences' question speaks directly to a longstanding cultural anxiety about the presence of the past in contemporary Russian culture. This is an anxiety that has been most effectively addressed by the founders of the Russian NGO Memorial and their ongoing efforts to preserve the historical memory of the Stalinist era.

Bring up the bodies

On 30 October 1989, more than a thousand people gathered outside KGB headquarters near the centre of Moscow to commemorate the deaths of their loved ones who had lost their lives to Soviet authoritarianism. The peaceful demonstration was organized by the newly formed civil rights organization and so-called 'historical enlightenment society', Memorial.

Demonstrators surrounded the Lubianka, a building famous for having accommodated the torture and murder of thousands of prisoners throughout the Soviet years, and, candles in hand, shared a moment of silence in honour of the deceased. Exactly a year later, an even larger crowd returned to the Lubianka to mourn the loss of their relatives and to bear witness to the unveiling of the Solovetskii Stone, a national monument to the victims of Soviet repression. The stone had been transported to Moscow from the infamous Solovetskii prison camp, one of hundreds of labour colonies that made up the Soviet Union's extensive Gulag network. The following year 30 October gained official recognition as the 'Day of Political Prisoners'.[4] Annual commemorations have continued outside the Lubianka where every year since 2007, from 29 to 30 October, the relatives of victims of Soviet terror come together to read aloud the names of people who were killed under Stalinism during a ceremony now known as 'Vozvrashchenie imen' (Return of the names). The list of names is compiled by Memorial and is read in alphabetical order for twelve hours by volunteers who often queue for hours in order to participate. Even after reciting name after name for twelve hours straight, participants hardly move through more than a small percentage of the victims' names and have to pick up from where they left off the following year.

According to Memorial's website, the organization was initially created to 'preserve the memory of the victims of political repression in the country's recent past'. In an early article entitled 'The Birth of Memorial' the founders describe their initiative: 'Memorial – is the search for truth both in the past and in the present. Memorial – is work in the archives, it is recording the stories of the repressed and the creation of monuments. The democratization of our society is Memorial's most important task' (Ianovskii, 1989: 1). One notable factor in Memorial's description of their mission as quoted here is the explicit connection the organization draws between the preservation of memories of the Soviet past and the possibility of a democratic future. Since 1987 Memorial has set up regional offices throughout Russia and other former Soviet countries. The organization has become increasingly involved in human rights activism and in efforts to raise public awareness about human rights violations throughout Russia and the former Soviet states.

Most pertinent to this book are Memorial's efforts to commemorate the victims of Stalinism and to make the details of Russia's twentieth-century history accessible to the public. Since successfully commissioning the Solovetskii Stone in 1990, Memorial has established dozens of other monuments to Gulag victims. They opened the first and only on-site Gulag museum, Perm-36, which was in operation from 1995 to 2014, when the museum closed due to withdrawal of support from regional organizations. In 2015, the museum grounds were taken over by local authorities and the territory was soon reopened as a museum that tells the story of the Gulag system, commemorating the work of the prison employees.[5] Information about Stalin's crimes was removed and the museum was converted from a space commemorating the victims of Stalinist terror to one that tells the story of its perpetrators (Khapaeva, 2016: 68).

Memorial continues to collect, record, and archive people's personal recollections of Soviet totalitarianism. Their local chapters have also overseen the process of identifying and exhuming scores of mass graves throughout Russia, Ukraine, and Belarus. According to Oleg Golovanov, coordinator of Memorial's mass grave-discovery efforts, there are approximately 100,000 unmarked mass graves on former Soviet territory which contain the remains of millions of victims of Soviet terror. In other words, as Golavonov phrased it in a 1989 interview with the Associated Press, 'This is a country built on bones' (Golavonov, in Adler, 1993: 95).

Memorial declares its dedication to the discovery and revelation of historical truth. In her article documenting the exhumation of a mass grave in Vinnytsia, Ukraine, Irina Paperno writes that Memorial is in search of 'What *really* happened' and 'how [we are] to live with it today' (2001: 109). In a country where the tragedies of the past have been constantly though incongruously hidden by the ruling party, Memorial's efforts to uncover the details of Russia's past have proven invaluable. It is largely within this space, between the unofficial uncovering of the past and the state's official concealment of the past, that the scholarly study of cultural memory in contemporary Russia has emerged.

In his 2013 book, *Warped Mourning: Stories of the undead in the land of the unburied*, Alexander Etkind introduces the terms 'hard' and 'soft' memory. Hard memory, according to Etkind, is signified by city monuments and architectural forms of commemoration that indicate a broad social consensus about the meaning of the past in the present. Soft memory, Etkind argues, is expressed primarily through texts and conversations in which public opinions about the meaning of the past are created and debated over time. According to the author, these two types of memory function interdependently to shape a society's relationship to the past. 'The hardening of memory is a cultural process with specific functions, conditions, and thresholds', Etkind writes. 'In a democratic society, it requires a relative degree of consensus in the public sphere. Such consensus follows after, and because, the intensity of the "soft" debates has reached a certain threshold' (2013: 246).

The notion that critical conversation can lead to a greater understanding of the past both within a community and within one's self is, of course, nothing revolutionary. In Russia in 2010 however, very little consensus had been reached about the meaning of the past in the present and that which was forming was heavily influenced by the Putin administration's approach to memory politics. This is one of the reasons that the 'soft debates' that took place after each performance of *Legacy of Silence* were especially significant at the time. According to Etkind, the lack of social consensus in Russia in the 2000s blocked the hardening of memory. 'Memory without memorials is vulnerable to a cyclical, recurrent process of refutations and denials' (246). Calling upon the work of Sigmund Freud, Etkind writes, 'If the suffering is not remembered, it will be repeated. If the loss is not recognized, it threatens to return in strange though not entirely new forms, as the uncanny. When the dead are not properly mourned, they turn into the undead and cause trouble for the living' (2013: 16).

Russia's inability to lay the past to rest, both literally and figuratively, has been a dominant theme in recent studies of the country's memory culture. According to Etkind, it is, in part, the lack of public engagement with the horrors of Russia's twentieth-century history that has riddled the country's current memory practice with a state of melancholia in which the country and its people appear unable sufficiently to distinguish between past and present, and are therefore prevented from processing their historical loss. Persistent reference to 'the undead' in Etkind's work evokes a particularly morbid resonance when considered in the context of Memorial's ongoing efforts to exhume the hundreds of mass graves found under forests and fields all across the former Soviet Union.

Legacy of Silence portrayed two German characters speaking with an Israeli psychologist about the impact memories of their personal and national pasts have had on their perceptions of themselves in the present. As the post-show discussions demonstrate, these conversations proved especially evocative for contemporary Russian audiences who, despite the apparent differences, often interpreted the performance of German cultural memory as an invitation to consider their own personal and national pasts. In this way, discussion of Germany's relationship to the atrocities of its twentieth-century history became an effective path to considering the complexities Russians face in their efforts to understand their relationships to their own country's totalitarian past.

Of course, there are certain points of dissonance that are important to consider in any comparison of the process Germany has undergone in its efforts to reconcile the country's past and present with the chance for a similar opportunity in Russia and the former Soviet Union. One major difference that cannot be overlooked is the fact that Stalinism began far earlier and lasted far longer in Russia than the Nazi regime did in Germany. Furthermore, distinguishing between victims and perpetrators can be significantly more difficult in Russia than in Germany. Many Gulag prisoners were politicians who had previously served under Stalin. And, perhaps most importantly, even though the Stalinist repressions brought terror to the country's citizens for years on end, a majority of citizens remained faithful to the Soviet ideology that facilitated those repressions even after Stalin's death in 1953. In fact, as historian Nanci Adler describes in her 2012 book *Keeping Faith with the Party: Communist believers return from the Gulag*, in distinction to Holocaust survivors, many political prisoners of the Stalinist era maintained their loyalty to the Communist party long after their release from the labour camps.

Adler's study testifies to the depth of commitment to the Soviet ideology many citizens experienced. Belief in the communist narrative persisted for many people throughout the late and post-Soviet years. As a result of this enduring attachment to Soviet mythology, many members of Russia's post-Soviet generation have faced the complex task of navigating not only the loss of their relatives to the violence of Stalinist terror, but also the loss of investment in the Soviet ideology that had dominated the public sphere for multiple previous generations. Those who came of age in the late and post-Soviet years were thus bridled with the necessity to process what Etkind has called 'double mourning' (2013: 12), i.e., the necessity to mourn the loss of their country's revolutionary ideals, and simultaneously to mourn the millions of lives that were taken as a result of the implementation of those ideals.

In other words, one of the risks of uncovering the past and commemorating the dead in Russia is that the process is likely to bring up even more than the hundreds of thousands of unidentified bodies Golavonov and his colleagues continue to uncover with every passing year. For many Russian families, it is not only belief in and understanding of the past that is at stake in a commemoration of the deceased, it is in fact the very nature of belief that is called into question through exploration of the Soviet past. Though most people in Russia are well aware of the atrocities committed under Stalinist rule, many people maintain investment in certain elements of Soviet ideology to this day.

By welcoming the stories of the dead into the living space of the present, the creators of *Legacy of Silence* asked audience members to join them in their attempts to sort through those narratives and to articulate the tragic aspects of their own pasts at the risk of raising difficult questions about the present. Does Gerda's denial about her father's knowledge of the Nazi persecution of the Jews, and her need to construct a protective barrier around her memories of him, in some way mirror the complexities of how Russians might relate to their families' Soviet pasts? How does

Rudolph's confession of his former need to believe in a totalitarian system responsible for the murder of millions come to bear on the stories the play's Russian audience members may have heard from their parents and grandparents? These are among the primary questions raised by performances of *Legacy of Silence* and are also central to an understanding of the next play in the cycle, *Second Act. Grandchildren*.

Second Act. Grandchildren

After approximately a year of performing *Legacy of Silence* at the Sakharov Center, Kaluzhskii and Polivanova began again to approach the living relatives of former members of the NKVD and KGB. The successful results of those interviews premiered as a full production in 2012. Upon arrival at the Sakharov Center for a performance of *Second Act. Grandchildren*, each audience member receives a ticket with a seat number. The chairs are set in a large circle, each with a small number taped to the armrest. There are two television monitors set up on stands on either side of the circle. Though, like all of the Sakharov Center theatre programming, the production is free, admission is limited to thirty-five audience members per performance: everyone must reserve a place in advance. One audience member described the experience in a blog,

> You enter the space and they give you a ticket with your seat number on it. You look around the circle for your seat (the seat numbers aren't in order). Sit down. Someone is already seated, someone is looking for their seat like you were just doing. Someone is buried in their telephone, someone is chatting, someone goes outside for a smoke. There are no actors. Only people, just like you.[6]

The impression that 'there are no actors. Only people, just like you' is an essential element to the atmosphere of the performance. Before the play even begins, the audience is posited within the same space as the performers.

When all the seats are occupied, digits begin to flash on the two television screens set on either side of the circle, eventually settling on one number. A woman in the circle begins to speak: 'When I talk to my daughter about her relatives, it's not always simple. She never asks me about it herself, never asks about any of it. But I tell her anyway' (Kaluzhskii and Polivanova, 2012: 1). The speaker continues to share with the audience how she once told her daughter that her great-grandfather worked for the railroads that transported millions of people to their deaths. After a few minutes, the numbers begin to flash again and another speaker is called upon to continue with the story of his or her personal family history.

There are nine monologues in the original production. The actors speak them in short segments interspersed with one another. Depending on the performance, some of the actors may appear on video only, shown on the same screens where the numbers flash. The content of the monologues varies from those that are more factual to those that are more self-reflective. What they have in common is that they are all reports of intergenerational conversations about the Soviet past in Russia. There are moments of great weight, and moments of shared laughter. The mood in the room shares something with that of a twelve-step meeting. The speakers appear to unburden themselves through their acts of confession, and gain acceptance through the practice of shared conversation.

One of the speakers recounts how as a child he and his family used to go to visit his grandparents at their dacha. 'They always had guests', the speaker remembers, 'Everybody would be eating and singing. There were these wonderful dogs there,' he recalls, 'and horses, and these people – zeks – who looked after everybody. Grandpa was an officer on the Moscow-Volga canal project in Iakhroma. And, well, this so-called "dacha" was actually a prison camp. Dmitrovlag' (2012: 2).

Another speaker, Evgeniia, recounts how fondly her mother remembered her time as a student in the Law Faculty at Moscow State University where she enjoyed the lectures of Professor Andrei Ianurevich Vyshinskii, the state prosecutor of Stalin's Great Purge trials of the 1930s. 'She always used to tell me how he was a real professor and how he even knew Latin! And I would try to tell her that Andrei Ianurevich was not only a "real professor".' To which Evgeniia's mother would respond, 'But he gave such great academic lectures. He was always well-shaven, his grey hair was so handsome. He always wore a well-pressed suit, and he gave his lectures in a big communist auditorium.' As Evgeniia describes it, she would then ask her mother, 'Mum, how can you talk about him like that? He's an executioner responsible for the deaths of millions.' To which her mother would respond, 'I know. But he gave such great lectures' (2012: 9).

The stories the actors recount in the production are both beguiling and familiar. *Second Act. Grandchildren* highlights the ubiquitous nature of these narratives by calling out the seat numbers of not only the actors, but also those of the audience members. As the seat numbers flash on the screen, you soon begin to realize that yours could be next. In this way, members of the public are invited to contribute their family histories as well. According to my 2013 interview with Kaluzhskii and Polivanova, it is admittedly rare for an audience member to speak up when his or her number appears on the screen, though it has been known to happen. Nonetheless, the mere invitation for audience members to speak their own narratives draws attention to the fact that the stories the audience members hear from the actors are no more or less remarkable than their own. The way the performance is staged draws audience members' attention to the fact that whether your relatives were among the repressors, the repressed, or, as was often the case, both, everyone whose family lived through the Soviet years has a story worth telling.

One of the actors describes the conflicted nature of remembering the past in the post-Soviet context when she admits, 'It's not clear how we should feel about it. Should we be proud of it? Who the hell knows?' She goes on, 'Can you be proud of the fact that your relatives murdered people? But on the other hand, you think, well, they basically built the country. It might have been screwed up, but they had a dream, and they were ready to die for it, to sacrifice their children' (28). Such a sentiment is a clear example of precisely the 'double mourning' Etkind describes. The speaker is attempting to reconcile the destructive actions of her relatives with their deeply held belief in the ideals of Socialism. The texts in *Second Act. Grandchildren* depict a generation of Russians who are not always sure what to believe when it comes to certain sides of their Soviet pasts. This inner conflict is one of the contradictory but common sentiments depicted by the actors in *Second Act. Grandchildren*.

Figure 7: *Vtoroi akt. Vnuki*, directed by Mikhail Kaluzhskii (2012)

Another central paradox of Russian cultural memory depicted in the play is discussion about whether individuals were or were not aware of what went on under the Stalinist regime. After her father's death, Evgeniia, for example, whose mother studied law under Andrei Vyshinskii at Moscow State University, began asking her mother questions about the repressions, to which her mother would respond, 'We knew nothing. We didn't know anything about the repressions.' Evgeniia reports asking her mother, 'How could you have known nothing about the repressions? Half your family was in prison' (28). Evgeniia's questions speak directly to the intricacies of Russian cultural memory, the fact that many families include both victims and perpetrators. And in truth, there were many individuals who personified such a contradiction even within their own experiences.

In her review of the production, *Radio svoboda* cultural critic Maria Shubina describes her experience of watching the play and trying to think of what she might say about her own family if her number were to come up on the screen. 'I never had anything like that', Shubina writes, 'My great-grandmother and great-grandfather were wonderful people. He [sic] built bridges and roads' (2012). Shubina recounts how she decides that if her number comes up on the screen she will keep silent. Meanwhile she waits in horror for that flashing number 34. But then, she suddenly remembers her great-grandfather on the other side who she describes as a 'gloomy and stingy man' and who she had somehow learned once worked for the civil service. This memory which had been dredged up from underneath those more pleasant memories of her family narrative inspired her to think about new questions of injustice and evil. 'And then,' she says, 'at that moment when the thirty minutes had passed and we'd already come to the end, I wanted to be with them, with those who spoke out and told their different histories. I was looking forward to the moment when number 34 would light up – I was ready to say that I too could finally speak up' (Shubina, 2012).

The narratives the actors speak in the play are full of personal details that lend each story elements of irony and humour alongside notes of melancholy and contemplation. Each history is different of course, and yet they all share a common theme, the experience of living adult lives in post-perestroika Russia and taking on the responsibility of an attempt to sort through the complexities embedded in the country's relationship to its Soviet past. *Second Act. Grandchildren* does not try to make sense of or set straight such complexities. It is rather an attempt to interrupt the silence about Stalinism and the country's twentieth-century history. In other words, it is an enactment of precisely the type of 'soft debate' Etkind identifies as necessary for the building of consensus about the past.

Analogous conversations about Soviet history do take place in other cultural spheres including film, literature, and art in twenty-first-century Russia. However, to enact such conversations in the context of the theatre, I argue, provides an unusual opportunity for the transmission and representation of cultural memory that is unique to the physical practice of performance. In its characteristically ghostly approach, theatre facilitates an embodiment of historical narratives by staging a live intervention between past and present. The actors perform the texts from the past and act as stand-ins for those who spoke them first. 'To perform in this sense', as Joseph Roach writes, 'means to bring forth, to make manifest, and to transmit.' Although, as Roach reminds his readers, 'To perform also means, though often more secretly, to reinvent' (1996: 1). How then, it is important to ask, does the physical process of performing the past in *Legacy of Silence* and *Second Act. Grandchildren* both reify and reinvent narratives of the past through its live intervention into the present?

Embodying the archive

Memorial provides an invaluable resource for the preservation of cultural memory in contemporary Russia. In order to maintain the memory of the victims of Stalinism, the organization has sought to create a reliable and accessible archive of Russian historical artifacts. In many ways, the techniques applied in documentary plays like *Legacy of Silence* and *Second Act. Grandchildren* are analogous to those used by Memorial and their efforts to build monuments, establish archives, and open museums all for the explicit purpose of uncovering and preserving historical truths. Like Memorial's initiatives, many documentary plays are also concerned with the veracity of documents from the Soviet past and the validity of their evidentiary status in the present. Both Memorial and documentary theatre artists use documentation and representation of personal narratives to tell a national history. By revealing the intimate connection between private memory and public history, both practices confront the contradictory impulses inherent to 'double mourning', and challenge certain beliefs that sometimes go unquestioned in Russia's post-Soviet interpretations of the past.

It is clear, then, that there are commonalities between Russian documentary theatre and rituals of commemoration. The notion that theatre can come to constitute a ritual space is, of course, an idea at the foundation of performance studies. In their initial investigations into the pathways between theatre and anthropology, Richard Schechner and Victor Turner argued that, '"Experimental" theatre is nothing less than "performed," in other words, "restored" experience, that moment in the experiential process – that often prolonged and internally segmented "moment" – in which meaning emerges through "reliving" the original experience' (Turner, 1982: 18). As Turner and Schechner extended this line of thinking they explored how theatre and ritual are two performance practices that have the potential to construct a liminal space in which, 'entities are neither here nor there; they are betwixt and between the positions assigned and arrayed by law, custom, convention, and ceremonial' (Turner, 1977: 95). That is to say that theatre, like ritual, creates a space for transformation.

As this chapter has sought to demonstrate, Russian documentary theatre productions like *Legacy of Silence* and *Second Act. Grandchildren* occupy a liminal space in which both artists and audiences are invited to participate in a ritual of remembering. By coming together to share in the re-telling of historical narratives, the participants of Russian documentary theatre both remember and re-negotiate their perceptions of their national history. In this sense, the ritual performance of *Second Act. Grandchildren* mirrors Memorial's annual gathering outside the Lubianka in which volunteers read out loud the names of the victims of Stalinist terror. In the words of memory scholars Warwick Frost and Jennifer Laing, both gatherings are 'staged so that society may remember and reflect upon past occurrences and their relationship to today' (2013: 1). However, there are also some essential differences between these two types of commemorative rituals that are worth noting at this time.

Unlike the commemorations staged by Memorial, documentary theatre practice employs a uniquely embodied form of remembering that extends beyond the preservation of memory through the collection and recitation of archival sources. The practice of performing texts and narratives from the past in the present in Russia's documentary theatre repertoire offers participants an opportunity to engage in a ritual of remembering that not only recalls the narratives of the past but also enacts the past in such a way as to make it operable in the present. In the case of *Second Act. Grandchildren*, for example, artists and audiences gather in memory of the deceased. Together they embody and thereby interact with the narratives of the past that are spoken in the present. In this way, the creators and performers of the play use the practice of repetition and surrogation to make manifest a uniquely theatrical form of commemorative ritual. They both recollect the event in the past and welcome the ghosts of that past into the present.

In differentiating between these two types of commemorative practices, we are reminded of Diana Taylor and her discussion of embodied memory as detailed in the introduction. Taylor, we recall, shifts her readers' attention from the popular notion that knowledge is transmitted through the written word and toward a belief that alternative bodies of knowledge can also be transmitted through performance practice. She distinguishes what she calls 'archival memory' from what she identifies as 'embodied memory'. In doing so, Taylor observes how embodied commemorative practices offer an alternate route to remembering, one enacted through embodied experience and co-presence. In this way, she writes, 'people participate in the production and reproduction of knowledge by "being there", being a part of the transmission' (2003: 20). In the case of *Legacy of Silence* and *Second Act. Grandchildren*, audiences bear witness to the personal narratives shared and, in both productions, are invited to contribute stories of their own. It is not necessarily the way the actors move that qualifies these performances as forms of embodied remembering. It is rather the fact that their stories about the past are reenacted in the live space of the theatre and, in that sense, serve to recall moments from the past into the ritual space of the present.

The concept of embodied memory is also at the centre of Rebecca Schneider's argument that historical reenactment stages the possibility of a 'twenty-first-century body interacting with traces of acts of history' (2011: 33). As Schneider observes, Civil War reenactors often approach their performance practice with an obsessive attention to material detail. Their commitment to material accuracy, she suggests, grows from a desire to *feel* what their historical predecessors are thought to have *felt* in the past. By reconstructing historically accurate costumes and enlisting the use of period-specific objects, Schneider's book argues that historical reenactors create the possibility for the past and present to *touch*. Not unlike historical reenactors, the actors (or perhaps more accurately reenactors) of *Legacy of Silence* and *Second Act. Grandchildren* bring events from the past into the present moment in order to make manifest contact between past and present. However, in distinction to historical reenactment, performances like *Legacy of Silence* and *Second Act. Grandchildren* make no attempt at material accuracy in that they consciously reject any effort towards verisimilitude. It is therefore important to ask: if there is no attempt to mimic the original speakers and thus no effort to accurately reproduce a material moment from the past, can these plays really be said to *touch* history in the manner that Schneider suggests?

As critic Pavel Rudnev wrote in his review of *Legacy of Silence* for the website *Chastnyi correspondent*, 'There is essentially no event, no extra direction, no "roles". We don't see actors playing their parts – we see people onstage' (2013). Speaking from my experience, as one of those people onstage, I can confirm that the performers in these plays have no intention of playing parts in the traditional sense. We rather aimed to speak the texts in such a way as to bring the narratives of the past into the mutable space of the present. By speaking without any pretence of playing a character and simply welcoming the texts into the physical space of the theatre, both artists and audiences were offered access to an alternative body of knowledge, that of embodied recollection.

In Russia's twenty-first-century documentary theatre repertoire, it is the narratives themselves that are brought forth in performance through embodied practice and made materially present in the space. In other words, it is the act of both speaking and hearing the texts, within the live context of the theatre that lends the words their materiality, their embodied relevance in the moment of performance. The plays under discussion in this chapter are therefore not only made up of constative utterances, to use Austin's terms, they are performative. They not only describe and reflect the speakers' experiences of the past; the act of performing these plays has the capacity to transform individuals' perceptions of the present. According to Austin, words spoken in the context of the theatre are 'infelicitous' and lack the capacity to be performative. However, as this chapter has demonstrated, *Legacy of Silence* and *Second Act. Grandchildren* are performative in that they create the space for change. By virtue of gaining literal contact with the narratives spoken onstage, participants of both productions do indeed gain the opportunity to *touch* history through their theatrical practice.

It is in this moment of contact between past and present that Russian documentary theatre transforms the narratives of the past into something operative in the present. By reenacting the spoken narratives of the past and creating the space for past and present to *touch*, Russia's documentary theatre artists enact precisely the type of critical public dialogue about the past that the actors onstage simultaneously seek to represent. In this way, their performance of history can be said to make manifest the narratives of the past, simply in the new context of the present tense. The actors and audiences of *Legacy of Silence* and *Second Act. Grandchildren* do not merely gather to remember the past and thereby mark it as absent. They rather recall, re-present, and recuperate the narratives of the past so as to bring them into the here and now. In other words, the stories told by both actors and audiences in performances of *Legacy of Silence* and *Second Act. Grandchildren* are spoken not only in memory of those who first recounted the narratives, they are indeed spoken in anamnesis of them.

As this chapter's analysis of *Legacy of Silence* and *Second Act. Grandchildren* has demonstrated, Russian documentary theatre artists use archival material to construct a new kind of cultural repertoire. They employ the liminality of theatrical representation in order to create a ritual space in which the narratives of the past are made mutable in the present. In their efforts to depict a culture of commemoration, one that may not be reflected in the artists' and audiences' everyday lives, Russia's documentary theatre repertoire manages to enact precisely the process of critical inquiry it seeks to represent. The cumulative effect of Russia's uneasy relationship to documents and historical archives, in combination with the culture's penchant for non-linear approaches to historiography, has made Russian documentary theatre a particularly potent space for the performance of memory in contemporary Russian culture.

Uncovering the hidden and forgotten

As Freddie Rokem wrote, 'the notion of performing history can clearly be distinguished from documents exhibited in a museum, where something from the past, instead of being reenacted on the stage, is preserved, displayed, and perhaps even constructed like an archeological site' (2000: 6). Kaluzhskii notably also uses the metaphor of an archeological site to describe his plays, but rather than conceive of them as a static or completed display of archeological findings, he compares the act of both creating and performing the plays to that of excavation. In his March 2012 talk delivered at the University of Cambridge entitled *Performing Memory*, Kaluzhskii claimed that it is the 'active process of uncovering the hidden and forgotten, that makes performing memory so productive' (Kaluzhskii, 2012).

This 'active process' of which Kaluzhskii speaks is one that extends from the conception and production of the play through to the ritual of performance. The actors of *Legacy of Silence* and *Second Act. Grandchildren* extend an invitation to the audience to re-experience the narratives of the past and in that sense bear new witness to their significance in the present. Through the repetition of their texts, and the embodied reenactment of conversations from the past, both artists and audiences take up their archeological tools and set to work uncovering memories, some inescapably haunting and some long forgotten, but all brought to life again within the bare brick walls of Moscow's Sakharov Center.

Since the premiere of *Legacy of Silence* in 2010, several other projects have appeared in Moscow's documentary theatre repertoire that look explicitly at national narratives of the Soviet past and their relationship to the present. In the spring of 2012 Memorial began its own programme for the development of documentary theatre projects. Polivanova, who is also the curator for cultural programming at Memorial's Moscow office, began collaborating with Georg Genoux, Pavel Rudnev, and a number of local artists to establish Memorial's small lecture hall and gallery space as a new documentary theatre venue. The space opened in June 2012 with the 'Memory Drama' festival, an event that featured lectures, performances, and master-classes from many of Russia's leading documentary theatre practitioners. The festival also premiered a collection of new documentary theatre projects including one play that staged the trial of Joseph Brodskii, another composed of texts from recorded conversations between police radios during the storming of the White House in 1993, and a third which explored the relevance of nineteenth-century philosopher Petr Chadaaev's writings to the history of political prisoners in Russia. Though the repertoire of Memorial's documentary theatre venue appears to largely have faded since the festival, a number of the plays which premiered in the space continued to run in other venues in Moscow and tour to cities around Russia and Eastern Europe.

Teatr.doc has also premiered several important productions that incorporate Soviet historical documents as source material since that time. Boris Pavlovich's 2013 production *Viatlag*, for example, stages a reading of entries from the diaries of the Soviet political prisoner Artur Stradin. In 2016, director Anastasiia Patlai premiered her production *Kantgrad*, a play that uses texts from interviews with the residents from the German city Königsberg which was occupied by the Soviet army in 1945 and renamed Kaliningrad in 1946. Patlai's play features the story of a German man and a Russian woman who fell in love at the time of the occupation and reflect in their interviews on their experience of sharing their lives together as supposed enemies in contested territory ever since. Patlai also curates a theatre programme at the Sakharov Center entitled 'The Archeology of Memory'. Founded in 2015 in collaboration with theatre critic Daria Aksenova, the initiative hosts a series of ongoing documentary theatre laboratories dedicated to exploring the significance of the Soviet past in the present.

The task set out by Kaluzhskii, Polivanova, and Genoux may have seemed a simple one: to begin a conversation about the past. However, in practice the journey from the opening of *Legacy of Silence* through to the premiere of *Second Act. Grandchildren* required a strong commitment from many contributors. From the actors and artists involved in the plays to the production teams, from the Sakharov Center staff to the support of those at the Goethe-Institut, it can be surprising how many supporters it took to create the space for a 'soft debate' about Russia's Soviet history. Though Polivanova and Kaluzhskii do not yet have plans for a third production, they chose their title of *Second Act. Grandchildren* to leave the option open for future projects to follow within the series. For though the progression from *Legacy of Silence* to *Second Act. Grandchildren* is significant, and the appearance of further documentary programming that explicitly addresses the country's relationship to its past is a sign of progress, it is clear that in many ways the critical conversation about the Soviet past in twenty-first-century Russia has only just begun.

Notes

1 In my discussion of the post-show conversation I draw on my own experience of having attended all of the post-show discussions between May 2010 and June 2011, and also the benefit of access to the complete video archive from 2010 to 2012.
2 As spoken during a post-show discussion and recorded on a video shared with me by the play's directors. Here and throughout *Witness onstage* I include quotations from the audio and video recordings of post-show discussions to illustrate the way audience members articulate their reactions to documentary theatre productions.
3 This was a process Polivanova described to me during our interview held on 25 May 2013 at the *DNK* New Play Festival in Krasnoiarsk.
4 The date of 30 October was initially marked as an unofficial day of remembrance in 1974 by several political prisoners who began a hunger strike while imprisoned in Perm and Mordovia as a simultaneous press conference was held in the home of Andrei Sakharov to call attention to their protest. Though the day was commemorated privately throughout the late Soviet era, it was only recognized officially by the state after perestroika in 1991.
5 For more on the new museum, see the Russian language *Radio svoboda* video at https://www.svoboda.org/a/26885761.html (accessed 24 August 2018).
6 This text is excerpted from a blog post by an author who is identified as Agata B. (2012), 'Vtoroi akt. Vnuki' (26 February), http://agata-w.livejournal.com/80808.html (accessed 4 February 2017).

3

Evidentiary hearing
The pursuit of justice in Russian documentary theatre

The year 2010 was an important turning point for Russian documentary theatre practice. Until that time, the works of Russia's documentary theatre artists were primarily focused on giving voice to otherwise marginalized members of society. Many of Teatr.doc's best known productions from the collective's early years were focused on specific communities or subcultures which would not otherwise have been represented on the Russian stage. For example, *Bezdomnye* (*The Homeless*, 2001–03) by Maksym Kurochkin and Aleksandr Rodionov, and *Voina Moldovan za kartonnuiu korobku* (*The War of the Moldovans for a Cardboard Box*, 2003) by Rodionov were both constructed from interviews with Moscow's homeless population. Vadim Levanov's *Sto pudov liubvi* (*A Hundred Pounds of Love*, 2002) portrayed the lives of pop-star fanatics. Elena Isaeva's play *Pervyi muzhchina* (*The First Man*, 2003) was constructed from interviews with women who were emotionally abused by their fathers. And Olga Darfi's *Trezvyi PR* (*Sober PR*, 2004) depicted the lives of media specialists, political technologists, and television producers. These plays, along with many others, were constructed in such a way as to offer audiences insight into the mechanics of everyday life in different subsections of society. In this way, the plays served to bridge the space between the stories of those commonly thought of as abnormal or social outliers and the so-called 'normal' discourse of everyday life. Such works were not constructed to express an overt social stance, although their attempts to represent the realities of everyday life in twenty-first-century Russia were, as this book argues, an inherently political practice.

The 2010 production *One Hour Eighteen Minutes* extended the methodology used in the plays described above. However, in distinction to those projects, the creators of *One Hour Eighteen Minutes* used their documentary approach explicitly to speak out against institutional corruption and the frequent disregard for human rights among Russia's network of political elites. The play resembled earlier verbatim works in its stripped-down approach to performance and in the way the speakers onstage spoke their texts directly to the audience with no illusion of a fourth wall. In distinction to the earlier works described above, however, *One Hour Eighteen Minutes* made no attempt to blunt or obfuscate its purposeful political edge. Since that time, and particularly since the 2011–13 protest wave in Russia, Teatr.doc and Russian documentary theatre more broadly have become widely recognized as symbols of political opposition. The company has produced several controversial works such as the production *Dvoe v tvoem dome* (*Two in Your Home*, 2012), which portrays the house arrest of Belarusian poet and activist Vladimir Nekliaev, and the project *Bolotnoe delo* (*Bolotnoe Case*, 2015), a play built from interviews with the relatives of imprisoned political protestors. In this sense, *One Hour Eighteen Minutes* can be seen as the start to a new chapter in Russia's documentary theatre practice as the form became increasingly associated with the country's

Figure 8: *Dvoe v tvoem dome*, directed by Mikhail Ugarov (2012)

opposition movement, particularly following Putin's return to the presidency in 2012.

Described by its creators as 'a trial that never was but should have been' (sud kotorogo ne bylo, no kotoryi dolzhen byt), *One Hour Eighteen Minutes* uses a combination of imagined, reconstructed, and verbatim texts from statements, articles, and interviews with the doctors, judges, and prison employees involved in the days before the murder of Russian attorney Sergei Magnitsky. After uncovering the biggest tax fraud in Russian history, Magnitsky was arrested on fabricated charges in November 2008 and held in government custody for over eleven months before he died on 16 November 2009 (eight days before the Russian legal limit of one year's detention without a trial). Magnitsky was detained after having testified against a group of corrupt government officials who initiated and participated in the theft of $230 million from the Russian government. He was arrested by the very officials he had testified against.

Though it was clear for years from his prison diary that he had been severely mistreated throughout his imprisonment, the details of Magnitsky's abuse have since been published in a 2012 report commissioned by Hermitage Capital (the investment company that had hired him as outside counsel for the case that led to his arrest).[1] The report details the human rights violations that took place, including repeated denial of medical care and beatings by prison staff in the hour preceding his death. Despite the international outcry from human rights groups, no one was held legally responsible for Magnitsky's death. In September 2011, two doctors were dismissed from the Butyrka detention centre for having failed to diagnose Magnitsky with diabetes and hepatitis, two illnesses he never had. In April 2012 the charges against the former prison doctor Larisa A. Litvinova were dismissed. Two years after Magnitsky's death, Russia's Interior Ministry declared that it was in fact Magnitsky himself who had stolen the $230 million of tax receipts from the government; and, in the summer of 2013, Magnitsky was found posthumously guilty of this theft, thus making Putin, in the words of legal historian Sadakat Kadri, 'the first western leader in a thousand years to prosecute a dead man' (2013).

The injustice of Magnitsky's arrest, imprisonment, and murder, as well as repeated attempts to cover up the institutional corruption in the handling of his case, were the initial inspiration for the artists of Teatr.doc to begin work on their production. The play consists of a series of 'testimonies', monologues performed sequentially in the style of a trial. *One Hour Eighteen Minutes* was the first Russian documentary play to use the construct of the courtroom format, a sub-genre of documentary theatre-making that has been widely practiced internationally since the early twentieth century. Following the premiere of *One Hour Eighteen Minutes*, several other Russian documentary theatre projects arose that used the trial structure to explore and expose injustice in the civic sphere. With *One Hour Eighteen Minutes* at its centre, this chapter explores the culturally specific connotations of documentary trial plays in twenty-first-century Russia. It illustrates how Russia's documentary theatre artists appropriate core elements of Soviet judicial methodology in order to address corruption in the country's current legal infrastructure. In this way, Chapter 3 investigates the interdependent relationship between the performance of testimony and the constitution of justice in Russian documentary theatre practice and uncovers the ominously intimate association between theatre and trials in contemporary Russian culture.

The trial begins

As they enter Teatr.doc's small black-box theatre for a performance of *One Hour Eighteen Minutes*, audience members each receive a 'briefing on the play' (instruktsiia k spektakliu). Included in the briefing are a summary of the events that immediately preceded Magnitsky's death, a note from director Mikhail Ugarov about why Teatr.doc felt it was important to create a performance on the subject, and a list of the play's 'characters' in order of appearance. The list begins with Magnitsky's mother, followed by the prison and medical staff who were directly involved in her son's last days. They are each identified by name and surname, 'so that', Ugarov writes, 'they can come to the theatre and see themselves'.[2] While the audience files in, the actors sit casually onstage, waiting, as is later revealed, to be called to the stand.

Once seated, the audience members of *One Hour Eighteen Minutes* are directed by one of the actors onstage to read the briefing. 'Item one,' a second actor firmly announces, 'Natalia Nikolaevna Magnitskaya, Mother' (Gremina, 2010: 1). The actor representing Magnitsky's mother stands and steps to the front of the stage. In her verbatim monologue the actor speaks the words of Magnitsky's mother as she recalls the experience of going to see her son's body in the morgue. She describes how she noticed bruises on his wrists and knuckles and wondered with whom he had been fighting. The speaker proceeds to state her accusations against the government officials responsible for her son's arrest, the prison employees liable for his torture, and the medical staff accountable for his final days. In this opening monologue, Natalia Magnitskaya specifies each person by name, thereby introducing the series of monologues to follow. Included

Figure 9: *Chas vosemnadtsat*, directed by Mikhail Ugarov (2010)

in the list of defendants are Oleg Silchenko, the head of the criminal proceedings against Magnitsky; Judge Elena Stashina, who repeatedly ruled to prolong Magnitsky's detention and refused her prisoner's request for medical care four days before he died; and Aleksandra Gauss, the doctor in charge of his medical treatment.

The actors appear onstage in everyday clothes. There is no set, except for a row of chairs lining the upstage wall. True to the theatre's slogan, 'Theatre without acting' (Teatr, v kotorom ne igraiut), the actors in *One Hour Eighteen Minutes* do not play characters or attempt to mimic the real-life figures they represent. They speak directly to the audience with no pretence of a fourth wall and, in this way, cast their audiences in the roles of judge, jury, and prosecutor. Actors present their evidence to the individuals in the audience who are asked to judge for themselves not only the figures represented onstage, but also the state system that facilitated their actions. Each time the testimonies are presented, which is to say each time the play is performed, audience members are presented an opportunity to engage in a collective process of judgement and to bear witness to the events under discussion.

Given that so many of the events surrounding Magnitsky's murder were concealed behind the closed doors of the prison and the courtroom, *One Hour Eighteen Minutes* offers both audiences and artists a unique opportunity to come together and to see for themselves the sinister corruption and the abundant apathy that led to this innocent man's death. The (primarily imagined) monologues spoken onstage stand in as surrogates for testimonies the defendants were never required to perform. The texts resemble courtroom testimonies in that the speakers defend their actions and attempt to verify their innocence. However, the testimonies also serve a secondary function in the context of this performance.

As legal-literature scholar Jan-Melissa Schramm writes, 'Testimony is a richly multivalent term' (2010: 478). Performed 'in the first person by those who seek to bear witness to the role of traumatic events in the formation of larger historical narratives', testimony has come frequently to signify an act of justice in and of itself (2010: 478). In the courtroom it is regarded as one of the most influential forms of evidence. Outside the courtroom, testimony means the practice of confessing one's personal and historical narratives. In both instances, testimony requires a witness (eyewitness, character witness, material witness, and so on) and a body of judgement (in the courtroom this usually means a judge or jury, or both). For justice to be served in the juridical sense or in the historical sense, a testimony must be both spoken and heard.

The necessity for testimony to be both spoken and heard is a feature the practice shares notably with the theatre. As Jerzy Grotowski argued in development of his 'poor theatre' model in the late-1960s, the only essential elements of the theatre are an actor and a spectator. At that time, Grotowski believed that while one could strip away all other elements of theatrical performance (design, director, text) and still call it theatre, without at least one performer and at least one spectator there would be no theatre. 'We can thus define theatre', Grotowski writes, 'as that which takes place between the actor and the spectator' (Grotowski, 1968: 32). That is to say that theatre is, in part, created through the exchange between an actor and a spectator, in the relationship and interaction between the two.

In the courtroom, it is as a direct result of the judge or jury's consideration of evidence as provided through testimony that a defendant is found either guilty or not guilty. Directly, through shared testimony, a society uses the rituals of the courtroom to define a code of societal ethics. In this sense, the speaking and hearing of testimony, whatever the verdict, enacts its own mode of justice. In other words, to use Grotowski's model, one could argue that *justice* is that which takes place between a speaking witness and a listening juror. Now, if we are to accept the notion that the speaking and the hearing of testimony has the capacity to make justice manifest, then how are we to interpret the ambiguity of representation in Teatr.doc's 'trial that never was'?

In the absence of an official legal trial, the artists at Teatr.doc collected evidence and assembled a jury in order to carry out the judicial proceedings the Russian government never managed to arrange. The actors stand in for the defendants, and the audience members act as surrogates for the jurists. A theatre trial may not carry the legal repercussions of a court trial, but there is no doubt that testimonies are spoken and judgements are made. The notion that justice can be constituted through the proclamation and reception of testimony sheds new light on Teatr.doc's 'trial that should have been' – a trial that is arguably enacted each time the play is performed. The actors of *One Hour Eighteen Minutes* present their testimonies for judgement and in this way use their performance to construct the atmosphere of a trial. Though, in another sense, *One Hour Eighteen Minutes* actually constructs a trial.

Reasonable doubt

Despite the fact that many of the figures represented are directly implicated in the crimes against Magnitsky, they deny any responsibility for the events that led to his death. Showing more concern for their own wellbeing than for any idea of justice, the defendants continually point to the depravity of the system as a whole as justification for their actions. In this way, the testimonies presented begin to complicate the question of who, or even what, is on trial. One such monologue is spoken by an actor representing Dr Gauss who, after diagnosing her patient with acute pancreatitis, called the emergency medical team and then waited in her office for one hour and eighteen minutes, only returning to the prison cell to verify that Magnitsky had already died. The title of the play is derived from this precise interval of time between the moment when Gauss reported Magnitsky's potentially critical condition and when she returned to the prison cell to find that he had already died. She describes the unhygienic conditions in the prison to justify her aloof attitude towards her job. 'It's dangerous just to be here at all', the doctor claims. 'You think all we have is a little dust floating in the air? Hepatitis. And that dirt there, under your feet? Tuberculosis. And bites? Bites, bites! A prisoner bites you, and you get HIV. We've had that happen. And after all that, we still make three times less than civilian doctors' (Gremina, 2010: 8). Gauss adamantly defends her handling of the case; she is one of numerous figures represented in the play who cites her salary as a primary reason for her lack of investment in her work.

Investigator Silchenko's monologue also includes discussion of his salary as he charges the wealthy with responsibility for Magnitsky's death and claims that he and his colleagues in the Interior Ministry are victims of the corruption of an elite business culture. 'They are the ones who are guilty,' he tells the audience, 'those in prison, their friends and relatives … You know, he was the lawyer of criminals … You spell it "businessmen" but it's pronounced "thieves"' (5). As Silchenko's text indicates, the spread of corrupt legal and financial practices has become ingrained in so much of life in contemporary Russia, it can be difficult to parse degrees of responsibility and complicity.

Later in the play, Judge Elena Stashina answers a series of questions that she reads from a document onstage. At first, the questions appear to be completely unrelated to the case. Questions like, 'Are you ever late for a hearing?' 'Did your grandfather fight in the war?' 'In the morning, do you have your eggs hard or soft-boiled?' (11). The questions become increasingly absurd until both the audience and the speaker appear to realize what is happening. 'Oh, well then, thank you. I understand. But why all these questions? … You want to find out if I'm a human being? Just ask me … No, I'm not a human being. I'm a judge. And in the courtroom judges aren't considered to be human beings. They carry out the will of the state. That's it' (11). Here Stashina points to one of the fundamental dysfunctions of Russia's judicial system. As in every testimony in the play, Stashina's is essentially a claim that she was simply doing her job, one which is undervalued, and that therefore she cannot be expected to perform with personal commitment or a sense of integrity. This, it is suggested, is a pervasive attitude among many of Russia's civil servants. Nobody involved in *One Hour Eighteen Minutes*, not the creators, not the audience, not even the defendants themselves are claiming that the country's legal practices are just. The question is not whether or not the system is corrupt. The question that *One Hour Eighteen Minutes* poses to its audiences is rather: how can people begin to be held responsible for such expansive corruption?

In exploration of this question, the play extends its trial to include defendants beyond the most obvious culprits. For example, one of the monologues is spoken by a girl who was sitting in the front seat of the ambulance that drove Magnitsky, along with two officers from Butyrka prison, back to Matrosskaia Tishina prison on 16 November 2009, three hours before he died. She responds to an unseen interlocutor when she says, 'I have nothing to do with this. Seriously, nothing at all. To tell you the truth I don't know why you even called me here. I never once turned around. I turned on the radio, so I didn't hear a thing. If there's one person who has nothing to do with this, it's me' (9). As this testimony reveals, the girl appears to have no understanding of why she is being questioned in connection to the case. She points to having turned on the radio as evidence of the fact that she has nothing to contribute to the investigation, and no inside perspective on whether Magnitsky was beaten while in transport that day.

A similar statement comes from Sasha, a young medical attendant at Matrosskaia Tishina prison, who, as we learn from the briefing on the play, was asked to 'take a walk in the hall' when the 'emergency medical team' arrived to attend to Magnitsky's fatal medical condition. Sasha then paced up and down the hall for one hour and eighteen minutes before the medical team left their 'patient' dead on the floor of the prison cell. Sasha emphasizes how little he knows about who Magnitsky was or what happened to him that day and spends the rest of his monologue discussing the supposed benefits of Samsung versus Nokia phones.

These two testimonies are of particular interest because neither of the defendants took direct action against the victim; and yet their actions, or lack of action, did permit the crimes that led to the prisoner's murder. By including these fabricated testimonies in their presentation of evidence, the creators of *One Hour Eighteen Minutes* ask their audiences to consider who exactly ought to be held responsible for Magnitsky's death.[3] As testimonies these two monologues call attention to how many people were involved, both officially and unofficially, in perpetuating a societal system of corruption and neglect. As the creators of the play write in the briefing, 'If the system responsible for Magnitsky's murder continues to murder others, if it remains as powerful as it has been then, at the very least, we in the theatre will testify against it.' In other words, the judicial proceeding staged in *One Hour Eighteen Minutes* is a trial not only of the individuals involved in Magnitsky's last days. It is also a trial of the system that facilitated his murder.

Trials onstage

Putting the past on trial through the re-staging of court transcripts is a practice that first came to prominence in modern theatre through the works of German writer and director Peter Weiss in the 1960s. As discussed in Chapter 1, directors such as Weiss, Heinar Kipphardt, and Rolf Hochhuth were important innovators in their staging of court documents as a path towards re-processing historical injustices in the present. In a society struggling to recuperate from the events of its totalitarian past, the works of these directors drew directly from court transcripts, news reports, and verbatim testimonies in their efforts to stage the collective judgement of their country's historical and cultural narratives. This movement in 1960s German documentary theatre inspired two later sub-genres of documentary theatre, 'theatre of testimony' in the US and 'tribunal theatre' in the UK. Developed by American director Emily Mann, theatre of testimony creates the space for a community of artists and audiences to come together and re-negotiate the narratives of their recent pasts. Mann's repertoire includes verbatim and fictional plays, but her play *Execution of Justice* (1984–86) made an important contribution to the form by staging the trial of Dan White, assassin of both Harvey Milk and San Francisco mayor George Moscone. Since the 1980s, London's Tricycle Theatre has taken to staging court documents in its series of works known as tribunal theatre. These plays include *Half the Picture* (1994) a dramatization of the Scott Report, an investigation into the Arms-to-Iraq inquiry, and *Nuremberg* (1996) which marked the fiftieth anniversary of the 1946 War Crimes Tribunal. Another vital addition to the development of documentary trial plays was the 1997 production of Jane Taylor's *Ubu and the Truth Commission*, a production that combined puppetry, folklore, and verbatim testimonies from South Africa's post-apartheid Truth and Reconciliation Commission.

In distinction to the stagings of court documents by Weiss in the 1960s, Taylor in the 1990s, and the directors of London's Tricycle Theatre in the 1990s and 2000s, the artists at Teatr.doc have no official court documents or testimonies from which to gather their documentary texts. This is why most of the 'testimonies' in the play are either imagined or constructed from accounts found in other sources such as blogs, articles, interviews, and public statements. For Peter Weiss, 'documentary theatre stands for the alternative that reality, however inscrutable it may make itself appear to be, can be explained in every detail' (see Irmer, 2006: 18). In the case of *One Hour Eighteen Minutes*, however, the play-trial serves in part to demonstrate the inscrutability of the proceedings around Magnitsky's case and the fallout since his death.

Anxieties about the authenticity of legal documentation and the sincerity of oral testimony are heightened in Russia as a result of the country's long history of political corruption in the courtroom. By pulling texts from various published and unpublished sources, using those sources to compose monologues that blend fact and fiction, and then proceeding to present these texts as evidence, the creators of *One Hour Eighteen*

Minutes exploit the suspect nature of documentation in contemporary Russian culture and confront the complexities of theatrical testimony as an instrument of justice. The courtroom as a venue for the transmission of cultural narratives has a complex history in twentieth-century Russia, and by setting their performance of justice in a theatrical courtroom the artists of *One Hour Eighteen Minutes* call up the country's unusually intimate, and occasionally lethal, association between judicial and theatrical practice.

Soviet trial practices

The connection between theatre and Russia's troubled legal history dates back to the early twentieth century, with the proliferation of Soviet mock trials directly following the 1917 Revolution. Though the use of mock trials as a tool for education and propaganda was not a strictly Soviet innovation, the early Soviet years saw a marked increase in judicial performance practices. As both Julie Cassiday and Elizabeth Wood note in their respective studies of trials and drama in twentieth-century Russia, mock trials became a favourite mode of propaganda immediately following the revolution. Trials were staged representing farmers who resisted collectivization as well as peasants who did not maintain appropriate sanitary habits. In these years, mock trials were meant to represent the ethical stance of the Communist party and were performed for the express purpose of reshaping the public moral consciousness. As Cassiday writes in her book *The Enemy on Trial: Early Soviet courts on stage and screen* (2000), 'The theatre and cinema that came into public trials after the revolution were part of a larger modernist movement in which art did not merely reflect or comment upon life but actually helped to reform, to redirect, and ultimately to revolutionize the lives of artists and spectators alike' (5).

Early Soviet trial organizers believed that the process of judgement enacted by a trial's audience could have a genuine impact on the beliefs and behaviours of society. As Wood argues in her 2005 study *Performing Justice: Agitation trials in early Soviet Russia*, '[T]he new "soviet" practices were acted out and enacted not so much in the conscious sense of someone "acting a part" but rather in the more complex sense of a parent who tells his or her child to "act your age."' Here Wood articulates a crucial distinction in her assessment of early Soviet theatrical practices. 'To act a part is to act something one knows to be fictional', Wood writes. 'To act one's age is to adopt a series of behaviours that one feels are appropriate and correct to the situation' (5). In other words, through their representation of revolutionary 'ideals', early Soviet trial plays were intended to construct a society in which such beliefs were held. By playing the roles of upstanding Soviet citizens, or morally sound spectators, the participants of early Soviet mock trials were learning how to perform new modes of accepted behaviour. These early amateur Soviet theatrics were thought to be an essential tool in the Communist party's efforts to create its Socialist values. The narrative structure of confession, conversion, and repentance as portrayed in theatrical courtrooms throughout the 1920s became so familiar to early Soviet audiences that it was soon seamlessly transposed onto the very real prosecution of citizens throughout the country in the 1930s.

In fact, as early as 1928 in the first Stalinist show trial, the Shakhty Affair, trial organizers applied precisely this script of confession and conversion to the prosecution of fifty-three mining engineers accused of treason and charged as enemies of the state. Of the fifty-three accused, only sixteen performed their confessions of admitted guilt, thirteen equivocated and the remaining twenty-four pled not guilty; nonetheless forty-nine were found guilty and five were executed. According to historian Mathew Edward Lenoe, the event was thought to be so effective that it was soon replicated in cities throughout the country, though reportedly with less finesse in the provinces (2004: 94). After seeing the confession and repentance of 'criminals' on trial, spectators were thought less likely to consider any dissent among the ranks (see Getty: 1999, 49–70). As Stalin's show trials became more common throughout the 1930s, the intimate relationship between trials and theatre in Russia became increasingly threatening. The courtroom was not only a venue for the propaganda of the Bolshevik party, but also a primary setting for the enactment of state terror.

In the case of mock trials, the representation of Soviet justice and Bolshevik courtrooms played an important role in the creation of a new code of socially accepted ethics in which truth and justice were tied to the class struggle against bourgeois enemies of the state. Of course not everyone who participated in these trials as either an artist or a spectator was converted to Bolshevism through their representational practice, but there is no doubt that the post-revolutionary performance of judicial proceedings and the 'self-reflection' (samokritika) such proceedings aimed to 'inspire' contributed to a major shift in the perception of what came to constitute notions of justice in Soviet Russia. The self-reflection of the early Soviet trials involved a forced prescription of right and wrong. The defendants, regardless of their crime or the evidence, were portrayed as enemies of the state; and only through the process of confession, conversion, and reintegration into society were they able to redeem their moral standing in the Soviet system.

Scrutinizing the Magnitsky case brings to light some unnerving similarities in comparison to the history of Soviet criminal proceedings. Though Magnitsky's case was never actually brought to trial, his arrest, imprisonment, and murder were meant to send a signal to people who might otherwise have been inclined to speak out against the corrupt practices of the Russian government. 'In court, as in documentary theatre,' writes Carol Martin, 'the forensic evidence stored in the archive is as much constructed as it is found. Not only do the police frequently fabricate evidence, but also both the prosecution and the defence do everything they can to credit/discredit evidence that might support/destroy their case' (2006: 11). At Teatr.doc, the artists use their constructed theatrical practice to spin the history of Magnitsky's case in such a way as to reveal the seams of the Putin administration's constructed attempt to silence possible whistle-blowers. They confront the artifice of their crafted trial, thereby consciously incorporating and reimagining the theatricality and terror of Russia's twentieth-century courtroom history.

In one sense, *One Hour Eighteen Minutes* promotes a process of self-reflection analogous to that which was intended to take place in early Soviet mock trials. It applies the construct of the courtroom to raise fundamental questions about justice and morality in the cultural consciousness. Whereas the self-reflection of the early Soviet trials left audiences with a compulsory sense of moral superiority, however, the trial at Teatr.doc leaves its audience members with a sense of discomfort. The self-reflection of early Soviet mock trials completed a cycle of redemption for their audiences with a clear narrative of who had done what wrong. *One Hour Eighteen Minutes* conversely leaves its audiences with questions unanswered, thereby encouraging each audience member to consider for themselves how a case like Magnitsky's could have become as common as it has in contemporary Russia.

The trial structure of the play achieves its pursuit of justice, in one sense, in that those who were never legally held accountable for Magnitsky's death are finally called to answer for their actions. In another sense, however, it is the system itself that is submitted to the strictest scrutiny in Teatr.doc's trial. The lack of civic concern expressed by the state employees represented onstage resonates far beyond the walls of Teatr.doc's underground theatre. In coming together to discuss the country's widespread lack of civic justice, the artists and audiences of *One Hour Eighteen Minutes* have created a venue in which to begin a new public dialogue. By engaging in the (albeit theatrical) judicial process, the artists and audiences of *One Hour Eighteen Minutes* use their performance practice to reinscribe their own relationships to justice. They apply the method of reenactment to make the intricacies of past injustices legible in the present. By reenacting the events surrounding Magnitsky's death, and calling upon the country's long history of judicial corruption in the process, the creators of *One Hour Eighteen Minutes* use their theatrical testimonies to, in the words of Rebecca Schneider, create the space for the past and present to *touch* (2011: 77).

After the trial

In the last scene of the first act of the play Judge Krivoruchko is portrayed as if he had, according to the briefing on the play, 'appeared on the other side and got what he deserved'. In the original 2010 production, this monologue was the final scene of the play. In 2012, Teatr.doc premiered a new version of the production that included a second act addressing the events that took place in connection to Magnitsky's case after his death. In the original production, actor Aleksei Zhiriakov portrays the judge as though he himself had been imprisoned and is now in Magnitsky's position, having to bribe and beg for basic amenities such as a cup of hot water. Hot water, and the fact that Magnitsky was denied it, is a theme that runs throughout the play. In her opening monologue Magnitsky's mother refers to her son's having been refused a cup of boiling water, a distillation of the inhumanity of his treatment in prison. And, in his first monologue, the actor representing Krivoruchko reads from Magnitsky's diary, citing his fruitless request, day after day, for a cup of hot water.

The 2010 version of the production culminated in Krivoruchko's fictional monologue in which the judge is represented begging and bribing for his own elusive cup of hot water. Once his bribe has been accepted, and a second actor returns with a steaming kettle, Krivoruchko realizes he has no cup in which to receive the water and nothing left with which to bribe the prison guard. 'I'd give you something else,' he begs, 'but I don't have anything, I gave you everything. I had a watch, but they took it from me. I don't have anything!' (Gremina, 2010: 14). Zhiriakov looks at the actor standing in for the prison guard and holds out his hands in a gesture of hopelessness. The guard pours the water from the steaming kettle into Krivoruchko's bare hands. The lights suddenly go out as the audience hears Krivoruchko scream in pain.

Figure 10: *Chas vosemnadtsat*, directed by Mikhail Ugarov (2010)

This moment in the play, when the audience bears witness to boiling water pouring over a helpless man's hands, approximates the extreme inhumanity Magnitsky and other victims of the Russian penal system suffer as a result of the corruption embedded in the country's legal structure. As the Lithuanian-born Russian director Kama Ginkas wrote, 'There are a great many things you can't grasp with your hands but if you make a poetic gesture around them, so to speak, you can see them approximately' (2003: 142). The sound of Krivoruchko's scream in conjunction with the brutality of the image onstage evokes a visceral response. The theatrical representation of violence intersects with the knowledge that the disturbing reconstruction as presented onstage pales in comparison to what really happened to Magnitsky. In this moment of rupture, the audience gains new insight into the one hour and eighteen minutes Magnitsky spent behind the closed doors of that prison cell on 16 November 2009. Though *One Hour Eighteen Minutes* may not lead to any immediate institutional changes in the Russian legal system, those who witness and participate in the trial that wasn't but should have been are given the opportunity through this practice of theatrical reenactment to both *touch* and be *touched* by the past.

Since the 2010 premiere of *One Hour Eighteen Minutes* Magnitsky's case has received international recognition as an instance indicative of the deeply embedded corruption of Russia's judicial and financial structure. Six months after Magnitsky's death William Browder, CEO of Hermitage Capital, presented his testimony before the US Human Rights Commission claiming that the 'story of what happened to Sergei Magnitsky is so medieval that it is hard to imagine that it could have taken place in today's world. But it did happen and it will continue to happen so long as the United States and the rest of the civilized world – and indeed, Russia itself – allow corrupt Russian officials to act without consequences.' This testimony was the start of a concerted effort led by Browder and his Hermitage Capital affiliates to institute a series of sanctions against specific Russian officials who, according to the bill that has since been passed, are 'responsible for the detention, abuse, and death of Sergei Magnitsky and other gross violations of human rights'.[4] Their initiative has come to fruition as what is commonly called 'The Magnitsky Act', a law first passed by the US congress in 2012 that instituted visa bans and the freezing of offshore assets for specific individuals considered guilty of human rights violations not only in connection to Magnitsky's case but in other instances as well. Since that time similar laws have been passed in several other countries, including the UK and Canada. In this way the bill is intended as a reaction to a 'broader pattern of disregard for the numerous domestic and international human rights commitments of the Russian Federation'.[4]

The bill was signed into law in the US on 14 December 2012 and precipitated the series of judicial absurdities in the Russian court system that led to Magnitsky's posthumous prosecution in 2013. Before this 'verdict' was reached, Teatr.doc amended their production in 2012 to include a second act in which the creators of the play incorporated events that took place after Magnitsky's death, including the passing of the Magnitsky Act and the construction of the retrospective case against him. Notably, the production does not include mention of the 'counter-sanctions' instituted by the Russian government in reaction to the passing of the Magnitsky Act, an appalling example of politically motivated legislation that bans US citizens from adopting Russian orphans.

One adjustment made in the revised production is that Judge Krivoruchko does not make a sound when the boiling water hits his hands. Instead, the lights go out and there is a brief moment of silence. After a few seconds of darkness the lights come up to reveal the actor standing nonchalantly onstage, holding the steaming kettle. Another actor stands and addresses the audience with a lighthearted attitude, 'Dear friends,' he pronounces warmly as he steps to the front of the stage.[5] 'Don't worry,

I have some good news. From now on we'll give you only good news. And the first piece of good news is that, you're not going to believe it, death doesn't exist anymore, at all, for anyone.' The actor points to individual audience members: 'It doesn't exist for you, lovely lady, or for you.' He points to another audience member: 'Or for you, by the way,' he says, approaching the actor who plays Magnitsky's mother. 'Or for your son, which is why we can put him on trial, and we will try him again and again and again.' At this, the actress who portrays Natalia Magnitskaya exits the stage and the remaining characters continue to discuss how pleased they are to have suffered no consequences for their actions. 'By the way,' one actor says to Krivoruchko, 'how are your hands?' 'My hands are completely fine,' the second actor responds. 'This is theatre. It's not even good theatre.' Krivoruchko then takes the steaming kettle into his own hands and pours the real contents out onto the stage floor. 'There's no boiling water. It's dry ice.' The pieces of dry ice scatter across the stage. 'It's just one of those so-called "special effects".'

In this sequence, the creators of *One Hour Eighteen Minutes* call attention to their own use of theatrical stagecraft in order to expose the 'stagecraft' executed by Russian government officials and their systematic refusal to hold anyone responsible for Magnitsky's death. In publicizing the artifice of his own performance and those of his stage partners, the actor playing Krivoruchko also draws his audiences' attention to the constructed nature of the Russian Interior Ministry's case against Magnitsky. 'This is theatre,' Krivoruchko announces, 'and it's not even good theatre.' That is to say, the manufactured nature of both these scenarios is obvious. Neither the actors at Teatr.doc nor the government officials responsible for Magnitsky's murder have bothered to conceal the constructed nature of their undertakings.

Krivoruchko's assertion that 'this is theatre' is a point often contested during the post-show discussions which immediately follow every performance of *One Hour Eighteen Minutes* in which audience members frequently declare that 'this is not theatre' (eto ne teatr), or rather, 'not simply theatre' (ne prosto teatr).[6] These two phrases appear again and again in the recorded conversations that follow the play and, I would argue, are an indication of cultural tensions around the relationship between everyday life and its theatrical representation in contemporary Russia. The phrase 'this is not theatre' was actually a frequent criticism of the work at Teatr.doc in the company's early days. At that time people used this formulation to express dissatisfaction with the work taking place there. Many audience members in the early 2000s maintained a desire for theatre to represent life not as it is but 'as it ought to be', a longing identified by Pavel Rudnev as a holdover from Stalinist aesthetics.

In the case of the *One Hour Eighteen Minutes* post-show discussions, however, 'this is not theatre' is a phrase generated by audience members to express the relevance the play has to their contemporary life. In asserting that *One Hour Eighteen Minutes* is not theatre, audience members attempt to articulate the intermingling of everyday life and its theatrical representation as performed in the Russian documentary theatre repertoire. Moreover, they are confronted with the artificial and constructed elements of everyday life as they bear witness to the cynically contrived nature of the Russian Federation's handling of Magnitsky's case. In this way, the creators of *One Hour Eighteen Minutes* play an important paradox of life in contemporary Russia and call up the country's historical apprehension around the interplay between theatre and trials since the early Soviet years.

While Russia's archives may open and close, and documents may be altered and concealed, the experience shared between the artists and the audiences in performances of *One Hour Eighteen Minutes* is exclusive to the embodied practice of documentary theatre. Though the audience remains fully cognizant of the fact that the actors are merely surrogates, perhaps apparitions, of the original speakers, the actions of those involved in Magnitsky's last days are presented and their presence fills the performance space as *One Hour Eighteen Minutes* makes clear the unchangeable consequences of the events of the past. While one's perception of and access to the past may be altered through the experience of participating in the theatrical trial, one thing that is demonstrated in the performance is that the horrors of the past did indeed happen. Despite any official effort to cover up the record of Magnitsky's death, and the deaths of countless others, their stories will, at least in this venue, still be both spoken and heard.

Summing up

In the years since the premiere of *One Hour Eighteen Minutes*, there have been several other documentary theatre projects in Russia that also call up the efficacy of the courtroom setting in their performances of justice. The 2012 theatre laboratory *Memory Theatre* at Memorial included a staging of the transcript from Joseph Brodskii's 1964 trial. Directed by Evgeniia Berkovich, *Chelovek kotoryi ne rabotal: sud nad Iosefom Brodskim* (*The Man Who Didn't Work: The trial against Joseph Brodskii*, 2012) used verbatim text from Brodskii's own writings, as well as from his hearing, as recorded by writer Frida Vigdorova, who attended the proceedings.

One of the most notable theatre trials to have come out of Moscow's documentary theatre repertoire since *One Hour Eighteen Minutes*, however, is undoubtedly the three-day event held at the Sakharov Center in March 2013 entitled *Moskovskie protsessy* (*The Moscow Trials*).

Co-organized by Mikhail Kaluzhskii and the Swiss director Milo Rau, *The Moscow Trials* draws its title from a series of Stalinist show trials that were performed between 1936 and 1938 and led to the executions of millions of defendants, primarily leaders of the Old Bolshevik party and top officials of the Soviet secret police. In their modern reimagining of the trials, Kaluzhskii and Rau staged a re-creation of three of the best-known political trials of the Putin years. The cast members were not actors but real-life artists, curators, religious activists, lawyers, witnesses, and jurors who were asked to argue their cases and judge for themselves whether the defendants were guilty of violating Article 282 of the Russian Criminal Code, which prohibits the purposeful 'offending of feelings of Orthodox believers'. This three-day event was produced under the auspices of Rau's International Institute of Political Murder and documented by a professional film crew who would later edit the footage into a film-length documentary intended for Western audiences.[7]

The first trial staged was the hearing against curators Yurii Samodurov and Anna Alchuk, organizers of the 2003 art exhibition 'Caution, Religion!'

Figure 11: *Moskovskie protsessyi*, co-created by Mikhail Kaluzhskii and Milo Rau (2013)

at the Sakharov Center. The collection featured works by over forty artists, each exploring the role of religion in contemporary Russian culture. The exhibition included a number of works later deemed to be controversial, such as Aleksander Kosolapov's painting *This is My Blood*, depicting an image of Jesus in front of the Coca-Cola logo. Four days after the opening of the exhibition, the Sakharov Center was attacked by a gang of Russian Orthodox activists who stormed the gallery and destroyed a number of the works by spray-painting slogans across the artworks and the walls of the gallery space accusing the artists and organizers of being heathens, bastards, and enemies of the Orthodox Church. The offenders were apprehended and charged with hooliganism but were later acquitted by a judge who appeared sympathetic to their cause and claimed their actions had been incited by the content of the exhibition. The following month the Procurator General opened an investigation against the curators of the exhibition who were eventually charged, tried, indicted, and each sentenced to a 100,000-rouble fine (approximately £1,300), although Alchuk was later acquitted.

On day two of *The Moscow Trials* the organizers turned their attention to a similar case in which Samodurov again, this time together with co-curator Andrei Erofeev, were taken to court for offending the feelings of Orthodox believers with their 2007 exhibition 'Forbidden Art'. In distinction to the previous exhibition, 'Forbidden Art' was not explicitly connected to the topic of religion, but again agitated a number of Orthodox activists who decided to take legal action against the organizers of the exhibition. As Lena Jonson discusses in her book *Art and Protest in Putin's Russia* (2015), the original trial of Samodurov and Erofeev dragged on for over two years and included numerous 'eyewitnesses' who were later revealed never even to have seen the exhibition in the first place. Again, the defendants were found guilty and had their prison sentences suspended in favour of issuing them with significant fines.

It was the third and final day of the event that caused the biggest stir, as *The Moscow Trials* team began their restaging of the 2013 trial against three members of the punk-rock activist collective Pussy Riot. In a protest action that has since become world famous, five members of the activist group entered the Cathedral of Christ the Saviour in central Moscow on 21 February 2012. Once inside, the women famously took off their overcoats to reveal brightly coloured clothing, unpacked their instruments, and climbed up onto to the platform in front of the altar where they began dancing, kicking their legs in the air, and falling to their knees for approximately forty seconds before they were apprehended by church employees and swiftly ushered off the premises. The thirty seconds of video footage of these activities was later edited together with video taken in a different church and released online as the music video for the group's protest song, 'Virgin Mary, Chase Putin Away'. Two weeks later, three members of the group were arrested and placed in pre-trial detention for five months. Maria Alekhina, Nadezhda Tolokonnikova, and Ekaterina Samutsevich were all found guilty of organized hooliganism with intent to offend the feelings of Orthodox believers. Samutsevich was later acquitted in appeals court and released, while Alekhina and Tolokonnikova were sentenced to two years in medium-security penal colonies.

On 3 March 2013, approximately one year after her arrest, Pussy Riot member Ekaterina Samutsevich was called to the stand at the Sakharov Center in the theatrical re-creation of her original trial. Suddenly, the performance was interrupted by several state officials who entered the gallery, claiming to be from the Office of Immigration. Swiss director Milo Rau and members of his film crew were asked to hand over their documents to prove they were legally permitted to be taking part in such an endeavour. While the so-called migration officials were busy checking documents inside the gallery, a small group of protestors dressed as Cossacks began gathering on the street outside. Next a number of police officers joined the commotion, ostensibly in order to make sure nothing was getting out of hand. Eventually the 'immigration officers' left and a few of the Cossack protestors agreed to watch the proceedings and see for themselves the substance of what was taking place. The performance continued and no further legal action was taken, aside from that which had been previously planned by the project's creators.

In an interview on the radio station *Ekho moskvy* following the performance of *The Moscow Trials*, Kaluzhskii described a conversation he had had with one of the police officers who arrived at the scene. 'I was explaining to him what documentary theatre is because he was taking notes in his little notebook and he sincerely didn't understand what was happening', the director recalls, 'If it's a play then why are there real people in it, and if there are real people then how can you call it theatre?' (*Ekho moskvy*, 2013). This police officer's question, as Kaluzhskii recounts it, points directly to the way documentary theatre blurs the boundaries between that which is real and that which is fabricated, a quality I argue is even further complicated in the contemporary Russian context.

The Moscow Trials was a very different endeavour from *One Hour Eighteen Minutes*, of course, and yet both projects are important examples of how Russian theatre artists use documentary forms to explore the intricacies of injustice in the civic sphere and its correlation with the country's Soviet past. Of course, not every documentary play in Russia is as concerned with the pursuit of justice as these two projects. However,

I argue that any attempt to reenact or revive the events of the past in Russia is inherently tied to questions of justice, and, conversely, any attempt at the constitution of justice in contemporary Russia necessitates an acknowledgement of and engagement with the events of the past. In the case of *One Hour Eighteen Minutes* and *The Moscow Trials*, Russia's documentary theatre artists utilize the efficacy of the theatrical courtroom to reappropriate a societal process of judgement.

As director Mikhail Ugarov once said in an interview about his production, 'I understand that a little play in a theatre isn't going to change anything, but the word will be said,' (2010). The significance Ugarov ascribes to 'the word' in this statement is indicative of a central value of verbatim theatre. The emphasis Ugarov places on the speaking of words, however, is only part of the equation that makes documentary theatre a viable space for transformation. What Ugarov leaves out is that in addition to the impact of the words' being spoken is the necessity for the words to be *heard*. As this chapter has illustrated, the efficacy of the theatre as a venue for social change and as a practice of anamnesis lies in precisely this space between the actors' speaking of the words and the audience's reception of the words. Through their shared experience of both speaking and hearing the testimonies provided, the participants of *One Hour Eighteen Minutes*, and of Russia's documentary theatre repertoire more broadly, negotiate collaboratively a renewed conception of justice and initiate dialogue about the country's complex relationship between the injustice of the past and the corruption of the present.

Notes

1 The report can be accessed in full at http://russian-untouchables.com (accessed 24 August 2018), where it is described as 'a 75-page report with new documentary evidence showing how Sergei Magnitsky was murdered in Russian Interior Ministry custody and how the Russian government has consistently lied in public about Sergei Magnitsky's false arrest, torture and death to cover up the criminal liability of the Russian officials involved'.
2 Translated and excerpted from the 'Note from the director' included in the 'briefing on the play'.
3 The documentary materials for the play were collected by Ekaterina Bondarenko, Anastasiia Patlai, and Zosia Rodkevich. The text includes reports from the journalists Dmitrii Muratov (*Novaia gazeta*), as well as Valerii Borshchev, Olga Romanova, and Evgeniia Albats (*Novaia vremia*). Excerpts from Sergei Magnitsky's prison diary are also read in the play as provided by his family. The script was subsequently written and constructed by Elena Gremina based on the documentary materials listed above. For more details on how the documentary materials were collected and edited into monologues for the play see the interview with Anastasiia Patlai and Zarema Zaudinova from 5

August 2018 at: https://www.svoboda.org/a/29412625.html (accessed 18 August 2018).
4 The bill was sponsored by Senator Bill Cardin and was attached to a House bill regulating new trade agreements with Russia and Moldova. The law's full name as signed into law in December 2012 is the 'Russia and Moldova Jackson–Vanik Repeal and Sergei Manitsky Rule of Law Accountability Act of 2012'. The full text can be found at http://www.treasury.gov/resource-center/sanctions/Programs/Documents/pl112_208.pdf (accessed 21 July 2017).
5 The following quotations from the revised version of the play are translated and transcribed from the video recording shared with me by Victoria Kholodova, Manager at Teatr.doc.
6 Here I refer to the complete video archive of post-show discussions from the play's premiere in 2010 through to January 2012, shared with me by the creators of the play.
7 For more information on this project visit Rau's website at http://international-institute.de/en/the-moscow-trials/ (accessed 18 August 2018).

4

Material witness
History, belief, and the theatre of enactment

Russia's twenty-first-century documentary theatre artists draw upon the legacy of their country's twentieth century in their search for new methods with which to stage collisions between theatre and everyday life. Chapter 2 illustrated how the artists of the Joseph Beuys Theatre and Moscow's Sakharov Center use documentary theatre to make meaningful interventions in Russia's culture of commemoration. Chapter 3 showed how the artists at Teatr.doc draw out important connections between the performance of justice and the reconciliation of historical narratives in contemporary Russian culture. Both of these case studies support the premise set out in the introduction to this book: the notion that through the process of reenacting texts and events from the past, Russia's documentary theatre artists seek to create a renewed sense of agency and engagement in the present.

Chapter 4 extends this exploration of the relationship between memory, justice, and belief in Russia's documentary theatre repertoire through analysis of a 2008 production of the autobiographical play *Pavlik – my God*. First published in the journal *Isskustvo kino* in 2007, the concept for the play grew, in part, from a laboratory for playwrights and directors held at Iasnaia Poliana, writer Lev Tolstoy's former estate, organized by Mikhail Ugarov. It was during this 2006 laboratory that playwright Nina Belenitskaia began her collaboration with director Evgenii Grigoriev, a partnership that would prove crucial to the play's realization in the years to follow. *Pavlik – my God* tells the story of a young woman named Tania Zharova, Belenitskaia's self-professed alter ego. In her efforts to come to terms with having been abandoned by her father as a teenager, Tania turns to the mythology of the past and finds inspiration in the legend of the Soviet adolescent-martyr Pavlik Morozov.

As the story goes, Pavlik Morozov was a 13-year-old boy who was murdered by his relatives after denouncing his father to the Soviet authorities in 1932. In *Pavlik – my God*, Tania sets off on a journey across the Russian and Soviet historical landscape in order to, in her words, *become* the so-called 'pioneer 001', as he was identified in Stalin's 1955 Book of Honour of the Moscow Pioneer Palace. Once she arrives in Pavlik's hometown of Gerasimovka on the far side of the Ural mountains, Tania invokes the spirit of the boy hero, whose monument is brought to life onstage. The Pavlik Morozov of Belenitskaia's play appears to the protagonist and to the audience in various incarnations throughout the show. The two characters, Tania and Pavlik's statue, make up the entire cast of the play; the five screens lining the stage become the virtual set for the production and the primary means through which the audience is transported from modern-day Moscow to the timelessness of Pavlik's rural hometown in Sverdlovsk region.

Of all the Russian documentary plays included in this study, *Pavlik – my God* is the one that most challenges traditional notions of documentary. Not only does it feature a statue that comes to life, but the play's plotline and its staging are noticeably more theatrical than most other plays in Russia's documentary theatre repertoire. In this way, *Pavlik – my God* deviates stylistically from the other plays discussed in this book and raises questions as to whether it can be said to represent events from actual everyday life. Nonetheless, the stories and scenarios in the play can be interpreted as documentary materials in that they are drawn directly from the playwright's autobiography. Moreover, the production integrates documentary video footage, archival sources, and published interviews – all of which reveal the artists' investment in exploring the use of materials from real life onstage. Despite its differences from the other plays included in this study, and in some ways because of its differences, *Pavlik – my God* is an essential component of this book's consideration of the development and significance of Russian documentary theatre, for its unparalleled capacity to make the narratives of the past operable in the present is an especially elegant illustration of this book's argument that Russian documentary theatre artists enact a process of anamnesis through their performance practice.

Chronologically, *Pavlik – my God* is the earliest of the plays to undergo in-depth analysis in this study.[1] Dedicated discussion of *Pavlik – my God* follows here, however, because of how thoroughly and intricately it depicts the key themes so far introduced in this book. This 'pioneer-play concert', as Belenitskaia describes it in the script, was the first Russian documentary play to feature narratives of Soviet history and their continued resonance in the culture of the country's present. As the following close reading makes clear, *Pavlik – my God* presents a confluence of Russian documentary theatre's simultaneous investments in the practice of commemoration, performance of justice, and enactment of historical narratives within the theatre space.

In analysing the production, this chapter will explore how it weaves across the porous boundary between fact and fiction, now and then, and here and there, as it freely traverses the seventy-five years between Pavlik's death and the play's premiere in 2009. By blurring the boundaries between what is real and what is imagined, *Pavlik – my God* makes clear important nuances of Russia's relationship to its twentieth-century history. The transformation of Pavlik Morozov's monument into the boy-legend himself is one of a series of transformations in the play exemplifying a distinct temporal, spatial, and material flexibility that, I suggest, is central to Russian documentary theatre's efficacy as a practice of anamnesis. By tracking the processes of transformation as experienced by the author, the protagonist, and the audiences of *Pavlik – my God*, this chapter explores how Russia's paradoxical relationship to its past has come to shape the notion of belief – be it religious or ideological – in the country's present.

Pavlik Morozov lives

Tania begins the show alone, entering the space and politely asking audience members to switch off their phones. She then pulls out her phone to demonstrate how whenever she calls her father he predictably neglects to answer the call. The actress holds up her phone above her head as the rhythmic sound of the ring tone reverberates through the theatre's sound system. 'He sees my number' Tania tells the audience, 'and doesn't pick up. I usually call him from another number' (Belenitskaia, 2007: 1).[2] These lines are spoken in a matter-of-fact tone, without the sentiment one might expect in a discussion of such personal matters. Next, the young woman exits the stage and returns right away, dragging a large leather suitcase from which she pulls a series of household items. In lieu of child support, Tania explains, she is trying to earn enough money to supplement her mother's income and provide her family with the necessary resources to get by.

The first item for sale is a man's suede jacket that she persuasively markets to a man in the front row. The next piece of merchandise presented is a unisex bathrobe that Tania models enticingly before approaching another audience member and pleading with him, 'my mother's been wearing it around the house for seven years. She hasn't taken it off ever since he left. Buy it from me, please' (2). Occasionally the actress actually manages to extract cash from her more willing customers. As Belenitskaia described to me in our 2013 interview in the canteen at the Moscow Art Theatre, the props in the original production were taken directly from the playwright's home.[3] These material objects from Belenitskaia's real life stand in as those of her theatrical surrogate. The audience, of course, could not have known that the bathrobe Tania modeled had actually belonged to the playwright's father, or that Belenitskaia's mother had in fact been wearing it around the house for the past seven years since the father of her children left her. Nonetheless, the item's significance both onstage and off contributes to the play's intermingling of what is real and what is imagined. This indefinite line between Belenitskaia's biography and that of her onstage alter ego mirrors the uncertain correlation in the play between the historical figure, Pavlik Morozov, and the cultural mythology that was built up around him in the decades succeeding his death.

The legend of Pavlik Morozov has undergone countless revisions since it first appeared in the Soviet press in 1932. As historian Catriona Kelly discovered in her extensive archival research on the topic, very few of the details of Pavlik Morozov's case are verifiable and indeed, many parts of the popular account of his story have been disproven. Nevertheless, as Kelly details in her book *Comrade Pavlik* (2005), morality tales about the boy were reproduced in books, plays, poems, and even an opera throughout the Soviet years. As legend variously had it, the young Pavlik Morozov discovered that his father was illegally hoarding grain, or forging documents, or colluding with 'kulaks', or perhaps all of the above, and proceeded to write a letter of denunciation that he hand-delivered to his schoolteacher, or the village commissar, or the closest representative of communist authority, depending on which sources you consult. Pavlik's father was subsequently tried and sentenced to ten years' hard labour but was ultimately executed before his ten years were up. Not long after the trial, Pavlik and his younger brother Fedia Morozov were killed in the forest on the outskirts of Gerasimovka. Two months later, the boys' paternal grandparents, two of their uncles, and one of their cousins were put on trial for the homicide. Four of the five defendants were convicted and sentenced to death.[4]

Beginning with a 1932 article in the newspaper *Pioneer pravda*, the denunciation, the murder, and the trial were all nationally publicized. The boy's heroic deed swiftly became a parable of dedication to the state for young communists across the Soviet Union and was subsequently converted into the stuff of cultural legend when it caught the attention of Maksim Gorky in 1933. As Sheila Fitzpatrick describes, Gorky became the leading advocate for the erection of a monument in honour of Pavlik and cited the boy's story as an example of Soviet heroism at the 1934 Soviet Writers Congress (Fitzpatrick, 1996: 225). Monuments to Pavlik were built all over the Soviet Union and the martyred boy became the namesake for schools and kindergartens across the nation's eleven time zones. His story was retold in poems and children's books and later became the inspiration for Sergei Eisenstein's unfinished and unreleased feature film *Bezhin lug* (*Bezhin Meadow*). Production of the film was halted in March 1937, leading to a scandal in which the Party Central Committee 'declared the film anti-artistic and politically quite unsound', according to Boris Shumiatskii's article 'O filme Bezhin lug' ('About the film Bezhin Meadow') published in the newspaper *Pravda* in 1937.

Pavlik Morozov held a prominent place in propaganda parlance for decades. In 1965 the Soviet government funded the erection of a monument to the boy in his hometown and founded a Pavlik Morozov schoolhouse museum which remains open to this day. Groups of schoolchildren used to make regular pilgrimages to Sverdlovsk region where they visited the essential sites and wrote letters to the long-dead teenage hero. The tale of Pavlik's heroism was used to promote various ideological agendas throughout the Stalin and post-Stalin years; and, as Kelly writes, the few verifiable facts about the boy's murder became gradually 'absorbed into the world of fiction' (2005: 123). In other words, the Pavlik Morozov legend became, over time, a malleable mythology employed to 'represent Soviet society as it wanted to show itself and to see itself' (Kelly, 2005: xxxiii).

In the late 1980s, the boy's somewhat mythical reputation began to turn when a number of publications appeared claiming to debunk the heroism of Pavlik's story as it had been constructed in previous decades. Iurii Druzhnikov's *Voznesenia Pavlika Morozova* (*The Apotheosis of Pavlik Morozov*, 1988) suggested an alternative narrative in which Pavlik's denunciation of his father was not motivated by loyalty to the state but was rather an act of familial revenge. Druzhnikov's research revealed that the boy's father, Trofim Morozov, had (like Belenitskaia's father) left his wife and children and taken up residence with another woman. The

Apotheosis of Pavlik Morozov argues against the notion that Pavlik Morozov was a national hero and suggests that he was, in fact, little more than an insubordinate child. The boy's reputation continued to decline throughout the 1980s and 1990s, a development leading to the toppling of a Pavlik Morozov statue by crowds in August 1991. By 1999 the Morozov legend was popularly acknowledged to have been fabricated.

To the protagonist of Belenitskaia's play, however, Pavlik Morozov remains a hero set apart from the reality of the everyday, a figure representative of precisely the revenge and righteousness she misses in her own day-to-day experience of life in modern Moscow. Tania does not mind that the details of Pavlik Morozov's story are generally thought to be fictional. Her conviction is not shaken by the knowledge that the alleged denunciation, the show trial, and all that came after were likely constructed for the explicit purpose of propaganda. And she appears to have no interest in recognizing the ways in which her hero's reputation was marred in the late 1980s and early 1990s. Between attempts to market her father's bathrobe and sell the very slippers off her feet Tania announces, with the audience as her witness, that she will no longer call her father 'papa' but only refer to him by his surname. 'Are you listening, Papa?' She speaks straight to the audience, 'I don't love you anymore – that's number one. I am turning you in – that's number two. I denounce you – that's two and a half ... Now Pavlik Morozov is my God' (2).

The figure of Pavlik Morozov in the play epitomizes Tania's longing for her idealistic image of the past, for a time in which, she imagines, it was possible to believe in something. She finds inspiration in the history of the pioneers and interprets Pavlik's story as representative of a moment in history when children were respected and had the right to impose justice on those who behaved irresponsibly. Tania's choice to believe in a past that never existed in order to make sense of the paradoxes of her present is made possible in part by common practices of memory-making in twenty-first-century Russia. As described in this book's previous chapters, the Soviet foundation myth of communism's historical inevitability, in combination with the constant and transparent revision of narratives of the past, has caused a bizarre feedback loop in contemporary Russian culture. Not yet having reached a popular consensus on the meaning of Soviet history in the present, many people's sense of Russia's twentieth-century history remains a point of contention and a source of anxiety in the contemporary civic space. By reimagining the Pavlik Morozov mythology and placing it in direct relationship to the social circumstances of the play's contemporary protagonist, *Pavlik – my God* thematizes precisely these tensions around the role one's perception of the past plays in their interpretation of the present.

Do this in memory of me

As soon as Tania invokes Pavlik Morozov as her 'God', a rustling is heard from the audience. A young man stands up from his seat, gathers up his belongings, and begins to move through the audience toward the aisle. As he enters the playing space he strolls casually toward the screen at the back of the stage where the word 'papa' has been projected in red letters on the centre screen. Tania attempts to continue her monologue as the young man starts making shadow figures on the screen with his hands and barking like a dog. He soon leaves the screen behind and begins harassing her, making crass comments, mocking her sincerity, and claiming that he is her Soviet-style hero. Tania tries to ignore the young man, as though he might just go away; but when that proves unsuccessful she refutes his claim with what appears to be sound logic.

Tania points out that Pavlik was 14 years old when he was killed, whereas the young man in front of her is clearly years older. Pavlik responds playfully, 'That was practically eighty years ago. Can't I grow up just a little bit?' (2). Next, the young man offers to show her his scars. He proceeds to unbuckle his belt and tug on the waist of his jeans in order to show her where he claims to have been stabbed to death all those years ago. Having reached the limit of her patience, and having resolved to maintain her belief in her falsified version of history, Tania attempts to dismiss her stage partner with the seemingly irrefutable fact that 'Pavlik is dead – and you are alive' (2). With this line, the boy's attitude changes from playfully antagonistic to solemn and serious as he walks up to Tania, looks her intently in the eye, and alleges, 'That's not a fact' (2).

The 'fact' that Pavlik Morozov is dead is no more reliable within the world of the play than the 'fact' that he denounced his father is in reality. The nonlinear logic in this sequence reflects the complex temporal loop of Soviet historical mythology. In *Pavlik – my God* the actors perform the paradox of Russian cultural memory by playing fast and loose with linear notions of chronological reason. The play fashions a process of temporal metamorphosis akin to what literary scholar Mikhail Iampolskii describes in his 1995 essay, 'In the Shadow of Monuments'. In his survey of the shifting and lasting impact of Soviet sites of memory in the post-perestroika urban environment, Iampolskii claims that 'Any monument creates around itself some kind of special temporal expanse in which time moves differently than in other places, a sort of mystical protective zone that surrounds the monument and is apparently connected with the experience of temporal metamorphosis' (1995: 96).

At this point in the play, Tania begins her journey to the small village where Pavlik's monument still stands today. Of course the audience members of *Pavlik – my God* know that they are sitting in a small black-box theatre in the centre of Moscow in the present day, but in another sense they are transported to the timelessness of Gerasimovka, which appears to them onscreen in its present-day state, though seemingly unchanged since the days of Pavlik Morozov's death in 1932. Once again we are put in mind of Rebecca Schneider's notion that 'lodged in the logic of reenactment' is a belief 'that the past is not (entirely) dead, that it can be accessed *live*' (2011: 11; original emphasis). If, as has been argued in earlier chapters, the creators of *Legacy of Silence, Second Act. Grandchildren*, and *One Hour Eighteen Minutes* stage a process through which past and present touch, then *Pavlik – my God* can be said to intertwine the narratives of the past with the turmoil of the present so intimately as to make them virtually indistinguishable.

Another important instance of temporal interlace occurs in the production through the projection of the documentary video footage shot by Grigoriev during a trip to Gerasimovka in preparation for the show. According to my interview with the playwright, Grigoriev (a Sverdlovsk native) had some reservations about Belenitskaia, a Muscovite born and bred, attempting to comment on or portray the realities of life in small-town Russia. Partly for this reason, in the early stages of writing the play Belenitskaia followed her own nascent protagonist's footsteps in order to see the village and Pavlik's actual monument. While in Gerasimovka, Grigoriev (whose career then was primarily as a documentary filmmaker) and Belenitskaia collected video footage and other documentary materials depicting the village, the people, and the landscape.

In autumn 2008 Grigoriev returned to Gerasimovka with a team of filmmakers to collect footage specifically for the five-screen set-up for the show. Grigoriev and his colleagues from the documentary film collective *Pervoe kino* were innovators in a style known as 'panoramic cinema' in which the images on the screens are coordinated in such a way as to give viewers the impression that they are moving through the space as it appears in the video.[5] The effect is striking and especially conducive to the temporal interlacing woven throughout the text. The video installation and the live action of the play interanimate one another and manage to encompass the audience in the process. The actors onstage interact with the images onscreen and the live audience in the space and, in this way, open up new pathways between past and present.

For example, the film crew's trip coincided with the anniversary of Pavlik's murder, and the video captures not only the life and landscape of Gerasimovka, but also features the annual commemoration of the local tragedy in which, ironically enough, congregants from the Orthodox

Figure 12: *Pavlik – moi Bog*, directed by Evgenii Grigoriev (2009)

church gather around the boy's monument to sing religious hymns in his memory. As the audience later discovers, the live action of the play also takes place on the anniversary of Pavlik's death. Thus, the original day of Pavlik Morozov's murder (the exact date of which has never actually been confirmed, but is traditionally thought to have been on 3 September 1932) is conflated in the play with the day when the video was shot (3 September 2008), as well as the present moment in which the audience watches the performance. The positioning of the screens and the close-up angle of the shots create the illusion that the elderly community of modern-day Gerasimovka occasionally join the audience in their observation of what takes place within the theatre space. Likewise, the live audience becomes implicated in the onscreen commemoration as the two interact via the live presence of the actors onstage.

The video elements of *Pavlik – my God* merge further images of past and present as the projected documentary footage of the town is spliced with old Soviet propaganda videos and dreams of a Soviet ideal. Old women in traditional Russian attire are shown standing outside their small wooden houses. A herd of cows wanders through the street, and the vast open space that characterizes so much of the country outside its city centres reminds the play's generally urban audience how differently time and linearity can function in this town over 2,000 kilometres from Russia's capital.

Real presence

In addition to the temporal instability of historical narratives, questions about the reliability of space also came under scrutiny after the end of the Soviet Union. As Emma Widdis describes in her essay, 'Russia as Space', streets and squares were renamed, monuments were removed, and as a result, notions of public space in the Soviet Union also became untrustworthy (2004: 31). It is precisely this distrust, I suggest, that lends verisimilitude to the play of space in *Pavlik – my God*. A close look at the nature of space in Belenitskaia's play reveals how, through the process of theatrical representation, the stage on which *Pavlik – my God* is performed, while never ceasing to maintain its corporeality as a stage, is simultaneously converted into the sprawling Siberian steppe of Pavlik Morozov's hometown.

Following Pavlik's challenge to traditional notions of historical linearity in his line, 'That's not a fact', a strobe light begins to flash and an ambient sound reminiscent of an aeroplane fills the room. The two actors perform a series of poses: one evoking Vera Mukhina's iconic Soviet-era Worker and Kolkhoz Woman statue and another in which Pavlik holds Tania lying lifeless in his arms. The sound and strobe lighting build in intensity and speed as Pavlik recites a few lines from Stepan Shchipaev's sixty-page romantic poem about the murdered boy-legend. The poem describes in detail how the sun shone down on the cold autumn forest and revels in describing the ripe, juicy berries the boys had ventured out to gather on that fateful day in 1932.

Next, Pavlik zips Tania into the large suitcase that had formerly held her wares for sale. He lifts the actress inside the suitcase and spins her in a couple of circles before placing the suitcase down gently and exiting the stage. The lights fade to black with only a soft pool of light focused on the suitcase with Tania still inside it. A few autumn leaves float down from the fly-space and the rhythmic clicking of an old film projector eclipses the ambient sound of the aeroplane. The word 'papa' which had been projected on the centre screen is replaced by an old-fashioned Soviet propaganda video detailing the legend of Pavlik Morozov. Shot by director Vasilii Alchikov, the film was originally released in 1977 and features re-created scenes of Pavlik's heroic deeds.

This strip of action, from Pavlik's line 'That's not a fact', through the evocative choreography and imagery of Mukhina's classic Soviet monument until the end of the video segment, initiates the temporal and spatial metamorphosis staged by the play. The distinction between past and present collapses and the theatre is converted into a mutable space where Tania's imagination of her historical hero merges with the reality of events that are taking place onstage. The movement sequence represents Tania's journey from Moscow to Gerasimovka but also serves to take the audience back in time and across several time zones to a space where one has the sense that very little has changed since the days of Soviet collectivization in the 1930s.

After the archival video footage comes to a close, Tania unzips the suitcase from the inside. Once freed from the luggage, the actress begins to uncurl herself and emerge, all the while describing the details of her journey. Soon, Pavlik returns to the stage, this time in the form of a statue. He appears in stiff white clothing, his face painted white, wearing a small red neckerchief. This red tie is a familiar symbol of the Soviet pioneer uniform, a set of garments almost every Soviet child was required to don at one point or another once they joined the obligatory version of the scouts, only with a distinctly Soviet twist. There is a comical irony to the statue's entrance, with his feet restricted by a cardboard pedestal. The actor inches ahead awkwardly as his false right arm and plaster-clenched fist wave about in front of him.[6] Despite the statue's apparent silliness Tania reacts to the figure with reverence and explains to him precisely why she has come to Gerasimovka to see him. 'Are you Pavel Morozov?' Tania asks. 'Yes', the statue responds drily. 'The son of the accused?' she confirms. 'Yes', Pavlik repeats. After a few more clarifying questions, Tania reveals to her stage partner why she has come. 'I want to become you', she informs the animated statue (3).

At first the vivified monument cannot comprehend why she would want such a thing. 'Have you seen the report on our dug-up bodies?' He begins to recite the police report describing where he and his brother were found after the murder. 'The victim was found lying in an easterly direction, his head covered by a bag. The flesh between his thumb and forefinger had been sliced through on the left hand. Fatal stab wounds were identified in his groin and abdomen. His insides spilled out. The second fatal incision was in the victim's chest area next to the heart. Cranberries were scattered underneath him ... .' He pauses and asks Tania, 'Why would you want that?' (4).

'I want to become you', she insists, ignoring his question. 'Your hands were cut because you were fighting back', she continues, to feed the image she has created of her imaginary hero. Pavlik responds, 'That was just a reflex to stop the blade.' He attempts to reason with her, 'I'm dead. Everybody hates me.' Tania listens to Pavlik's attempts to dissuade her and replies encouragingly, 'Well, hey, I'm not perfect either, but at least you're committed to something. That's so rare these days' (4). After a

Figure 13: *Pavlik – moi Bog*, directed by Evgenii Grigoriev (2009)

sufficient amount of convincing, Pavlik acquiesces to Tania's devotion and her request by leading her in a recitation of the traditional pioneer pledge. He clumsily ties a red pioneer scarf around her neck with his one functional hand and instructs her on the conversion ritual. 'I, Tatiana Zharova, do solemnly promise, in the presence of my comrades in the ranks of the Vladimir Ilich Lenin All-Soviet Pioneer Organization: to love and cherish my Motherland passionately and to live, study, and fight as the great Lenin bade us and as the Communist party teaches us' (4). The sound of Tania's pledge is absorbed by a recorded feedback loop that builds in speed and intensity until Tania and Pavlik are left facing the audience with their mouths gaping open, as the frenzied electronic echo of their declared commitment to Lenin resounds around them. Next, the two take their place on the platform centre stage as the projection screens are lit up with images of the local landscape.

Scenes of limitless fields and wide-open skies begin revolving on the screens around Tania and Pavlik. Some of the projections are sped up so that the clouds move quickly while the land appears to stand eerily still. Soon the centre screen settles on the image of Pavlik's statue which appears in the background behind the live monument onstage, a visual echo that further muddies the difference between reality and creative representation in the play. Tania treats the onstage monument tenderly as she brushes off some dust, straightens out Pavlik's pioneer scarf, and gently places her head on his shoulder. At this the boy looks around as if to see if anyone is watching before he places his cheek against her forehead in a moment of understated tenderness. With their eyes closed, neither Tania nor Pavlik notice at first as the townspeople appear, larger than life, on the screens all around them. After a small crowd has gathered, Pavlik suddenly realizes that they are being watched. He pulls Tania out of her reverie.

Shaking her hand in a falsely officious manner, Pavlik tells Tania there is something he needs to tell her. 'The colour red suits you,' he tells her, referring to her iconic pioneer scarf, a symbol of Soviet patriotism, 'but you know, I didn't have a scarf like that.' 'Did you lose it?' Tania asks him. 'No,' Pavlik says as he leans in and whispers in her ear, 'I was never a pioneer. Tatiana, I never denounced my father' (5). Founded in 1922, the Young Pioneer movement was thought to be an essential element of Communist education for young people across the Soviet Union by the early 1930s. However, the pioneer uniform and its iconic red tie were only elevated to the level of sacred symbolism in the mid-1930s. As Kelly describes, 'In the 1920s, ties had not been obligatory even on demonstrations, and Pioneer uniforms had been so scarce in rural districts that they were even awarded as prizes for good behaviour; ten years later, the past was reinvented to suggest that tie-wearing had always been an intrinsic part of Pioneers affiliation' (154–5). In 1939, Pavlik's portrait was retouched to include the red tie, an example of the type of Soviet historical revisionism that has given way to contemporary anxieties about historical narratives and authoritative discourse in twenty-first-century Russia.

Still holding Tania's right hand, Pavlik shares this controversial information with his stage partner. 'Yeah, right', she responds, refusing to accept what he has just told her. Tania then attempts to pull away from Pavlik who, with his functioning left arm, holds onto Tania's right hand. This leads to a small scuffle that dislodges Pavlik's false arm, which drops to the floor upstage, behind the platform on which the two are standing. Tania immediately stoops to the floor to retrieve the plaster arm as Pavlik continues to speak with purpose, 'Only two things are real: I was born, and I was murdered in the forest where Fedka and I were gathering cranberries to make winter jam. I was killed, but the truth is, I wanted to live. I'd be over 90 by now. I'd have lost all my teeth. I'd be deaf, and probably blind. Though actually I'd probably have died in the war, like half the village did, because I'd have been so brave' (5). Tania refuses to hear him and continues in her veneration of the boy as the righteous hero she so desperately wants him to have been, despite the fact that he tells her repeatedly how he never wrote a denunciation and that he would have preferred to live. Tania has nothing to say about Pavlik's declaration. In fact, she begins the next scene alone on stage, reciting the details of his supposed written denunciation and gesturing enthusiastically with the statue's right arm which she held onto at the end of the previous scene.

Soon Pavlik re-enters the space, no longer constrained by his cardboard pedestal, having shed his statue-like shell. This time his status as a statue is indicated by white clothing and white face paint, on top of which the actor has donned a false moustache and a tattered brown sports jacket. He leans on a single crutch, though he moves with agility as he performs his best crotchety-old-man impression. He plays at performing himself as the 90-year-old man he never came to be. As Tania revels in the fantasy of how Pavlik wrote the denunciation against his father with his own hand, shaking the statue's detached right arm, Pavlik storms the stage. 'Have you seen the denunciation yourself?' he yells at Tania with disdain. 'No,' she responds. 'But …', he interrupts and shouts forcefully, 'that's because I never denounced my father!' (5).

Pavlik attempts to reason with the young woman by describing the absurdity of the scenario and the impossibility of the legend as it has been reported over the decades, but Tania will have none of it. She pulls off his moustache and backs him up against the stage wall. Pavlik continues explaining how his father's trial unfolded farcically as Tania tries tirelessly (and fails) to reattach the monument's fallen arm. When this effort proves futile she throws the arm aside, takes out a knife from the suitcase that has been left in the corner, and proceeds to stab Pavlik in the abdomen three times with force. His reaction is minimal. 'Stone', he says, knocking on the white plaster wig that sits atop his head, implying that Tania cannot kill a statue, someone who is already dead, or conversely, someone who may have never even lived.

Tania does not want to know what really happened to Pavlik; she feels she has found something to believe in and is willing to ignore all historical data in order to maintain that belief. Her imaginary idol is falling down around her and Tania will do almost anything in her attempt to keep the fantasy in place. For Tania the Soviet images in the play represent an ideal, something in which one can truly invest one's self without the cynicism she sees as inherent to the culture of today. In this way, Belenitskaia explores her own relationship to symbols of the Soviet past as an expression of a genuine longing for the ideals such symbols were meant to represent, while simultaneously discovering the fact that many of the ideals such images symbolized not only failed to come to fruition but were actually instrumental in the systematic state terrorism of Stalinist Russia.

In order to achieve this multivalent exploration of both the desire for, and terror of, symbols of the past in the present, Belenitskaia calls upon an established Russian literary tradition of bringing historical monuments to life. We have observed the uncertain nature of time and space in the post-Soviet Russian context and considered the process of transformation undertaken via Tania's journey to Gerasimovka. Next, this chapter analyses the mutability of matter in Belenitskaia's play. It illustrates how the vivification of Pavlik's statue characterizes an important pattern of metamorphosis in Russian art and culture and explores how this instance of theatrical enactment resonates within the broader Russian documentary theatre repertoire.

This is my body

The tradition of transforming monuments from inanimate to animate holds a prominent place in Russian literary history. As Roman Jakobson details in his essay, 'The Statue in Pushkin's Poetic Mythology', three of Aleksandr Pushkin's best-known works feature statues that come to life – *The Stone Guest* (1830), *The Fairytale of the Golden Cockerel* (1835), and perhaps most famously, *The Bronze Horseman* (1837). The title character of Pushkin's *Bronze Horseman* is brought to life yet again in Andrei Bely's 1913 Symbolist novel *Petersburg*. And, more recently, author Vladimir Voinovich, who is best known as a late Soviet satirist, published his novel *Monumental Propaganda* (2000), in which a small-town bureaucrat takes home a discarded Stalin monument and proceeds to build an unusual lifetime partnership with the statue, making it her own private icon. Like her literary predecessors, Belenitskaia brings Pavlik's monument to life, in part, to explore the relationship between the country's present-day circumstance and its history of political power. In the case of *Pavlik – my God*, however, the convention undergoes a major revision. The 'weighty, sonorous' power of the Bronze Horseman, as he races his way through the pages of Andrei Bely's *Petersburg* (1978) and exercises total power over Pushkin's Evgenii, as well as the menacing presence of Pushkin's *Stone Guest* and even Voinovich's comical comment on the longevity of political power, all stand in direct contrast to Belenitskaia's Pavlik who ultimately, despite Tania's insistence to the contrary, represents an innocent casualty more than a historical hero.

Nonetheless, in each of these works the trope of bringing a monument to life follows a precedent for the possibility that the constructed likeness of a person might contain within it some dormant element of the person it claims to represent. That is to say that the tradition of bringing monuments to life in Russian literary history exposes a distinct flexibility when it comes to the corporeality of representation. Literary monuments are brought to life outside the Russian context; however, this book suggests that cultural investment in visual representations as active agents of change is heightened in cultures with a strong history of Orthodox influence, where many believe that icons embody elements of the saints they depict. In her modern interpretation of this familiar literary tradition, Belenitskaia consciously exploits a legacy of investment in the belief that representation can lead to incarnation.

At this point in our consideration of the play, it is important to keep in mind that the figure of Pavlik Morozov as historical legend bears little to no resemblance to any actual person from the past, and that the mythology constructed around the boy's name exists almost exclusively in poems, operas, films, and in the cultural imagination. Thus, there is a sense in which the invocation of the cultural myth of 'Pavlik Morozov' as embodied through the performance of Leonid Telzhenskii in the play could be said to be as *real* a 'Pavlik Morozov' as any other. In other words, I suggest that through the theatrical representation of their legendary martyr-hero, the creators of *Pavlik – my God* manage to stage an actual incarnation of Pavlik Morozov onstage. If, as this chapter has shown, the theatrical space holds the possibility to convert past into present, and reality into fiction, then the leap of faith required to believe in the conversion of an actor into embodied cultural legend is not far-fetched.

The notion that the act of theatrical representation contains within it the possibility of incarnation recalls this book's previous discussion of the Russian Symbolists and their investment in theatre as a religious act in which audiences and artists were meant to become one through their efforts to recreate existing reality (see Peterson, 1986). For the Symbolists, theatre was a craft that had the capacity to transform one's experience of the everyday. Through the process of theatrical representation, the Symbolists sought to provide both artists and audiences access to a transcendental realm. In his 1908 essay, 'Theatre of One Will', for example, Fedor Sologub compares the act of performance to a 'liturgical act' and a 'mysterious rite' (Sologub, in Green, 1986: 180).

In noting these parallels between the performance of *Pavlik – my God* and the Symbolist investment in theatre as a 'liturgical act' we also must inquire into what the contemporary analogue to the Symbolists' higher consciousness might be. For a generation of Russians struggling to reconcile the incredulity of historical narratives and their encroachment upon the ambiguous ideology of the present, documentary plays like *Pavlik – my God* offer audiences a chance to think critically and collectively about the nature of their country's contemporary civic sphere. The live embodied practice of performance involves each of its participants in, as Mikhail Kaluzhskii describes it, 'an active process of uncovering the hidden and forgotten' (Kaluzhskii, 2012). By representing the narratives of the past within the live theatrical space of the present, participants of Russian documentary theatre are provided a venue in which to interpret the past and reconsider its influence in the present. Artists and audiences alike are directly implicated in the process of interrogating how one's perception of the past comes to bear on one's ability to believe in the present. As the incarnation of Pavlik Morozov in Belenitskaia's play makes especially clear, the country's documentary theatre artists perform not only in memory of the events of the past but, additionally, in anamnesis of them. They recall aspects of their history in such a way as to make them, quite literally, operative in the here and now. They stage opportunities for audiences and artists to interact with the events of the past through their embodied performance of those pasts in the present.

The creators of *Pavlik – my God* evoke the flexibility of time, space, and material in contemporary Russian culture to full effect in order to join audiences and artists in precisely this kind of collective exploration of their national historical narratives and the role such narratives play in each person's individual life in the present. When it comes to historical narratives like that of Pavlik Morozov, of course, one never knows which elements of the story are real and which parts are imagined. The autobiographical nature of *Pavlik – my God* inspires an analogous process of questioning in its audience: one can never be sure which parts of the play are drawn directly from the playwright's experience and which have been fabricated. In its confusion of the distinction between what is real and what is imagined, *Pavlik – my God* confronts key concerns in contemporary Russian culture and embodies core elements of the country's fraught relationship to its Soviet past.

And they believed me

In Pavlik's heyday, when groups of young Pioneers from all over the country used to travel to Gerasimovka to pay their respects to the 'Pioneer 001', there was a tradition that, in addition to visiting his monument and the town's one-room schoolhouse, children would also visit the place in the forest where his body was found. A small gate protects the sacred spot, and it was at this gate that children were encouraged to leave notes for Pavlik Morozov with the belief that the young martyr could grant wishes from beyond the grave. In the play, Tania also has a wish which she tries to tell to Pavlik during the performance; but he insists she follow the protocol by writing it down on a piece of paper and leaving it for him, as everybody else was required to do.

At this point in the play, a large glass jar filled with folded pieces of paper descends from the fly-space. Pavlik explains to the audience members that they each have a piece of paper and a pencil under their seats and that if they would like to leave a wish, he will do his best to grant it. As audience members reach under their chairs and begin to write, Pavlik reads off examples of the type of handwritten notes he has received in the past. 'I wish for mama, papa, and Vovka, my bunny, to live forever in happiness and health.' 'I wish papa would quit drinking.' 'I wish to graduate from high school with honours' (9). What are we, the audience, to make of this sequence, in which we learn that the wishes of several previous generations have been entrusted to a mythical historical figure, a child who was murdered by his own family? And how do the implications of such an irony inform our perception of Tania and her personal transformation over the course of the play?

Tania's last day in Gerasimovka has arrived. She has struggled to reconcile her own memory of her father and of the events of her past with the memories of him she has created for herself. Here again, she reflects upon the nature of truth and fiction as she tells a story, taken directly from the playwright's own biography, 'There are three things that I'll never forget: How my sister begged him to come home and said that she didn't want to live without him. She had only just turned nine. How, when he left, mom ran after him in her slippers in the snow. And how, when I knew he had gone forever, I lied to them telling them he'd be back soon. And they believed me' (7). This passage is a direct reference to the complications of truth and lies, reality and fiction embedded in the heart of the play. The protagonist, who is known to be a surrogate for the playwright, tells the audience of how in a moment of crisis she lied to those closest to her, and they believed her.

How is the audience to interpret such a confession, especially after having just spent the evening bearing witness to her journey and her story, which have been presented to the public as the playwright's own autobiographical truths? Why did she tell her mother and sister that her father would return, even though she knew it to be a lie? Was it for the express purpose of comforting her loved ones in their moment of need, or was it because she too simply needed to believe it was true? And, if it was out of her own desire to believe, then who is to say she has not been telling the same kinds of lies to her audience throughout the previous hour? In this passage Tania attempts to scrutinize the essential difference between belief and reality as she sorts through her own relationship to both. She speaks the lines with the attitude of someone who has come to understand and acknowledge her wounds in life, and thereby encourages her audience to do the same.

In the final scene of the play, Pavlik invites Tania to share a toast in honour of his Jubilee and offers to listen as she tells him her wish. Glass in hand, Tania tells Pavlik what she wants most, 'I wish I had a father' (10). She and Pavlik clink their small glasses, Pavlik takes his drink quickly, looks down at the floor and says flatly, 'You did.' It is important to note, however, that there is an ambiguity to these lines in the Russian original which is not fully realized in the English translation. In Russian, Tania's line could be interpreted also as 'I wish there was a father', not only wishing for her own father but also for the realization of the very concept of 'father'. In this sense Tania's wish is a reflection of her desire for a father figure, but it also represents her desire for the realization of an essential mythology, of a history that never was. In this way Belenitskaia acknowledges the complexity of accepting her personal circumstance; but she also implies through the words of her alter ego that clinging to a mythology of the past without admitting the intricacies of actual historical events only serves to keep one further from one's self.

When Tania wishes for a father, she is simultaneously wishing for the realization of her ideal of justice and responsibility. When Pavlik answers her with, 'You did', or alternatively, 'There was', he is reminding Tania, himself, and the audience that while there are elements of Soviet history that represent such a mythical ideal, it is crucial to remember the contradictions, violence, and tragedies contained within it. In the final lines of the play, Belenitskaia makes clear her intention to show how Tania's personal journey of reconciling her past with her present reflects a necessity she sees in Russian culture more generally. As Tania undergoes her process of self-examination and excavation in the play, the audience of *Pavlik – my God* is given the opportunity to construct their own archeological project in order to investigate their relationships to history and themselves.

This final scene is indicative of the way *Pavlik – my God* traverses the limits between reality and representation. As each of the previous chapters in this book have demonstrated, shifting conceptions of time, space, and material stability in Russia throughout the twentieth century have paved the way for an onset of cultural anxiety in which paradox and scepticism became a way of life. The murky territory of 'documentary theatre', a form of performance which is essentially a contradiction in terms, has proven an ideal form for Russian theatre artists to reenact and to enact the paradoxes embedded in their day-to-day lives. Though on the one hand, Russia's documentary theatre artists' interest in the form is born out of their dedicated pursuit of truths and the revelation of justice, I suggest that the vivacity of documentary theatre in contemporary Russia is also closely connected to the genre's capacity to address the ambiguities of representation that have come to dominate so much of Russia's post-Soviet social space.

In a country where, as writer Peter Pomerantsev has claimed, 'Nothing is true and everything is possible' (2015), Russian theatre artists use their performative practice in an attempt to decipher and distinguish that which is constructed from that which is actually happening. At a moment when the past is still shrouded by mythology and the present remains muddied with cynicism, Russian documentary theatre artists are inquiring into the possibility of belief in contemporary culture. 'To believe or not to believe', as Mikhail Ugarov stated in a recent interview, 'has arisen as an important problem not only for those of us in the arts but for society as a whole' (Lisitsina, 2012).

The question of belief in the context of this study is closely tied to the related notions of truth, trust, and sincerity in contemporary culture. Through the performance of documents and the staging of verbatim texts, as Daniel Schulze argues, '[a]udiences seek to hold onto or even rescue the notion of truth, which seemingly is lost in contemporary society' (2017: 195). In other words, the live performance of documentary materials speaks to the anxieties and interests of our specific historical and cultural moment in that it signifies a desire to access an experience of authenticity. This is also the dynamic Janelle Reinelt observes when she writes, 'Living in a world of simulation where everything is understood to be only a copy of a copy of a copy and nothing is for sure, public rehearsal of facts becomes one way of holding on to the very notion of facts and of building a meaningful narrative around them' (Reinelt, 2006: 81–2).

The revelation and representation of facts is a central element of many productions included in Russia's documentary theatre repertoire, as it is in realty-based theatre worldwide. However, as indicated by the plays analysed thus far in this study, the rehearsal of facts is not as prominent a feature in the specifically Russian version of the form as it is, for example, in the UK or the US. In Russia, documentary theatre relies less on the revelation of a single or verifiable 'Truth' as it does on the exploration of individual and subjective truths. In fact, as my research suggests, the specifically Russian version of documentary theatre as a genre is often less concerned with presenting a provable or definitive historical narrative as it is with the exploration of how cultural narratives are constructed in the first place. In the case of *Pavlik – my God*, for example, the play makes no claim to portray the 'real story' of Pavlik Morozov. In fact, it can hardly be said to tell the 'real story' of its author Nina Belenitskaia either. Instead, the documentary nature of the play is located in its attempt to uncover the truth of how the historical and cultural narratives we tell ourselves about ourselves come to shape our perceptions of and relationships to the societies in which we live.

While tensions around justice, belief, and memory are crucial to documentary theatre practice as it appears across the globe, plays like *Legacy of Silence, Second Act. Grandchildren, One Hour Eighteen Minutes* and *Pavlik – my God* point directly to a number of questions located at the heart of documentary theatre as it has arisen in its specifically Russian historical and cultural context. To what degree can one believe in or trust the value of the spoken or written word? How can a community, nation, or society truly invest in its present without first acknowledging the complexities of its past? And, how does the uniquely post-Soviet Russian experience shape the unusual pairing of the theatrical and the real as practiced in contemporary Russian documentary theatre? In *Pavlik – my God*, Tania undergoes a transformation by investigating her own desire to believe in a past that never was and by coming to terms with the circumstances of her everyday life. In their performance of the play the actors and creators of *Pavlik – my God* invite their audiences to follow Tania's lead by looking closely at their own beliefs about the past and by questioning how they have come to influence their interpretations of the present.

Notes

1 *Pavlik – my God* premiered in October 2009 at Moscow's Project Fabrika and continued to run at Teatr.doc and at the Sakharov Center as a co-production of the Joseph Beuys Theatre and the documentary film collective Pervoe Kino. The original production featured actors Donatas Grudovich and Maria Kostikova as Pavlik and Tania. The roles were later recast with Leonid Telzhenskii and Maragarita Kutovaia, respectively. All references to the production in this book are based on the second casting. In March 2015, Grigoriev opened a third staging at the Gogol Center featuring Igor Bychkov in the role of Pavlik and, alternately, Anastasiia Pronina and Aleksandra Revenko in the role of Tania.
2 As there were some changes made to the text between the 2007 publication of the play in *Isskustvo kino* (No. 3) and the 2009 production discussed in this chapter, I have provided page numbers from the most up-to-date text, an unpublished script shared with me by the author.
3 The suitcase and its contents were subsequently stolen from the backstage area at some point during the production's first-year run, at which point the

props were replaced by surrogates, also taken from the personal collections of the actors and production team.
4 For more on the details of the Morozov trial see Kelly, 2005: 98–109.
5 The details Grigoriev's method and work were featured in a short news segment on a local Tavda television report in September 2008. This video can be viewed at https://www.youtube.com/watch?v=JYFKel-tDmU#t=25 (accessed 24 August 2018).
6 Costume design by Anna Selianina and makeup by Elena Demidova.

5

Burden of proof
New Sincerity and the performance of post-Soviet national identities

Questions about the nature of trust, sincerity, and belief in contemporary Russian culture run throughout the country's twenty-first-century documentary theatre repertoire. In their varied interpretations of the form, Russia's documentary theatre artists create performances that speak directly to the country's cultural tensions between history, memory, and national identity. Each of the plays discussed in this book explores the contours of how Russia's conflicted relationship to its Soviet past continues to influence and shape the experiences of people's everyday lives in contemporary culture. Though the majority of Russian documentary plays are focused on the events of the present rather than those of the past, they nonetheless reflect a cultural legacy of doubt and disbelief that has grown directly from the circumstances of Russia's Soviet history. In this penultimate chapter, *Witness onstage* considers how Russian documentary theatre artists use a peculiar blend of irony and sincerity in their explorations of twentieth-century history. By zeroing in on the interplay between cultural memory and national identity in Russia's documentary theatre repertoire, I consider how artists use the practice to express an earnest desire for both a past and a present worth believing in.

Chapter 5 focuses on the 2012 autobiographical solo show *Uzbek*, written and performed by actor-director Talgat Batalov. *Uzbek* tells the story of how Batalov emigrated from Tashkent to Moscow at the age of 19. The play is performed in the style of 'documentary stand-up', a designation conceived of by the artist himself. *Uzbek's* style of performance recalls that of renowned Russian playwright and performer Evgenii Grishkovets, whose solo shows in the 1990s helped pave the way for the emergence of New Russian Drama. As Beumers and Lipovetsky describe, Grishkovets' solo show *Kak ia sel sobaku* (*How I Ate a Dog*, 1998) 'created a new aesthetic convention and a new kind of relationship between playwright and actor, theatre and spectator' in Russia (2009: 179). Like Grishkovets, Batalov exploits the singular intimacy of autobiographical solo performance and employs a satirical tone in his expression of his personal history. Interestingly, Batalov does not cite Grishkovets as a major influence, even though their works share many important qualities. In my 2012 interview with Batalov during the Drama New Code Festival (DNK) in Krasnoiarsk, the artist told me his style of performance is primarily inspired by American stand-up comedians like Lenny Bruce, George Carlin, and Bill Hicks. He describes the tradition of stand-up comedy in the US as 'social therapy' and asserts that Russia has not yet developed its own culture of stand-up where people can go to 'laugh at their own taboos' (see Fedorovskaia, 2013).

In his invocation of some of the most groundbreaking and controversial comics in recent history, Batalov draws clear connections between his work and the biting social satire of his American predecessors. He places his performance of *Uzbek* within the structure of Western stand-up, a performative genre, as Ian Brodie writes, 'predicated on the *illusion* of intimacy [and] a disregard for the distancing of the stage' (2008: 156). Batalov's performance seeks to replicate the direct communication and occasionally antagonistic relationship between comedian and audience that is characteristic of the 'kings of comedy' cited above. *Uzbek* deploys a distinctly sarcastic tone in its depiction of the corruption and absurdity of modern Russian bureaucracy and its satirical critique of xenophobia and prejudice against Central Asian immigrants in Moscow. In this way, Batalov's play addresses a number of pressing sociocultural issues in Putin's Russia, including immigration, xenophobia, and the performance of post-Soviet national identity.

In addition to its sardonic overtones, *Uzbek* also voices what I argue is a distinctly sincere sentiment in its attitude toward certain elements of the Soviet past. My use of the word sincerity in this study draws on Lionel Trilling's definition of the term as one used to describe 'a congruence between avowal and actual feeling' (1974: 2). However, it is also important to note that in the years since the publication of Trilling's seminal study *Sincerity and Authenticity*, the connotations of the word 'sincerity' have shifted as contemporary notions of selfhood are newly negotiated within what some scholars have termed our post-postmodern society (see, for example, McLaughlin, 2004; Trimmer, 2010). Moreover, as Ellen Rutten discusses in her book *Sincerity after Communism* (2017), the notion of a 'New Sincerity' is especially nuanced as it arose in the late and post-Soviet period in Russia because of its direct connection to the processing of the country's twentieth-century historical traumas. Batalov's performance embodies many of the ironies and paradoxes of national identity in the post-Soviet context alongside its honest expression of the performer's lived experience. Through its close reading of *Uzbek* in performance, this chapter inquires into what exactly is at stake in the contradiction between the style of irony to which the performer credits his work, and the apparent sincerity observed in Batalov's radical effort to express candidly the complexities of his own cultural heritage onstage.

Show us your papers

'Hi, everyone. My name is Talgat Batalov and today I'm going to tell you why I'm not an Uzbek' (Batalov, 2012: 1). Thus begins Batalov's comedic recounting of his own immigration process in the show that premiered in February 2012. *Uzbek* was one of a collection of new documentary plays featured in the theatre festival, 'Breaking Down Borders: Working with Documents' (*Razrushaia granitsu: rabota s dokumentami*), produced by Georg Genoux's Joseph Beuys Theatre and held at Moscow's Sakharov Center. For several years after the festival, *Uzbek* was included in the regular repertoire at both the Sakharov Center and Teatr.doc. It has been shown at the restaurant-club Artefaq and toured nationally and internationally to theatre festivals throughout Russia and Eastern Europe, as well as to Seoul and to London. In 2013 *Uzbek* was nominated for a Golden Mask award in the 'experiment' category.

Batalov was born and raised in Tashkent. He came up as an actor at the Ilkhom Theatre, trained by director Mark Weil. Like Batalov's family, Weil's had also relocated to Uzbekistan from elsewhere in the Soviet Union. Weil founded the Ilkhom theatre in 1976 and was internationally recognized for his innovative and socially engaged performance work. In 2007, Weil was murdered in the entranceway to his apartment building. Several years later, in 2010, three men were convicted of the murder, claiming their actions were in response to Weil's portrayal of the Prophet Mohammed in his production *Poderzhaniia koranu* (*Imitating the Koran*, 2006), based on a poem of the same title by Pushkin. Many people doubt the veracity of the conviction, however, and believe Weil's murder to have been politically motivated. It was following Weil's murder in 2007 that Batalov decided to leave his home and his family and begin the process of immigrating to Moscow (Chachko, 2012).

By speaking in the first person about his experiences as an Uzbek immigrant, Batalov's solo show creates space for the exploration of national identities in Russia and the former Soviet republics, a topic rarely raised in contemporary Russian dramatic practice. In Uzbekistan, Batalov jokes, everybody thinks of themselves as Russian: Jews, Georgians, Armenians, Tatars, even Koreans. Everyone who speaks Russian, he says, identifies as Russian. In the play's opening lines, Batalov describes his surprise at arriving in Moscow at the age of 19, only to find out that Russians saw him as Uzbek. 'When I lived in Uzbekistan I considered myself Russian because everybody there considers themself Russian', Batalov claims. 'When I came to Moscow I was considered an Uzbek', he continues. 'So you would say to someone, "You know, I'm from Uzbekistan." And they'd say, "That means you're an Uzbek." You'd say, "No, I'm not an Uzbek" – "What? It's Uzbekistan, everybody there's an Uzbek." And you'd think, "OK, now I'll explain what it means to live in a multicultural city where there are 160 different nationalities", and you start to list every nationality. Then you think, "Fuck it, that'll take too long", and you say, "OK, guys, I'm an Uzbek." The truth is, I'm just a regular old Tatar' (1).

In this passage, Batalov explicates the intricate nature of national identity in the post-Soviet context. He explores the historical legacy of a nation that allegedly sought to promote both the individuality of the varied nationalities it came to encompass as well as the mythology of the Soviet Union as a unified multi-ethnic nation with Russia at its centre. 'Of the many ambivalences and contradictions woven into the fabric of Soviet civilization,' according to Mark Bassin and Catriona Kelly, 'nothing was more ambivalent and contradictory than national identity' (2012: 3). In the opening lines of his show, Batalov details the lasting impact of the Soviet Union's so-called 'friendship of the people' ideology and shows how it continues to shape individuals' experiences of life in the post-Soviet region.

Batalov felt an incongruity between how he had previously defined his own national identity and that which was imposed upon him after moving to Moscow. An impulse to identify the performer's specific national heritage is especially problematic, as the audience deduces, because his appearance is neither traditionally Uzbek nor identifiably Tatar. However, neither his appearance nor his ethnic heritage were ever sources of contention for him in Tashkent, a city full of residents whose families were relocated from throughout the former Soviet republics, particularly during the early 1940s. By drawing his audience's attention to the clashes between

Figure 14: *Uzbek*, created by Talgat Batalov (2012)

how people in Uzbekistan identify themselves and how they are conversely categorized by the majority of Muscovites, Batalov reveals tensions around the longstanding cultural investment in the notion that Russia stands as a modern centre to Central Asia's premodern periphery.

In his book *Social Construction of International Politics: Identities & Foreign policies in Moscow 1955 and 1999*, political scientist Ted Hopf demonstrates how the social and spatial relationship between Russia and Central Asia has been an important factor in the construction of national identity in Russia for nearly a century (2002: 55). He explains how the 'hierarchical relationship between Russia at the top and Central Asia at the bottom' has become integral to the country's developing identity discourse throughout the Soviet and post-Soviet years. Hopf's study focuses on specific moments in Russia's twentieth-century history. However, as has become clear more recently, tensions around immigration and xenophobia became particularly lethal at the start of the twenty-first century in Russia, especially in Moscow, where the population of Central Asian migrant workers continued to grow. The rise of Russian nationalism in Moscow and around the country witnessed a notable shift. The revolution in Ukraine, the annexation of Crimea, and the subsequent war in Luhansk and Donbas have led to an unusual pivot on the part of many Russian nationalists who have maintained their allegiance to Putin partly by redirecting their violent intent toward the mythology of an encroaching Ukrainian fascism. Despite these shifting political circumstances, the influx of Central Asian immigrants in Russia remains a source of tension and underlying conflict in many cities throughout the country.

Precise statistics are, naturally, impossible to pinpoint, given the vagaries of legal documentation among many of Moscow's Central Asian immigrants, but some experts estimate that migrant workers make up no less than ten per cent of Moscow's current population. According to a study by the advocacy group Eurasia.net, there are roughly 500,000 Kyrgyz immigrants, one million Tajiks, and two and a half million Uzbeks who have taken up temporary residence in Moscow as guest workers since the early 2000s. The dominance of this sociospatial rhetoric in contemporary Russian culture is not only reflected in Batalov's text, but also in the staging of his show.

Uzbek is performed in a bare space without scenery. The audience sits in chairs clustered together in the middle of the room. In the original production, a collection of strip lights were laid out on the floor in the shape of Moscow's Metro map. The audience's seats were set within the boundaries of Moscow's circle line, otherwise known as the city's centre. In the premiere, Batalov stood outside the centre and travelled to various points on the map that coincided with the outlying regions he travelled to in his journey toward Russian citizenship. In its latest incarnation, *Uzbek*'s staging no longer includes the strip lights that indicate the city's Metro map; but Batalov's primarily Russian audience remains in the centre, while the performer presents his autobiographical story from numerous stations along the edge of the space. As Batalov describes the different locations to which his journey has taken him through the years, he moves around the room to various places, requiring audience members to adjust their seats and crane their necks if they care to see the action at all times during the show.

If, as Hopf argues, Russia has historically been perceived as the centre to a Central Asian periphery, then Moscow is thought to be the cultural hub within that national context. In fact, a similarly hierarchical relationship dominates the sociospatial dynamics within the city limits: many people who live in Moscow's outlying regions strive to take up residence within the Metro's central circle line. In *Uzbek* the audience inhabits the space of Moscow's crowded centre, whereas Batalov remains relegated to the periphery as he collects the documents necessary to provide him a way in. In this sense, the play embodies Batalov's experience of outsiderness and places the audience in a both literally and figuratively uncomfortable position within the structure of the play.

The only objects that share the performance space with Batalov are a couple of boxes that are revealed to contain collections of documents. These documents include his green Uzbek passport and military registration

Figure 15: *Uzbek*, created by Talgat Batalov (2012)

card, his red Russian passport, and his proof of residence for a small village in Tverskaia region with fewer than six hundred residents. As he narrates the darkly farcical shenanigans involved in acquiring many of these documents, Batalov hands them out to audience members, who pass them around so that each spectator can verify their validity.

One of the first documents Batalov presents for inspection is his red Russian military registration card, where it is written that he has been deemed temporarily unfit for military duty. As Batalov tells the story, he arrived at the army registration office assuming that he would be able to have his Uzbek registration card rewritten to exempt him from military duty. However, unsurprisingly, the administrators at the Russian registration office had a different idea and insisted that he return that evening for his military physical. It became clear to Batalov at that point that he needed to take action. Never having orchestrated a bribe before, he decided to exit the office to call a friend he knew to be an expert. As Batalov describes it, giving bribes was this friend's hobby. He gave bribes everywhere even when it wasn't necessary. 'Hi, I've got a big problem', Batalov tells his friend (2),

> – What is it?
> 'I'm being drafted into the army.'
> – What do you mean?
> 'Seriously, right now, I'm being drafted into the army.'

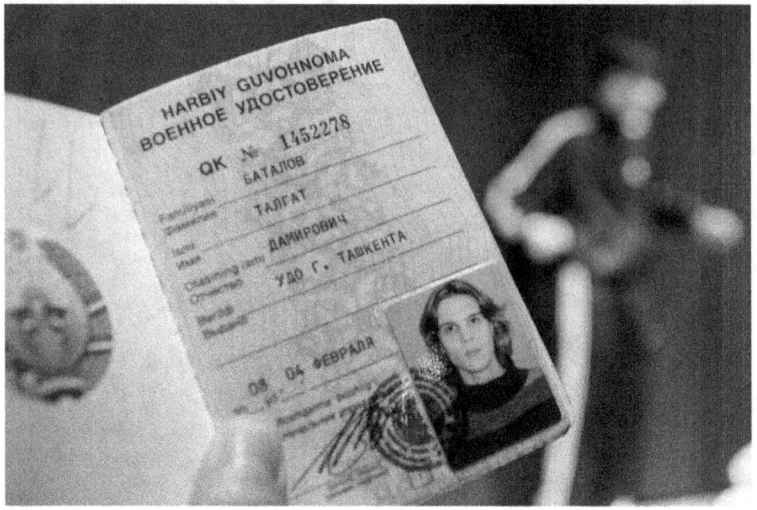

Figure 16: *Uzbek*, created by Talgat Batalov (2012)

– Where are you?
'Tverskaia region.'
– That's good news. And who is about to draft you?
'Women.'
– That's also good news.

Batalov's friend advises him to go to the closest store to buy cognac, vodka, and chocolates before returning to present them to the 'plumpest woman' in the office. As for the type of chocolates, his friend insists, '"Perfection" brand chocolates, only "Perfection" chocolates. None of those fucking "Inspiration" chocolates, they hate those' (2).

Batalov follows his friend's instructions precisely. He returns to the office, approaches the 'roundest looking woman' in the room, and asks her name. He then requests, 'Angelina Vladislavovna, may I speak with you for a moment?' At this she takes him by the arm and escorts him to a small office down the hall. She locks the door behind them, looks at Batalov and asks in confrontational tone, 'And?' 'I want to express my gratitude', Batalov tells the woman, to which she responds, 'Well, finally' (2). Having fully understood the implications of this statement, the woman instructs Batalov to return for the military commission at six o'clock that evening. Following this verbal agreement Batalov walks to the nearest supermarket to buy chocolates, cognac, and fruit before handing these goods to Angelina Vladislavovna shortly before his scheduled military physical.

By following his friend's advice and clumsily stumbling through his first official bribe, Batalov recounts how he walked away that night with the actual document the audience members hold in their temporary possession. The performer's comedic presentation of this story creates an atmosphere of inclusion. He speaks to the audience in a conversational voice and shares with them the types of personal narratives that are traditionally reserved for close friends. He even hands over the document under discussion, thereby expressing an apparent trust in the audience's implicit promise to return it. The rituals of such 'informal practices', as political scientist Alena Ledeneva calls them (2006), are well-known to Batalov's audiences; and it is, in large part, their familiarity that lends the narratives their humour.

As they laugh at the charade of Batalov's military physical and at the refined science of bureaucratic bribery, audience members are also invited to reconsider their own involvement in Russia's expansive network of informal exchange practices. Their position within the crowded centre of Batalov's 'peripheral' narrative posits them in the role of those who have relegated the actor to the outside. As they receive Batalov's documents they are also implicated as in some ways akin to those city officials who seek to challenge his right to the city. Such a simultaneous expression of intimacy and antagonism is a hallmark of stand-up comedy and one Batalov exploits to its fullest extent in his behind-the-scenes look into the inner workings of Russia's acceptance of everyday corruption.

In her study on the interpersonal exchange of perishable goods in contemporary Russia, anthropologist Jennifer Patico investigates how the country's patterns of 'gift-giving' are closely related to its socialist past. While the exchange of money for favours is clearly recognized as a bribe, certain items such as candy, flowers, and cognac have become recognized in Russia as appropriate gifts or 'signs of attention' (znaki vnimaniia) commonly given to teachers, doctors, or other people in service positions who have shown particular care to a consumer (2002: 351). In Batalov's case, the differentiation between bribery and 'gift-giving' is ambiguous in that he presents his 'signs of attention' to the women at the military registration office before he has completed his military physical; but, as Patico admits, the difference between the two can often be hard to distinguish. By calling attention to the absurdity of these exchange practices, *Uzbek* asks its audience members to reconsider their own complicity in a society where corruption is normalized and indeed embedded in the practices of everyday life. The familiar and habitual nature of everyday corruption in contemporary Russian culture is one of the central taboos Batalov submits to comedic interrogation.

In addition to exposing the farcical nature of everyday corruption in twenty-first-century Russia, the story behind Batalov's military registration also calls attention to the paradoxical status of the document he presents to the audience. On the one hand, the means of the document's acquisition affirms that Batalov's military registration card itself stands for very little. In fact, as Batalov tells his audience, his status as 'unfit for military duty' is contingent upon his returning to the same military registration office annually and repeating the same ludicrous ritual of informal exchange in order to maintain the 'validity' of the document. On the other hand, without this infelicitous document that the audience casually passes around for inspection, the actor onstage would surely have had a very different immigration tale to tell.

Each time Batalov recounts the unofficial methods with which he acquired his immigration documentation, his audience is reminded of the false testimony the documents claim to present. Nonetheless, at the start of the show, when the actor begins to pass them out, he politely requests that the audience not forget to return them. He emphasizes the particular importance of returning his red Russian passport as he smiles slyly, admits an apparent vulnerability, and reminds the audience that he still needs that one. In this way, we observe how the role the documents play in *Uzbek* is characteristic of the contradictory and ambiguous status of official documentation in twenty-first-century Russian culture.

Performing documents

In her 2013 article, 'Clean Fake: Authenticating documents and persons in migrant Moscow', anthropologist Madeleine Reeves investigates precisely these blurred boundaries between documentation and authentication, as she describes the intricacies of Russia's unwritten rules of fakery widely adhered to by migrant workers, their employers, and the civil servants who facilitate the country's expansive system of unofficial networks. Reeves suggests that consideration of the informal industry of immigration documents provides 'insight into a mode of governance ... that thrives less on rendering subjects legible than on working the space of ambiguity between life and law' (508). The article includes the story of two Kyrgyz women who, upon arrival in Moscow, purchased their residency permits for 500 roubles at Kazanskii station. They were later discovered to have been in possession of false documents and sent back to their village a couple of hours outside Batken. In their interview with Reeves, the two women reflect upon their experience and describe to her what they came to understand as the difference between documents that are 'fake' (falshivye) and 'clean fake' (chistye falshivye). They explain that 'fake' documents can be immediately identified as counterfeit, whereas 'clean fakes' can be passed off as the real thing, depending on one's capacity to prove their 'authenticity'.

As ethnic profiling is a common and, in fact, legal practice in Russia, it is common for Central Asian immigrants to be asked to hand over their passports and registration certificates to police officers looking to collect their supplementary income. In the likely scenario that someone of so-called 'non-Slavic' (see Lemon, 1998: 22–5) appearance is stopped in the street or the Metro, they are then required to prove the authenticity of their documents by, for example, describing the precise location of the address indexed on their residency permit. Such a request can be problematic, even for those who *have* acquired authentic documents, since the address on the permit often bears no connection to where the person actually lives. That is to say, the efficacy ascribed to immigration documents and residency permits depends crucially on the document's *and* the individual's capacity to appear authentic. Therefore, 'Being "legal"', as Reeves writes, 'depends on successfully performing a right to the city and a convincing knowledge of its geography.' In other words, if the validity of a document is challenged by the authorities, it falls to the individual to perform its authenticity.

To catch the complexities of Reeves' argument and its relevance to a play like *Uzbek* we ought first to contextualize her use of the word 'performance' as it refers to both theatrical practice and the experience of day-to-day life. To this end, we return to the tried and trusted formulation of Austin's distinction between an utterance used to describe or indicate (constative), and one that enacts an action through the process of being spoken (performative). Reeves' assertion that an individual's behaviour has the capacity to inscribe a document with varying degrees of validity is an apt illustration of the performative dynamic Austin describes. The efficacy with which one is able to reproduce or 'perform' the identity indexed on his or her immigration documentation determines the degree to which that document is transformed into something functionally authentic.

In considering Batalov's performance of his national identity in *Uzbek*, however, we must also take into account how the information indexed on one's documents has the capacity to inscribe and shape the behaviour of the individual who carries them. How does the necessity to perform an 'authentic' identity influence the way an individual comes to experience his or her nationality? In our efforts to understand how everyday practices come to influence an individual's performance of his or her national identity, we are again put in mind of Richard Schechner and Victor Turner's foundational notion of performance as a type of 'restorative behavior'. These scholars' definition of performance as any 'strip of repeated action' or, in Schechner's words, 'twice-behaved behavior' (2002: 28), encompasses the term's theatrical connotations and also refers to the act of adopting certain habits or behaviours one interprets as appropriate to someone of a specific social standing or national heritage.

In the scenario that Reeves describes, we observe how in order to make their documents effectively authentic, Central Asian immigrants in Russia are regularly called upon to perform their national identity as it is indexed in their official documentation. By effectively performing his or her immigration document, a person has the ability to transform it into one that is functionally authentic. Furthermore, failure to do so might render even a legal document insufficient. In our analysis of *Uzbek* and Batalov's theatrical performance of his experience of national identity, it is also important to consider the notion of 'twice-behaved behavior' and to inquire into how the types of documents the actor pulls from his boxes might inscribe and shape the behaviour of the individual who performs them.

As Reeves' study makes clear, the information contained within one's official documentation, authentic or not, can play an important role in how people represent themselves or, alternatively, are represented in the social sphere. Individuals are required to perform their documents and thereby enact their authenticity. Meanwhile, the repeated necessity to adopt a set of behaviours thought appropriate to the identities indexed on one's immigration documentation inscribes one's relationship to the city and its inhabitants. That is to say that, while people are required to perform their documents, so too can documents be said to perform their people.

Migrants like me

Also pulled from Batalov's boxes are transcripts from a collection of interviews the performer conducted in preparation for the show. The first interview, read verbatim by Batalov onstage, is with a man named Khamid, an Uzbek immigrant who describes how he left his university in Tashkent to join his father selling doner kebabs near Kurskaia Metro station. In accordance with the station's location along the perimeter of Moscow's city centre, Batalov approaches one of the audience members sitting along the edge of the circle and asks them to give up their seat. 'Just like any other immigrant,' Batalov teases the audience member, 'I've come to take your place' (3). He then proceeds to sit in the audience member's chair and recounts how, at the request of his father, Khamid somewhat reluctantly left his home and his girlfriend to start his new life in Moscow, where he has been selling kebabs ever since.

Khamid's conversation demonstrates how difficult life in Moscow can be for many migrant workers. Though they may be university-educated, many immigrants are unable to find work in their field, either in Russia or at home, and find that their best bet at making a living wage is by working as cleaners, construction workers, or in fast-food establishments which will hire them without looking too closely at the details of their legal employability. As Reeves describes, many of these migrant workers inhabit the space between 'being legible and illegible to the state' by sharing and forging documents, a practice 'fraught with social and moral uncertainty' (509).

Another conversation Batalov recounts in the play is with Sharipov Karomat Bakoevich, a so-called 'Tajik human rights activist'. Batalov's play premiered in the middle of Russia's 2011–13 protest wave, a moment referred to most explicitly when Batalov recalls Bakoevich's belief that Russia's political opposition consists entirely of Israeli Jews paid by the American government to fly in specifically for demonstrations. At the end of his conversation with Batalov, Bakoevich shares some ironic advice regarding the actor's attendance at a series of recent political protests. He instructs Batalov to stay away from the upcoming opposition demonstration to be held at Bolotanaya Square and encourages him to join other Central Asian migrants in support of the current administration at an upcoming pro-Putin rally to be held at Moscow's Luzhniki stadium. 'Don't go to Bolotnaya Square. Come to Luzhniki on the 25th, that's where the national diaspora will be speaking out in support of Putin. He's a decent person. You don't like him? You're keeping quiet? I understand, but he's a decent guy' (11). By exposing the prejudices of other immigrants in passages like this, *Uzbek* makes all national stereotypes fodder for its comedic immigration tale and exposes the ludicrous ways in which people across nationalities justify their positions. The audience laughs knowingly at statements like this, as the play provides the space for people to come together and acknowledge collectively the many bizarre rituals around politics and social life in twenty-first-century Russia.

Not all of the documents that come out of Batalov's boxes relay such a cynical message, however. One of the boxes also divulges a letter from

Batalov's father in which he commends his son for having the courage to move to Moscow on his own and applauds him for maintaining his own sense of self and resisting the cynicism of life in urban Russia. Before reading the letter, Batalov jokes about how often he had to meet random travellers from Tashkent at the railroad station or even the airport in order to retrieve these letters from his father, who does not trust the Russian postal service and is unskilled in the use of electronic communication. The note itself, however, is read without comment, leaving the audience to accept it as a genuine expression of admiration. Batalov's father provides his son a brief update about how the buttons in the lift in their building have been stolen again and admits there is little other news to share. 'Were you at the opening of the Moscow Film Festival?', the actor's father enquires, thinking his son might be schmoozing with other film-industry stars. 'Takeshi Kitano, Kusturica, Will Smith, and others were there' (7). At the end of the letter, Batalov's father confesses to having fallen into a 'strange depression' that he himself cannot fully understand. He tells his son how he misses him and asks very simply if he has any plans to come home.

The tone of this letter from Batalov's father stands in stark contrast to the ironic humour that has dominated the play up until this point. Unlike the official documents in the play, all riddled with ambiguity, the letter from Batalov's father is precisely what it claims to be. It stands out as an honest expression of one person's subjective experience, free from the duplicity embedded in each of the documents that appear to have been issued by the state. In contrast to the sarcasm that precedes it, the letter from Batalov's father actually represents what it claims to verify. Here we are reminded of David Levy's assertion as discussed in the introduction to this book, the notion that documents are something we use as stand-ins for ourselves and others, as those things 'we create to speak *for us*, on our behalf and in our absence' (2003: 23).

Though many of the documents presented in *Uzbek* may not be historically reliable, they are nonetheless important arbiters of influence in the lives of many. In the case of Batalov's Russian military registration, the audience's attention is drawn to the unreliability of the document's testimony. We read that Batalov is unfit for military combat, according to official sources, but we are told by Batalov himself that the document was acquired through less than honest means. The letter from Batalov's father, conversely, is presented to the audience as an object free from such duplicity. It appears as a genuine expression of longing, a testimony to one person's actual experience of everyday life.

Another document in *Uzbek* that genuinely characterizes what it claims to represent is an audio recording Batalov shares of a Skype conversation between him and his mother in which she describes how her grandparents were evacuated to Uzbekistan during the war, and why members of all subsequent generations have stayed. In this conversation Batalov asks his mother if she regrets having spent her whole life in Uzbekistan, to which she responds, 'No, I was born here. My mother was born here. I'm already the second generation in Uzbekistan. I've lived here my whole life and, to be honest, I don't want to leave. I like it here' (17). She claims that, throughout the Soviet years, the question of a person's ethnic background was never a problem and that tensions around national heritage arose for her in Uzbekistan only after the 1990s.

In distinction to the documents that came before them, this letter from Batalov's father and the recorded conversation with his mother reveal a sense of longing, a desire for certain truths associated with a time that has passed as well as a wish for simplicity in attempts to define one's idea of home. How are we to interpret the seeming sincerity of these two documents within the pattern of irony and sarcasm constructed in the first half of the play? And, what exactly differentiates these personal documents from the official documents that have come before them? In order fully to appreciate the significance of these two documents as reliable testimonies, as artifacts from the past made legible in the present, we must keep in mind the conflicted status of documents in the twenty-first century, in Russia and internationally.

The theatrical presentation of both personal and public documents in *Uzbek* highlights their paradoxical position as both articles of evidence and denotations of doubt. By regaling the audience with his narratives of 'informal exchanges', Batalov draws attention to his immigration documents as infelicitous artifacts that represent a system rife with corruption. In contrast, the personal documents from his mother and father depict a sincerity that prioritizes the subjectivity of personal testimony over any official attempts at objectivity. By staging such a juxtaposition between the reliability of personal testimony and the suspicious status of official documentation, *Uzbek* interprets and embodies cultural anxieties around the authenticity of documents and the sincerity of testimony in contemporary Russian culture.

The honesty of these two documents serves to soften the front of irony the actor presents to his audience and reveals a thread of sentimentality that is woven throughout the fabric of the text. As critic and fellow theatre-maker Nikolai Berman writes, 'Talgat, whom I feel like calling by his first name here especially since he's the only protagonist of the play, lets us in on his most private moments. He reveals those parts of himself that are seldom divulged to even our closest friends: the desire to share something truly important, a sense of genuine vulnerability, and the need to open up to another person' (Berman, 2012). In his attempt to reveal the duplicity and absurdity of so many social practices in post-Soviet life through irony, Batalov simultaneously discloses his own sincere investment in the topics his play intends to mock. He invites his audiences to join him in his comical examination of post-Soviet national stereotypes and also provides them the opportunity to engage with how such stereotypes impact each person's experience of day-to-day life in contemporary culture.

Uzbek is, in one sense, an expression of cynical detachment from the unreliability of official discourse in twenty-first-century Russia. It discloses an attitude of disillusionment with the ideologies of the Soviet past and undercuts the myth of order in the post-Soviet present. However, Batalov's play in performance is also an expression of yearning. It calls out for intimacy and for interpersonal connections that reach beyond the confines of national and cultural categories. Batalov shares the details of his personal history in close proximity to his audiences and thereby builds an atmosphere of closeness. He also casts his audience in the uncomfortable role of those who have continually tried to keep him out of the centre as he is continually required to perform his national identity in accordance with what is thought socially acceptable. In this way, Batalov performs the paradox of a concurrent irony and sentimentality that speaks to Russia's longstanding fascination with the rhetoric of sincerity as it has developed throughout the late Soviet and post-Soviet years.

New Sincerity

As Ellen Rutten describes in *Sincerity After Communism*, notions of sincerity have captivated Russian artists and intellectuals ever since the publication of Vladimir Pomerantsev's essay 'On sincerity in literature' immediately following Stalin's death in 1953. A new attitude toward and obsession with literary truth telling developed in the 1960s–70s with the proliferation of *samizdat* texts, illegally published literature and letters circulated underground below the radar of Soviet censors. In the late 1970s and early 1980s, the earnest interests of *samizdat* gave way to the cynicism and sarcasm of Sots-art, an artistic movement that melded the aesthetics of postmodernism as they appeared in the West with a distinctly Soviet style that played on a culturally specific relationship to authoritative discourse (see Yurchak, 2006: 238–81). In 1984, dissident poet Dmitrii Prigov published a collection of works entitled *Novaia iskrennost* (*New*

Sincerity). His use of the phrase signalled a shift in modern Russian literature as more and more writers sought out ways to articulate earnest expressions of their day-to-day experiences, which stood in contrast to much of the cynicism and irony of late Soviet culture. Since that time, the concept of a 'New Sincerity' has been used to describe such disparate works as the literature of Vladimir Sorokin and Dmitri Vodennikov in Russia, as well as the writings of David Foster Wallace and the songs of the indie-rock band Bright Eyes in the US.

New Sincerity rhetoric appears across the globe as it is often used in Anglophone writing to describe an aesthetic phenomenon that arose in reaction to the cynicism and citationality of postmodernism in the late twentieth century. Both in Russia and in the west, New Sincerity refers to a style of art, music, literature, architecture, and so on, that simultaneously incorporates the relativism and irony associated with a postmodern mindset while also seeking avenues for the earnest expression of everyday existence. Its frequent use in contemporary cultural discourse indicates a fascination with notions of truth and 'being one's self' a 'hard-to-monitor virtue' Rutten explores in depth in her study (2017: viii). Such abstract virtues of authenticity have become further complicated since the early 2000s with the onset of social media, as individuals have more opportunities than ever to construct and present images of their 'true selves' to an increasingly mediatized global audience. Indeed, the desire for a type of new sincerity in the twenty-first century is no doubt a reaction, in part, to the widespread sense of isolation and insecurity that goes hand in hand with the rise of social media and online cultures of self-representation.

The notion of a new sincerity in Russian art and literature has developed in connection to a series of related categorizations: new seriousness (novaia sereznost), new naivety (novaia naivnost), new authenticity (novaia podlinnost), and new realism (novyi realizm). What each of these (primarily literary) categorizations has in common is an implied investment in identifying and interpreting works that represent an attempt to renegotiate one's relationship to the irony of the late Soviet period. One author's work that is often attributed to the genre of new realism is that of Zakhar Prilepin, whose novels and short stories have been heralded as ushering in a return to psychological prose in Russian literature. Following the gradual rusting out of the mechanics of Socialist ideology in the late Soviet years, and the financial and social crises of the 1990s, many of Russia's twenty-first-century authors find themselves searching for something to believe in. As Mark Lipovetsky describes the phenomenon, these literary and artistic trends have represented an attempt 'to *reconstruct the edifice of humanism in the space of chaos*' (1999: 247; original emphasis).

While traces of poet Dmitrii Prigov's initial use of the term 'New Sincerity' are apparent in the way twenty-first-century cultural critics use it, the concept has collected rather different connotations since it first appeared in Russia in 1984. Often described as a cultural reaction to postmodernism, the term New Sincerity has more recently been applied to works that, in Rutten's words, 'are aware of the limitations of language and ideology, and the fact that everything has been said before. However – and here they profess to take issue with postmodernism – they accept these limitations. Instead of merely thematizing them, the *new sincere* author insists on using a critical, nostalgic irony as a coping strategy' (2008: 203). As it appears in Russian art and literature, New Sincerity is a trend that openly acknowledges the citationality of contemporary discourse, encompasses the cynicism of post-Soviet irony, and expresses a genuine investment in the search for alternative modes of interpersonal communication.

For example, in his essay on New Sincerity included in the collection, *What is Soviet Now?*, Alexei Yurchak analyses the series of pioneer girl paintings by Russian painter Dasha Fursei. The paintings under discussion feature young girls in pioneer uniforms who appear to be experiencing various kinds of youthful discovery; there is an innocence to the paintings and the girls depicted therein, a simplicity in the enthusiasm they appear to be experiencing. According to the artist, the pioneer girls in her paintings represent an innocence that cannot be found in Russia today and one that Fursei associates with certain aspects of Soviet life, though she was born in 1978 and, as Yurchak writes, 'never reflected much on her Soviet childhood' (2008: 257–76).

Yurchak explains this seeming contradiction as follows, 'Although the aesthetics of new sincerity implies an avoidance of cynicism in relation to the subject matter, this does not mean that the new sincerity lacks irony. Quite the contrary, as a post-postmodern phenomenon it is acutely self-aware and self-ironic. However, this is a particular brand of irony, which is sympathetic and warm and allows its authors to remain committed to the ideals that they discuss, while also being somewhat ironic about this commitment' (2008: 258). In other words, Fursei's use of Soviet imagery in her pioneer-girl paintings represents a sincere longing for ideals she associates with the mythology of the past, but she is using those images in a self-conscious manner in order to explore the origins of that longing. In the case of Fursei's paintings, as interpreted by Yurchak, there is, in other words, an underlying irony embedded within the earnest and innocent appearance of the images.

In the case of Batalov's performance of national identity in *Uzbek* we observe an inverse dynamic. The play is presented as an ironic and mocking depiction of national stereotypes in the post-Soviet cultural space; however, the sarcasm of Batalov's play in performance actually belies an attitude of sentimentality toward elements of his personal and national histories. In this sense, Batalov's play in performance aligns itself with both Lipovetsky's and Rutten's observations about sincerity in post-Soviet culture. The simultaneous expression of irony and sincerity in Batalov's play serves as a coping mechanism that seeks to create order from the chaotic fallout of Soviet history. In the case of *Uzbek*, the show's paradoxical play of irony and sincerity reveals a desire to communicate openly and honestly with those around us and, in that way, seeks to inspire hope in both the audience and the performer.

By sharing his paradoxical sentiments about the past and present, Batalov gives voice to the challenges he and his audience members face in their efforts to navigate the complexities of life in post-Soviet Russia. He uses humour and irony to expose the farcical elements of national stereotypes and lay bare the corrosive nature of the country's system of informal networks. Alone onstage, Batalov embodies an earnest vulnerability as he submits himself to the judgement of his audiences. *Uzbek* is unique among the plays discussed in this study in that Batalov presents himself as himself and seeks to articulate the contradictions of his real-life experiences. Through their laughter, audiences acknowledge the absurdities and the ironies inherent to the post-Soviet life Batalov describes. By speaking the details of his conflicted relationship to his personal and national pasts, Batalov enacts the interpersonal connections his play seeks to inspire. Together both artist and audience work their way through the dark narratives of bureaucracy and xenophobia, of corruption and antagonism, and at the end of the play they are left with one another and a genuine expression of one person's experience of day-to-day reality. In other words, in addition to the cynicism on the surface of the performance, Batalov's play also communicates an underlying belief, that despite the banalities and corrupt qualities of so many interactions in contemporary life, there are also some memories, narratives, artifacts, sentiments, and moments in life that are worth believing in.

You are not an orphan

The final segment of the play features a video clip from a film Batalov remembers watching as a child. In the video, a young Russian boy whose parents were killed in the war appears outside a family home in rural

Uzbekistan. In showing this video, Batalov reminds his audiences of the 16.5 million Soviet citizens who were evacuated to Uzbekistan between 1941 and 1942. The refugees included Russians, Ukrainians, Lithuanians, and Latvians. Among them were such familiar personages as Anna Akhmatova, Nadezhda Mandelstam, and Aleksei Tolstoy. According to policy analyst Paul Stronski, the unprecedented scale of wartime evacuation to Uzbekistan's capital 'fundamentally changed the course of Tashkent's urban development ... Its prewar urban plan for rational growth quickly went by the wayside as the city struggled to respond to its new wartime role as a vital industrial centre with tens of thousands of refugees trying to survive in a hungry, disease-ridden, and overcrowded city' (2010: 73).

Among this influx of wartime evacuees were approximately 43,000 children, many of whom had lost their parents in the war (see Saidova, 2013: 757–60). Orphanages were opened all over the country in order to accommodate the influx of parentless children, while others were taken in by Uzbek families who opened their homes to Soviet children of varying national heritage. Batalov asks his audiences to reflect upon this historical moment in the last scene of his play when he shows a video clip from the film, *Ty ne sirota* (*You Are Not an Orphan*, 1963). Directed by Shukhurat Abbasov, the film tells the story of the Makamovs, an Uzbek family that takes in fourteen children from different ethnic backgrounds during the war.

In the fragment of the film shown at the end of *Uzbek*, a small Russian boy approaches the home where he sees Makamov, his wife, and a group of children playing in the yard. The boy, whose face is covered with dirt and soot, quietly asks the man whether it is true that he takes in orphaned children.[1] Makamov tells him it is true and asks him his name. 'Kolia', the boy responds. 'Come over here, Kolia, have a seat, Kolia.' 'But I'm so dirty', the boy says to him. Makamov assures the boy that it is not a problem.

> 'Where have you come to us from?'
> – From Smolensk.
> 'Do you have parents?'
> – The Germans shot them.

Makamov treats the boy tenderly and invites Kolia into his home. After showing the clip, Batalov explains to his audiences the real-life story on which the film is based, that of an Uzbek blacksmith who took in sixteen Russian children during the war years. 'It turns out', Batalov informs his audience, 'that my family was also taken in by a family like that. That is my great-grandmother and my grandfather ... And so it's thanks to Uzbeks that I am standing here today, telling you my story. That's why I want to say thank you to Uzbeks, and thank you for coming' (20).

How are we to interpret this video as the final document revealed in Batalov's presentation of himself? Does the audience, along with Batalov, watch the video with scepticism, knowing full well that the idyllic Soviet images of diversity and abundance bear little resemblance to the actual circumstances of the time? Or, does the video represent a nostalgic longing for an idealized time when the complexities of Soviet national identity were not as taboo and divisive as Batalov experiences them to be today? I suggest that the film clip, and in fact the play as a whole, manages to communicate both at once. The play is simultaneously a sarcastic and comedic comment on the state of national identity in Russia and the former Soviet republics and an honest expression of longing for an imagined and idyllic past.

Clean fake

By placing himself, his history, and his papers onstage, Batalov exposes the inscrutability of his own performance of post-Soviet national identity. He interrogates his relationship to what Reeves calls 'the long arc of sociospatial incorporation' in the region and uses the embodied practice of performance to explore how notions of Central Asians as 'peripheral Others' to Russia's modern–urban identity have shaped his experience as an Uzbek immigrant in modern Moscow. By playing the paradox of a simultaneously ironic interpretation of the past in conjunction with sincere expression of its ideals, Batalov calls attention to the constructed nature of national identity. He exploits the blurred boundaries between authentic, fake, and clean fake in order to set the stage for his 'social therapy' and create the space for the renegotiation of cultural narratives surrounding the authenticity of documents and the sincerity of testimony in contemporary Russian culture.

In a country where 'documents are never entirely knowable and never completely transparent' (Reeves, 2013: 509), documentary plays like *Uzbek* have taken on particular relevance. By sharing the stage with one another and with Batalov's actual documents, *Uzbek* creates the space for artists and audiences to redefine the categories of centre and periphery and to generate a renewed investment in the value of telling the stories of one's personal and national pasts. The actor's documents are presented as signs of the infelicitous nature of official discourse in the country while the comedic and ironic delivery of the text expresses an acceptance of the absurdities of the everyday. By speaking the details of his conflicted relationship to his personal and national narratives, Batalov enacts the interpersonal connections his play seeks to inspire. In this way, the play presents an alternative mode of communicating and transmitting cultural memory, and uses the embodied practice of performance to build its own method of articulating and indexing identity.

In a historical moment when the restrictions on free speech in mainstream media sources are tightening, small stages around Moscow and the country are more vital than ever as venues for the open representation, discussion, and negotiation of current events and cultural narratives in twenty-first-century Russia. As access to the internet and alternative sources of information has proliferated in Russia and around the world, the type of documents used in Russian documentary theatre is also shifting. More and more plays have begun to emphasize the experience of individuals, and tend to privilege spoken narratives above printed sources. Commitment to the verbatim technique has loosened over the years, as Russia's documentary theatre artists continue experimenting with various structures to facilitate a collision between the action onstage and the experience of daily life. Nonetheless, the centrality of the spoken word has remained among the form's most salient features.

Having traced the first decade of documentary theatre in twenty-first-century Russia from the founding of Teatr.doc in 2002 to the performance of *Uzbek* in 2012, this book has thus far analysed a variety of methods the country's theatre artists use in their efforts to explore and interpret their experiences of everyday realities in contemporary culture. As we have seen, the style and themes of the productions included in Russia's documentary theatre repertoire are varied. While there are controversial and political productions among them, there are also plays on topics as varied as romance, family, history, and the banality of office life. One thing all of the plays included in this study share, however, is a commitment to considering precisely the questions set out in the introduction to this study: questions about the veracity of documents, the performance of justice, the sincerity of testimony, and the legacy of Russia's twentieth-century past in its twenty-first-century present.

Note

1 Abbasov's film in its entirety can be viewed at https://www.youtube.com/watch?v=rfSoBAoEav0 (accessed 15 December 2017).

6

A special verdict
Theatre and protest in Putin's Russia

The years between 2008 and 2012 were an exceptionally productive period for the development of documentary theatre forms in Russia. By 2008, the momentum of the form's early years had produced a lively and innovative community of young theatre artists dedicated to the exploration and explication of lived experience onstage. The socially engaged nature of their endeavour is apparent in the selection of plays analysed in this book. Russian documentary theatre's potential as a mode of civic engagement can also be observed in the dozens of regional verbatim theatre projects that have emerged across the country addressing local issues connected to institutional corruption, environmental concerns, and social welfare. So far, *Witness onstage* has analysed the active and transformative nature of documentary theatre during these years by focusing on the mechanics of individual plays in performance. Through close readings and performance analysis, this study has illustrated how Russia's twenty-first-century documentary theatre artists use the form as a way to address key cultural tensions and create new pathways to social change.

Since 2012, documentary theatre in Russia has become increasingly tied to the country's opposition movement. As I have argued elsewhere in this book, the practice of performing documents is an inherently political practice in twenty-first-century Russia. However, it was only after Vladimir Putin resumed his role as president in 2012 that the country's most socially engaged theatre collective, Teatr.doc, became the focus of a targeted campaign on the part of the administration to shut down the group's activities. In this final chapter, I recount the series of events that have befallen Teatr.doc's artists since that time, beginning with the initial eviction from their small basement black-box theatre on Trekhprudnyi Lane in 2014. Chapter 6 will locate those events within the broader sociopolitical context of Russia's protest movement and the overt return to authoritarianism under Putin's third term as president. In this way, Chapter 6 seeks to uncover what it was about the work at Teatr.doc in these years in particular, and about Russian documentary theatre more broadly, that posed a threat to the shifting political and cultural landscape in Russia under Putin's third term as president.

By drawing on Raymond Williams' oft-cited essay 'Structures of Feeling' (1977), this chapter explains how documentary theatre in Russia adapted to its specific historical and cultural circumstances in order to create the space for the exploration of experiences, ideas, and emotions not often represented in public media. Although the founding of Teatr.doc and the development of documentary theatre forms in the early 2000s were not initially intended as acts of political protest, both the venue and the form became closely associated with the opposition movement after 2011. Through consideration of the material the company produced in conjunction with certain changes in political discourse, this chapter illustrates the way specific forms of theatre and performance arose in reaction to and in conjunction with the prevailing structures of feeling of the era.

Additionally, this chapter marks the tragic loss of Teatr.doc's founders and artistic directors Mikhail Ugarov and Elena Gremina. Married since 1993, Ugarov and Gremina were the driving force behind the company. The two visionary theatre-makers passed away within six weeks of one another in the spring of 2018. In the wake of their passing, artists and critics have raised important questions about the future, the nature, and the value of Russian documentary theatre practice as it has developed in the second decade of the twenty-first century. Through exploration of these questions, I highlight how the productions analysed in this book's previous chapters represent a distinct period in the country's pioneering development of the form, and consider their relevance to a broader analysis of documentary theatre as a mode of civic engagement.

The Bolotnaya Square Case

Widespread concerns about electoral fraud in the Russian parliamentary elections in December 2011 set off a series of demonstrations that drew tens of thousands of protestors to the streets between 2011 and 2013. What began as a single demonstration about the elections soon galvanized into a country-wide opposition movement through which protestors expressed their disillusionment with both local and national politics in the months that followed. In March 2012, Putin was reelected to the presidency in an election that was marred by voter fraud and institutional corruption. Having served as president from 2000 to 2008, Putin spent a four-year interim term as prime minister while his close colleague and collaborator Dmitrii Medvedev occupied the presidency. In 2012 the power shuffle between the two men was revealed to be just that, as Putin prepared for his third presidential inauguration set to take place in Moscow on 7 May 2012.

The day before the inauguration, tens of thousands of protestors from across the country gathered for an opposition rally that took place on Bolotnaya Square in central Moscow. It was the largest demonstration since the start of the protest wave the previous December, with attendance estimates ranging from 20,000 to 60,000 (Gabowitsch, 2016: 3). During the rally, violence broke out between police and some of the protestors. Over 400 demonstrators were arrested on the spot. Additional protestors were arrested later in the day after the rally had already been dispersed. In the days, weeks, and months that followed, investigators continued to track down and arrest individuals who had attended the demonstration. Of approximately one thousand people who were arrested in connection to the Bolotnaya Square incident, thirty-four were subsequently held in pre-trial detention and charged with violating Articles 212 and 318 of the Russian criminal code, public disruption and violence against the police (Memorial, 2012). Twenty-eight of those charged in the case were found guilty; some were placed under house arrest while others were sentenced to two and a half years in prison. The Bolotnaya Square Case, as it has come to be known, symbolizes the rise of authoritarianism in Russia for many as the extended detainment of political protestors and the persecution of opposition leaders has persisted.

Increased restrictions on freedom of expression were put in place immediately following Putin's return to the presidency. In 2013 Russia's parliament passed a bill outlawing the representation of so-called 'homosexual propaganda' in the presence of minors. The vocabulary in the bill does not define the parameters of the restriction, an ambiguity which permits individual law-enforcement officials to impose the policy at will. This leaves any artists who represent homosexuality, what is commonly called in Russia a 'non-normative' lifestyle, susceptible to prosecution (*RIA novosti*, 2013). Next, in 2014, Putin signed into law a bill banning the use of profanity on stage, page, and screen. Any performing arts organizations found to be using words or derivatives from the banned lexicon are threatened with fines of up to 50,000 roubles (£600) (*Lenta*, 2014a). These two laws have not often been enforced; however, they serve an important purpose for the Putin administration: to generate an overall atmosphere of fear among the country's artists.

The third legislative development that has had particular impact on the artists whose works are discussed in this book is the 2012 law requiring NGOs that accept funds from sources outside Russia to register as so-called 'foreign agents'. A formulation reminiscent of certain Soviet designations, the term 'foreign agent' is used by the Putin administration to intimidate and threaten NGOs like Memorial and the Sakharov Center, two organizations that have been substantially supported by foreign funders, in particular by George Soros's Open Society Foundation, which has funded many of Russia's most progressive social initiatives since the early 2000s.

Once registered as a foreign agent, an organization becomes subject to a complex and poorly defined set of tax codes. In this way, the NGO is absorbed into a system of complicity in which the threat of closure due to personal grievances or political positioning makes the organization's future especially vulnerable. The Sakharov Center, for example, was fined 300,000 roubles (£3,800) in March 2015 for having failed to register according to the new policy. Memorial's inclusion on the list of groups required to declare themselves foreign agents threatened the closure of its St Petersburg anti-discrimination centre in 2013 (*Vedomosti*, 2014). While the centre has since reopened, it is difficult to say how the law might affect Memorial and the Sakharov Center in the future.

These are among the legislative changes that have contributed to the tightening of cultural policies in Russia since 2012. Such developments preceded the explicit targeting of individual artists and organizations that have become commonplace in the years that followed. The first nationally recognized instance of this type of targeted persecution in the theatre world was the scandal surrounding director Timofei Kuliabin's staging of Wagner's opera *Tannhäuser* at the Novosibirsk Academic Theatre of Opera and Ballet in March 2015. In his modern interpretation of the opera, Kuliabin imagined the singer Tannhäuser as a film director. In one of the sequences in the opera, a poster for one of Tannhäuser's films is projected onstage. Conceived as a parody of the poster for the 1996 American film *The People vs. Larry Flynt*, Tannhäuser's poster features the image of a crucifix between a woman's legs.

As a result of the production, both Kuliabin and the theatre's artistic director Boris Mezdrich faced a hearing in which they were accused by the head of the local diocese, Metropolitan Tikhon of Novosibirsk, of offending the feelings of Orthodox believers and inciting religious discord. The irony of the *Tannhäuser* scandal, as Rudnev describes in his essay on theatre and censorship in contemporary Russia (2017: 301), is that the production was built around a narrative of Christian martyrdom in which both the artist and the figure of the martyr are heralded as the passion-bearers of their time (2017: 301). Kuliabin and Mezdrich were both found not guilty. Nonetheless, the position of artistic director at a state-funded theatre is under the jurisdiction of the Ministry of Culture, and despite the court's findings, Minister of Culture Vladimir Medinskii decided to step in and remove Mezdrich from his post after the director refused to amend the production and publicly apologize for its content (Kaluzhsky, 2015).

Perhaps the highest-profile example of the Putin administration's attack on the arts thus far is the arrest of film and theatre director Kirill Serebrennikov who, at the time of writing, remains under house arrest while being investigated for embezzlement. One of the most influential Russian theatre directors of his generation, Serebrennikov took over as artistic director of Moscow's Gogol Theatre in 2012. After a total renovation, the theatre re-opened as the Gogol Center in 2014 under Serebrennikov's artistic directorship. The revamped multi-arts complex quickly became recognized as home to some of Moscow's most cutting-edge and stylish theatre productions. As part of his Gogol Center vision, Serebrennikov also ran what was known as the Seventh Studio, an offshoot of the Gogol Center that produced several large-scale productions between 2012 and 2014. In May 2017, the director and several of his colleagues who worked with him on the Seventh Studio project were placed under investigation for allegedly embezzling 68 million roubles (£870,000) from state funds allocated to the Seventh Studio project. The fabricated nature of the Serebrennikov case has drawn international attention as the prosecutors constructed falsified evidence in their search for a path to prosecution (*Lenta*, 2018). The project's managing director Aleksei Malobrodskii spent ten months in pre-trial detention before being released under house arrest in April 2018. Serebrennikov, as well as his colleagues Iurii Itin and Sofia Apfelbaum, spent close to two years under house arrest before being released on bail in April 2019. At the time of writing, the investigation against Serebrennikiov, Malobrodski, Itin, and Apfelbaum is ongoing.

Any assessment of the authoritarian atmosphere in Putin's Russia after 2012 must also take into account how the annexation of Crimea and Russia's military action in Ukraine have shaped the country's public discourse. Disinformation and propaganda dominated Russia's television coverage of Ukraine's Maidan Revolution. Following the ousting of Russia-allied Ukrainian president Viktor Yanukovych, Russian troops began appearing on Ukrainian soil, first in Crimea, which Putin successfully annexed after a controversial and unlawful referendum in March 2014. The annexation of Crimea by the Russian state has found wide support among Russian citizens as the conversation throughout the country's state-sponsored media sources increasingly turns to the topic of patriotism (Blakkisrud and Kolstø, 2016). Ukrainian political prisoners are being held in Russian prisons without access to a fair trial. Russian soldiers and Russian arms continue to fuel the ongoing military action between the Ukrainian army and the separatists occupying Ukraine's eastern regions. Putin and all state-sponsored Russian news sources continue to deny Russia's involvement in the conflict, which has claimed approximately 13,000 lives since it began in 2014.

As political scientist Maxim Alyukhov has argued, the gruesome and misleading coverage of the war in Ukraine on Russian television has 'significantly boosted the legitimacy of the Russian regime in the eyes of its citizens. One particularly skilful manipulation of facts and emotions induced viewers to accept the government's official stance on the conflict and led to the mobilisation not only among the regime's supporters, but also undecided and even critically-minded individuals' (2017). The annexation of Crimea and Russia's surreptitious involvement in the war in Donbas have paved the way for the persecution of individual artists and activists described above. By violating international law, persistently denying having done so, and suffering scant consequences, the Putin administration has proven itself capable of perpetuating even the most untrustworthy and destructive of cultural narratives in Russia. Questions about what is real and what is fabricated have faded for many Russian citizens as the myth of the 'reunification' of Russian-speaking territories has proven popular even among opposition figures like Aleksei Navalnyi, as well as supposedly liberal news organizations like TV Dozhd, Meduza, and RBK (Klimeniouk, 2017).

Given the brazen nature of the Putin administration's disregard for international law in these instances, it comes as no surprise that the regime has also since turned its attention to the persecution of individuals and of organizations that are thought to have overstepped their mark as designated safe spaces for the intelligentsia and opposition. Such was the case, it seems, for Teatr.doc. For years, Teatr.doc's artists had long promoted the line that nobody with any authority would have reason to bother with a tiny underground theatre producing plays on a shoestring budget and performing for crowds of a few dozen audience members. Unfortunately, it seems they were mistaken.

Theatre that is not afraid

On 15 October 2014, Teatr.doc received an unanticipated piece of correspondence from Moscow's Department of Property. This letter informed the theatre-makers that, at the start of the New Year, they would be evicted from their creative home of the past twelve years. The lease for their small basement studio space on Trekhprudnyi Lane in the centre of Moscow had been unexpectedly and unilaterally terminated. Gremina announced the news in a Facebook post that day, claiming that the theatre had never once, in its twelve years of tenancy, been late paying the rent, nor had the group ever been in violation of any fire or safety regulations. No reason for the eviction was stated in the letter but, following questions from journalists, the Department of Property officials later claimed the decision had been made in connection to unsanctioned renovations. Earlier in the year, the city had required the theatre to install an additional door in order to comply with fire-safety regulations. The installation of this new fire exit was subsequently deemed unauthorized and used as an excuse to issue the theatre with an eviction notice. It later came to light that the decision to evict Teatr.doc from the premises had been approved by the city administration in May 2014; however, the tenants were only informed of the decision six months later, after submitting their application, just as they had done for the previous eleven years, to renew the lease that was due to expire at the end of December.

As news of the theatre's situation spread, there was an outpouring of support for Teatr.doc, as evidenced by a torrent of posts on social media about the injustice of the city's decision. Actress Oksana Mysina and critic John Freedman began circulating online petitions that gathered over 5,000 signatures from artists, academics, and allies all over the world, including British playwrights Tom Stoppard and Mark Ravenhill. This pronounced reaction from international theatre artists stood in stark contrast to the silence of Moscow city officials. When questioned about Teatr.doc's tenancy termination Moscow Mayor Sergei Sobianin, for example, claimed he had never heard of Teatr.doc and knew nothing of the problems they were facing. 'There are a lot of theatres in Moscow who are doing god knows what', Sobianin was quoted as saying in response to questions from the press (*Colta*, 2014).

It was in direct response to these events that playwright and director Ivan Vyrypaev published an open letter following the news of Teatr.doc's eviction. Vyrypaev was one of the founding members of Teatr.doc in 2002. Together with a small group of dedicated theatre-makers, Vyrypaev helped convert the disheveled basement on Trekhprudnyi Lane into a working theatre space that went on to host many of Russia's most innovative productions since the turn of the twenty-first century. In his letter Vyrypaev explained to his readers the significance of Teatr.doc as an indispensable component of contemporary Russian culture. 'Doc', Vyrypaev writes, calling the theatre by its nickname used by artists and audience members who frequent the space, 'is a stage for real craft, true art. Artists gather there to speak out. I am not against commerce, I support commercial theatre. But as an audience member, as a citizen, and as an artist I see how important it is that the world has a space of absolute courage and open-mindedness. There are very few places like that in this world … And I truly hope', the playwright continues, 'that we as citizens of this country pay attention to and understand the fact that we are in possession of a true cultural treasure, one that we do not have the right to take and bury' (Vyrypaev, 2014).

In his letter, Vyrypaev refrains from expressing an explicit political stance. He claims not to know whether the decision to evict Teatr.doc was a purposeful attempt to shut the theatre down or simply a result of the residential tenants complaining about crowds gathering outside their building. However, he argues that regardless of the motives behind the theatre's eviction, the spirit of Teatr.doc must be kept alive. 'Because if we lose Doc,' according to Vyrypaev, 'then we lose hope that we still have

Figure 17: The original Teatr.doc on Trekhprudnyi Lane (2014)

a chance at becoming a real, conscious, society' (Vyrypaev, 2014). Here, Vyrypaev articulates precisely the features of documentary theatre in twenty-first-century Russia that this book has sought to elucidate. His letter testifies to the unique space documentary theatre had come to occupy in Moscow's public imagination at that time and points directly to the form's capacity to inspire hope and encourage civic engagement. As one of Russia's only independent theatre venues, Teatr.doc consistently produces plays and interactive community projects that challenge the status quo. As propaganda and disinformation flood the country's television channels, Russia's documentary theatre artists ask their audiences to question the veracity of those television reports, they invite artists and audiences to consider together the challenges of uncovering the 'micronarratives of truth' (Beumers and Lipovestky, 2010: 561) in today's media-saturated culture, and encourage participants to analyse their personal and national pasts in order to do so.

The last official day of Teatr.doc's tenancy on Trekhprudnyi Lane was 31 December 2014. The day before, audience members were invited to attend a free screening of the documentary *Silnee chem oruzhie* (*Stronger than Arms*, 2014), a film about the Maidan revolution by Ukrainian film collective Babylon 13. The screening was held, in part, as a fundraiser for one of the film's creators, Oleg Sentsov. A Ukrainian national and Crimea native, Sentsov was arrested by FSB officers in his home in Simferopol on 10 May 2014 following his participation in protests against the annexation of Crimea. Sentsov was later transferred to Russia, along with the Ukrainian activist Aleksandr Kolchenko and approximately 70 other detainees from the Russian occupied territory of Crimea. Found guilty of false terrorism charges, Sentsov was later sentenced to twenty years in a Russian penal colony. At the time of the screening at Teatr.doc, Sentsov was being held in Moscow's Lefortovo pre-trial detention centre, where he was severely abused while in custody.

The afternoon before the screening, Teatr.doc director Vsevolod Lisovskii informed his Facebook followers that a detective from the Central Administration had stopped by the theatre to investigate the circumstances of that evening's screening (Lisovskii, 2014). As the director describes, the officer advised him to cancel the screening of the Ukrainian documentary due to what he called 'complicated circumstances' that day in the city. In this the investigator was implicitly referring to the thousands of people who had already begun to gather on nearby Manezh Square in support of anti-corruption activist Aleksei Navalnyi. Navalnyi and his brother Oleg had both been falsely convicted of embezzlement, with sentences announced that day. The demonstration was in part a protest against their conviction and in part a march in opposition to Putin and to the corrupt system his administration had come to represent. Meanwhile, back at Teatr.doc, just up the road from the demonstration, Lisovskii assured the investigator that to show the film for free was not in violation of any licensing laws. The director invited the investigator and his colleagues to attend the screening that evening if they were curious to see what the film was about.

Lisovski's Facebook posts detailing the conversation were soon followed by an announcement from Gremina, also on Facebook, in which she informed her readers of that day's developments at the theatre. Gremina wrote that the visit from the investigator was likely just a scare tactic, but that to be safe, any audience members or Teatr.doc supporters without official documentation might want to refrain from attending that evening's screening. 'For those who do choose to attend,' Gremina wrote, 'a quick reminder',

> First – NO violence … Second – If the riot police do show up, the worst that can happen is that you'll be detained for a few hours. Document what happens, it will be an interesting experience. You can tell your friends and your kids. Third – The only person officially responsible for the event is me … Audience members are not at all guilty, we showed you and you watched … Fourth – There's nothing to fear. (Gremina, 2014b)

This notion that 'there's nothing to fear' subsequently developed into something of a credo for Teatr.doc's artists in the months after their eviction from Trekhprudnyi Lane. Following their unsuccessful appeal to the Department of Property, Teatr.doc's artists began a crowdfunding campaign to collect donations that would go toward the renovation of a new performance space. On the theatre's crowdfunding page, the theatre's logo appeared as it has on Teatr.doc's website since 2002. 'Teatr.doc' was printed in large white letters inside a black rectangle. When the page first appeared in mid-December 2014, the text below the theatre's name had been changed. Traditionally the logo read, Teatr.doc: Teatr, v kotorom ne igraiut ('The theatre without the acting') but, in its revised incarnation the logo read, Teatr.doc: Teatr, kotoroi ne boitsia ('The theatre that is not afraid').

There were fewer than two dozen audience members at the screening on December 30, 2014 when Moscow-based Ukrainian playwright Maksym Kurochkin gave a brief introduction to the film. Within minutes of the video beginning to play, voices were heard in the hallway before a team of police officers stormed through the door accompanied by a small camera crew, later identified as a news team from NTV, a conservative Kremlin-sponsored television channel. The officers claimed there had been a bomb threat in the building. They then proceeded to check the passports of everyone in the theatre before evacuating the space. Notably, the residents of the apartments on the floors in the same building above the theatre were never evacuated at all. According to Lisovskii's real-time updates on social media, the officers also demanded that everyone in attendance turn off their camera and phones in order to avoid inadvertently detonating the supposed explosive they claimed had been hidden somewhere in the theatre.

As the first group of officers continued their farce of an evacuation process, a second group of city officials arrived, this time from Moscow's Ministry of Culture. These men claimed to have been sent in order to determine whether or not the film was in violation of Russia's anti-extremism laws. While the first group of bomb-squad officers 'searched for explosives' backstage (damaging the theatre's property in the process), the second group of Ministry of Culture reps watched the full documentary on the screen in the theatre. Lisovskii, Kurochkin, and Teatr.doc's technical director Stanislav Gubin were taken to the station in police vehicles but were released later that evening. Gremina subsequently became the subject of an 'extremism' investigation which was dismissed approximately two weeks later.

This turn of events was indicative of the deepening tension between artists and the state at that time. The fact that the city's security team 'searched for explosives' in the theatre's office at the exact same time that the Ministry of Culture reps watched the full film in the next room is a clear example of how little effort the administration makes to conceal the fabricated nature of their accusations. As foreign policy expert Blair Ruble wrote at the time, 'The December 30 raid becomes even more disquieting, as the police were already quite busy that evening arresting nearly 300 of the thousands of demonstrators who had converged on the Manezh Square next to the Kremlin … One might have thought', Ruble continues, 'the gathering of a handful of theatre patrons would constitute too small a challenge for the regime at such a moment. Indeed, the mystery is, why does Vladimir Putin's government fear a minuscule drama company operating from a Moscow basement?' (2015).

After wrapping up their sinister satire on the night of the film screening, the bomb squad, the investigators, and the Ministry of Culture reps closed the theatre's door behind them, sealed it with police tape, and welded it shut. It seemed someone somewhere up in the city's administration had the idea that by fusing the theatre's heavy metal door to its frame, the work at Teatr.doc might cease. In fact, the company continued performing in the space for another week, simply leading audience members in through a back entrance.

It is impossible to say who exactly initiated this harassment campaign against Teatr.doc. Despite rumours, there is no evidence precisely indicating from how far up the 'power vertical' the decision may have come. It is possible the decision was discussed and planned in some sort of official manner and it is equally possible that an unknown individual in the city's administration decided to conduct the operation without any support from officials higher up in the Putin administration. What has become clear since the initial announcement of the theatre's eviction in October 2014, however, is that the aggressive actions described here were only the start of a concerted effort to close the theatre and intimidate its members.

On tour in Moscow

After vacating their homegrown theatre space at the start of January 2015, Teatr.doc's artists began showing their work at various theatres and galleries throughout the city. The company cheerfully advertised their dispersed repertoire with the slogan 'Teatr.doc goes on tour in Moscow!' the irony of which was not lost on the theatre's increasingly dedicated audience base. The positive spin Teatr.doc's directors put on this turn of inauspicious events is an example of their consistent identification as an institution that is not afraid and indeed, has nothing to fear. However, since their initial eviction in 2014 Teatr.doc has been consistently under threat of closure by Moscow authorities.

On 14 February 2015, after two and a half months 'on tour', Teatr.doc celebrated their thirteenth anniversary by throwing open the doors of a brand new performance venue. In the interim period between the closure of the original venue and the opening of the new space, the mission to keep Teatr.doc open had grown beyond a belief and investment in the value of the company's actual performances. Teatr.doc became, for many, a symbol for free speech in contemporary Russia. The need to keep Teatr.doc in existence coincided with a belief that the country had the potential to overcome its return to authoritarianism. I was one of the 200 people in attendance at the opening of the new venue, and the newly renovated, open-plan theatre was filled to capacity with the support of friends, followers, and Teatr.doc devotees. The theatre's directors had signed a lease with private owners for a rundown building just east of the city centre in mid-December. With 800,000 roubles (approximately £8,500) collected from online crowdfunding and a team of dedicated

A special verdict   153

Figure 18: Teatr.doc's second venue on Spartakovskaia Street (2014)

volunteers working under the direction of architect Oleg Karlson, the dilapidated building was, within two months, transformed into a bright and beautiful theatre space. The speed at which volunteers built the new Teatr.doc – with its bare-brick walls and pine-cathedral ceiling – was remarkable. The mood on the evening of the opening was triumphant.

Three months after the company opened their new venue at 3 Spartakovskaia Street, Gremina was set to premiere her latest work *Bolotnoe delo* (*Bolotnaya Case*, 2015). Devised by playwright Polina Borodina, the play's text is constructed from interviews with friends and family members of the individuals who were arrested and imprisoned following their attendance at the opposition protest at Bolotnaya Square on May 6, 2012. In my 2017 interview with Borodina, the playwright described walking from the Metro to the theatre the evening of the dress rehearsal on 5 May 2015 and noticing police officers with dogs sporadically placed along the street leading to the theatre. Not realizing their presence was connected to her play, Borodina was surprised to arrive at the theatre to find a small group of investigators questioning Gremina and a police van parked outside. Though nobody was arrested that night, police officers and city officials were frequently sent to Teatr.doc in the weeks that followed, for reasons that were never made entirely clear. On the evening of the *Bolotnoe delo* premiere, for example, a police officer had been directed to stand inside the theatre throughout the performance. Not knowing himself what he was meant to be doing, the officer was reportedly happy to accept the task from Gremina of distributing programmes to spectators as they entered the theatre space.

Shortly after the play's premiere, Teatr.doc's lease was terminated again. Though the building was rented to the group from private owners, it later came to light that the landlords had been instructed to revoke the rental agreement by a representative from Moscow's Department of Property. Despite the significant amount of money, energy, and dedication that had gone into creating the new Teatr.doc, the company began its search for a new performance venue with little more than a few online quips about changing the company's slogan to 'Teatr.doc: The theatre that's on the move'.

The group soon found themselves a new space to renovate, this one even closer to the city centre and with two small rooms they converted into separate stages. The renovations were carried out with little fanfare and the new venue opened in July 2015. In their new space, the company continued to confront the kinds of politically challenging topics that are rarely seen on any other stage across the country. Among the most socially engaged productions to appear in the company's repertoire in these years were, for example, Gremina's project *Voina blizko* (*War is Close*, 2016). A play in three parts, the project includes documentary materials from the trial of Oleg Sentsov, diary entries from a resident of Luhansk, and a reflection on brainwashing written specifically for the project by Mark Ravenhill. Director Anastasiia Patlai's play *Vyiti iz shkafa* (*Coming Out of the Closet*, 2016) also makes an important contribution to the repertoire as the one of the few theatre projects in Russia to speak openly about the experience of being gay. Straying from the documentary aesthetic somewhat, Ugarov's production *Chelovek iz podolska* (*Man from Podolsk*, 2017) is written by playwright Dmitrii Danilov and presents a dark and farcical picture of police brutality and corruption in Russia's law-enforcement agencies. In addition to these full productions, Teatr.doc also continued to host informal readings and discussions about political persecution, such as a reading of the prison diary written by openly gay Uzbek-Russian opposition journalist Ali Feruz, an event that prompted yet another visit from local law enforcement officials (*Mediazona*, 2017).

Three months after the reading, while Feruz was still in custody, Teatr.doc published a printed edition of the journalist's prison diary. The day the book arrived in the mail, Ugarov posted a picture of the edition on his Facebook page. 'The book is out', Ugarov wrote in his post that accompanied the photo, 'Attention! This is a DOCUMENT (document) [*sic*]! Future generations of lawyers and historians will laugh at the paper trail left behind by Putin's government, but this document will remain.

And it is through this document that a judgement about our time will be made.' Here Ugarov articulates an important element of the work at Teatr.doc and its historical significance. The pressure for artists to self-censor their work has grown in Russia as the threat of political persecution appears increasingly prevalent. Despite such threats, the artists at Teatr.doc continue to provide a space for freedom of expression, a place where the documents of the past and the present can be acknowledged, remembered, represented, and discussed. In this way, the artists at Teatr.doc and at other documentary theatre venues across the country use their creative practice to stage an important intervention in contemporary public discourse. Additionally, their work serves to document and to archive the changes they witness around them.

In the years since Teatr.doc's eviction from Trekhprudnyi Lane, the atmosphere of the organization has shifted. Prior to the onset of official bureaucratic bullying in 2014, Teatr.doc was known for its innovative aesthetic in theatre making and its independent approach to the development of theatre as a space for civic engagement. When the autonomy of the theatre collective came under threat by the Moscow city administration, the act of making socially relevant documentary theatre was transformed into an explicit act of political protest. As the previous chapters in this book have demonstrated, there have always been plays in the repertoire that posed politically charged questions, well before 2014. And yet it was primarily, my research suggests, the intentional intimidation on the part of city officials and the triumph of the theatre's survival that gave way to Teatr.doc's reputation as a space synonymous with the opposition. In their repeated attempts to shut the theatre down, the city administration effectively elevated the company's presence in the public imagination. The Teatr.doc collective became mythologized as one of the few remaining spaces for open artistic expression and uncensored political performance.

Since the events of 2014 and 2015, Teatr.doc has become an institution. Whereas in its early days, the theatre's small basement black-box studio was a place where many artists started out working for no money and little recognition, the company has since become a known entity, a place where young actors, writers, and directors strive to build a reputation as experimental theatre artists. The stripped-down non-illusory style of performance that was developed at Teatr.doc is now commonly referred to as 'doc-style' theatre (dokovskyi stil) and its influence can be seen on stages across Moscow and around the country. Twice a year, Teatr.doc hosts a work-in-progress festival that attracts documentary projects developed by Russia's newest generation of theatre artists. In this way, the company is revitalized by a steady flow of new actors, directors, and playwrights who work alongside the veterans of Russian documentary theatre to create an impressive number of new projects each season. The company has grown significantly both in the number of projects included in the repertoire and in the place the theatre holds within Russia's broader artistic environment.

Alongside these signs of growth, other changes at Teatr.doc have also emerged. According to some of the group's veteran members, the environment of artistic experimentation in recent years is not as lively as it once was. The tight-knit community of the collective's early days has dissipated as many of the theatre's founding artists have moved on and the political nature of the endeavour has, for some, eclipsed its creative allegiances. Several critics have argued that Russia's early twenty-first-century boom in New Drama and experimental theatre has since passed, and it is impossible to predict what may come next (Beumers and Lipovetsky, 2009; Freedman, 2014; Matvienko, 2014). When I asked Gremina in November 2017 if she thought the style or the quality of the work at Teatr.doc had been affected by the eviction in 2014 and all that had followed, she responded in her characteristically calm and thoughtful tone of voice. 'Well,' she said, 'we live in a different country now' (Gremina, 2017).

Emotional regimes under Putin

Among the changes Gremina is referring to in this statement is, I suggest, a shift in the emotional atmosphere throughout the country in the lead-up to and the aftermath of the 2011–13 protest wave. In his book *Protest in Putin's Russia* (2016) Mischa Gabowitsch argues that the opposition demonstrations in Russia were connected to a change in the way people both expressed and experienced emotions during these years. He discusses how the sentiment of 'stability' loomed large in the defining vocabulary of Putin's first two terms as president (2000–08). Images of Putin's masculinity and sobriety were purposefully promoted to stand in distinction to the perceived instability and humiliation of the Yeltsin years (1991–99). The frequent juxtaposition of keywords such as 'strength' with, for example, 'chaos' in state-sponsored media, was used to influence public perception and emphasize Putin's stabilizing role in society. These linguistic patterns in public discourse, Gabowitsch explains, are designed to dictate social norms to do with the expression of emotion in public. There were, of course, important economic and political developments that ran alongside the perpetuation of these emotional narratives; however, as

Gabowitsch describes, the use of emotionally evocative vocabulary played a key role in shaping the expression and representation of feelings in the public sphere in the early 2000s in Russia.

To contextualize the significance of this observation, Gabowitsch draws on the work of historian William Reddy and his study *The Navigation of Feeling: A framework for the history of the emotions* (2010). In an effort to establish a framework for the study of emotions throughout history, Reddy applies the term 'emotional regimes' to explore the ways different societies adopt certain sets of behaviours and expectations about the expression and representation of emotions in public (Reddy, 2010: 129). In doing so, Reddy argues, societies partake in a system of emotional management through which public customs and rituals either support or challenge a society's predominant emotional regime. In the case of the Russian protests, for example, Gabowitsch illustrates how the use of humour and irony by the opposition was a direct attempt to undercut official narratives about the Putin administration's strength, seriousness, and stability. The act of protest was, in this sense, according to Gabowitsch, 'as much a challenge to the emotional regime established under Putin as it was to his political regime' (2016: 68).

In his exploration of Reddy's notion of emotional regimes and its relevance to Russia's opposition protests, Gabowitsch points to several key events that, he argues, precipitated a change in the public expression of emotion about the country's leadership and thereby created the space for the mass demonstrations. The moral shock of the Medvedev–Putin swap was precisely one of these moments, Gabowitsch claims. Another noticeable shift in the country's emotional regime took place in November 2011 when Putin was vehemently booed by crowds on live television while making an appearance at a mixed martial arts tournament. 'For thousands of others, however,' Gabowitsch writes, 'the shock would be the direct experience of electoral fraud in December 2011' (2016: 74).

Reddy's concept of an emotional regime, and Gabowitsch's application of the term to the contemporary Russian context, offer important insight into the aesthetic, social, and political connotations of the work taking place at Teatr.doc. If, as Gabowitsch argues, the dominant media narrative throughout the early 2000s was designed to promote an experience of strength, stability, and singularity among Russia's population, the plays staged at Teatr.doc were constructed to encourage inquiry, curiosity, and plurality. Ugarov's notion of a 'nol pozitsiia' (zero position), as discussed in Chapter 1 of this book, for example, was a method documentary theatre artists of the era developed in order to stage the representation of a polyphonic collection of voices, views, and opinions thereby encouraging a more diverse process of questioning than that which was promoted by the Putin regime. Through the practice of performing documents, the artists at Teatr.doc provided a space for the public discussion and exploration of emotions and opinions that ran contrary to those supported by the Kremlin and state-sponsored media sources. Returning to Blair Ruble's text on the 2014 Teatr.doc raid as described above, the question of why Putin's government appears to 'fear a minuscule drama company operating from a Moscow basement' is, I suggest, directly connected to the challenge documentary theatre poses to the administration's effort to control Russia's emotional regime.

The idea of an emotional regime can be usefully understood in connection to an earlier work on a parallel topic, Raymond Williams' notion of structures of feeling. In his essay included in the collection *Marxism and Literature* (1977), Williams analyses how art, theatre, and literature help us discern certain social movements even before they have been recognized as such. He uses the term 'structures of feeling' to describe the patterns of thinking that emerge in society in reaction and in distinction to official discourse. Through the study of art, Williams suggests, we are able to observe the development of such historical and cultural shifts while they are still in process and before they have been defined by critics and historians as a distinct period of social development. By analysing the cultural conditions in which a work of art is produced, Williams argues, critics gain perspective on how alternative feelings, ideas, and beliefs gradually enter into public discourse, often in a diffuse manner, sometimes over several years. Such structures of feeling, according to Williams, develop in the gap between official narratives and constitute a space in which artists gradually renegotiate their understanding of and relationship to the society in which they live, even if they are not entirely conscious of the ways in which they are doing so at the time.

The founders of Teatr.doc did not begin their work with an explicit intent to destabilize official discourse or foster political opposition. They rather sought a creative space in which to develop a type of theatre that spoke to the social and historical conditions of their moment. Beginning with the introduction of verbatim theatre in 1999, Russia's theatre artists began experimenting in different approaches to staging documentary materials onstage. The emergence of interactive theatre and witness theatre in the years that followed are evidence of how the form grew and adapted to the broader cultural circumstances in Russia at that time. In hindsight, it appears clear that such practices were a challenge to the Putin administration's developing emotional regime, a restrictive environment built to diminish the space for free thinking and diverse points of view. However, as this chapter suggests, it was only after Putin's return to the presidency in 2012 that documentary theatre and the structures of feeling the form fostered posed an especially significant challenge to the Putin administration's emotional, and therefore political, regime.

Life after Doc

According to critic Marina Davydova, contemporary Russian theatre can be divided into two categories, before and after the founding of Teatr.doc. In the beginning, '[t]he very fact of its existence' Davydova writes, 'was seen by many theatre people as either a revolution or a rebellion' (Davydova, 2018: 94). At the helm of this theatrical rebellion were two artists whose names have appeared frequently throughout the pages of this book, Elena Gremina and Mikhail Ugarov. Both theatre-makers began working as playwrights in the 1990s before moving into directing following the founding of Teatr.doc in 2002. As writers, directors, and producers, Gremina and Ugarov were vital to the development of new Russian drama. Renowned artists in their own right, they also supported, encouraged, and mentored several generations of post-Soviet Russian theatre artists throughout the late-1990s and 2000s. The resonance of their passing in the spring of 2018 shook the international theatre community and left the fate of Russia's only dedicated documentary theatre venue in the balance.

When Ugarov died of a heart attack at the age of 62 on 1 April 2018, everyone involved in Russian theatre understood his passing to mark the end of an era. When Gremina, aged 61, passed away a mere six weeks later on 16 May, also of heart failure, the finality of that end appeared more tragic and conclusive than any of us could have anticipated. Writing from under house arrest in connection to the Seventh Studio case, friend and theatre producer Aleksei Malobrodskii described the two artists' influence when he wrote, 'Lena and Misha discovered dozens of talented playwrights and directors as well as hundreds of actors. They gave us a whole theatre movement. They educated thousands of audience members, thousands of citizens' (*Gorky media*, 2018). As Malobradskii articulates here, the influence of these two theatre-makers extends far beyond the walls of the theatre. Their creative work was not only an attempt to reshape the notion of what constitutes theatre in Russia, it was also a reimagining of what constitutes citizenship.

Naturally, the significance of their work shifted in accordance with the changing circumstances of the country. Critics wrote about Teatr.doc each time the company was forced to move, but in the years following

Figure 19: Elena Gremina (2014)

the initial eviction fewer and fewer reviews were published about the plays they actually performed (Solntseva, 2018). In the years leading up to Gremina's and Ugarov's deaths, the theatre's mission became increasingly associated with its persecution instead of its innovation.

In her editorial about the group and in tribute to its founders, Elena Kovalskaia reflects on the development of Teatr.doc and addresses the question of what could come next for the collective. 'Doc wasn't originally a political theatre but for Gremina and Ugarov, reality was political', she writes. 'Ugarov's well-known theory of the "zero position" is rooted in Roland Barthes' notion of writing degree zero. In discussion of his theory, Barthes cites Kafka as an example of this type of writer. Doc simply reflected reality. Is Doc to blame that Russia's reality became so Kafkaesque?' (Solntseva, 2018). Kovalskaia goes on to describe how many of the theatre's members have insisted that Teatr.doc must not give in to pressures to

Figure 20: Mikhail Ugarov (2017)

close the theatre down, that above all else Teatr.doc must be saved. 'But this very word "save"', Kovalskaia claims, 'sounds ridiculous in connection to the word "Doc" which is synonymous with evolution' (Solntseva, 2018). Articulating a controversial position, Kovalskaia argued it would be better to let Teatr.doc close and to create something new than to try to preserve a project whose time has passed.

In practice, the future of Teatr.doc hinges on factors that are largely out of the collective's control. The lease for their third venue was not renewed. The landlords claimed this was a result of the building's residential tenants complaining about noise and crowds. In September 2018, the company began another 'Moscow tour' performing a dispersed repertoire at various venues throughout the city. A planned partnership with the Gogol Center has initiated the renovation of a new space not far from Kurskaia Metro station and, in April 2019, Teatr.doc opened a mid-sized studio space on Bolotnyi Island in central Moscow. Known colloquially as 'Doc on the Island', this space will continue to house the company's repertoire until the Gogol Center stage is ready, at which point the Teatr.doc artists plan to maintain both stages as they continue to grow the repertoire in the years to come. As these developments illustrate, the company's artists appear committed to seeing the project through and continuing to grow the work which has brought the collective international recognition. Regardless of what happens next, it is clear that the sixteen years between the founding of Teatr.doc in 2002 and the loss of Ugarov and Gremina in 2018 was a uniquely vital and vibrant era in the history of Russian theatre and in the development of international documentary theatre forms.

Doc is life

In her opening remarks to the 2012 documentary theatre symposium *Witness onstage*, Gremina began with a seemingly simple statement. 'Documentary theatre is something that a lot of people practice these days, but nobody really understands, really knows, what it is' (Gremina, 2012). In this statement, the co-creator of Russia's most socially engaged theatre collective challenged her colleagues to consider the multivalent and multifaceted nature of a creative genre that has since become, in the words of Pavel Rudnev, Russia's 'most patriotic trend in contemporary theatre' (2018: 474). Through its collection of case studies analysing individual plays in performance, this book has tried to elucidate the mechanics of what documentary theatre in twenty-first-century Russia *does*; however, it has not lingered on this crucial question posed by Gremina in 2012, the question of what documentary theatre in twenty-first-century Russia *is*. One reason a clear definition of the form has been so elusive is for the very same reasons Elena Kovalskaia describes above. As a form, documentary theatre in Russia is always in progress as it develops in accordance with the needs of the society in which it is created.

For this reason, among others, I refrain from attempting to articulate a single definition for a performance practice that, as this book has illustrated, is varied in its style, structure, and meaning. Instead, I will take this opportunity to share some of the ways in which Russia's documentary theatre artists defined their own practice in the days and weeks following the news of Teatr.doc's first eviction from Trekhprudnyi Lane in 2014. As previously mentioned, many of the artists and audience members who have been involved with Teatr.doc over the years posted their reactions to the news and their sentiments about the space on the theatre's Facebook wall as the details of the lease termination unfolded. 'What is Doc to me?', wrote critic, curator, and producer Maria Kroupnik,

> It's real theatre about the present moment ... Doc is shows, seminars, round tables, social projects. It is work with vulnerable audiences and the most sensitive topics. Doc is a home, it is a group of playwrights who first became

> friends and then began working on projects together. It is a stage, one that I have cleaned myself ... Of course the theatre is not just a set of walls, these walls were made by people, with their own hands ... It may be a miniscule space but this is our place of strength, our atomic reactor. (Kroupnik, 2014)

In his response to the news Talgat Batalov, author of *Uzbek*, wrote, 'What do they think, Teatr.doc is just a building? Excuse the pathos, but Teatr.doc is people, it's an incredible community' (Batalov, 2012). Others recounted their memories of when they first discovered the work at Teatr.doc and how their experiences at the theatre have come to shape their lives since that time. For example, playwright Ekaterina Bondarenko wrote, that she had never seen theatre so alive and raw until she came to Teatr.doc. She recalls how, when on tour with the show *Two in Your Home*, a politically challenging play about the Belarusian poet and activist Vladimir Nekliaev, people would sometimes ask her how it could be that they were permitted to perform it at all. In her Facebook post, Bondarenko writes that she and her colleagues used to answer flippantly, citing the fact that their theatre only seats sixty audience members and claiming no one would have reason to bother with such a small venue. In the comments section below Bondarenko's recollection, Anastasiia Patlai shared a particularly resonant remark. As the community of artists and audience members at the centre of Russia's documentary theatre movement struggled to recover from the fallout of the news of their eviction, Patlai provided a succinct response when she wrote, '*Dok eto zhizn*' (Doc is life).

Several months later, on 30 December 2014, before the evening's now infamous raid had yet been foreshadowed, playwright Iurii Klavdiev posted an ode to Teatr.doc in the form of a letter to a past love. 'Well, my sweet DOC,' Klavdiev writes, 'It seems today and tomorrow are your final days ... And, well, I don't even know what to say' (Klavdiev, 2014),

> You're a good man, DOC. You came into my life at just the right time – half a year later and I'd probably have been in prison for robbery or assault. You taught me to not be afraid of thinking. You taught me to try to understand other people. You taught me that we're all equal in that we are equally fucked, but there is a way out – and in order to find it, you have to think.

Klavdiev goes on to describe how, when faced with the threat of bureaucratic closure, Doc smiled wisely and simply built a new space, even though it could have just as easily closed. 'In the last ten years, you have built hundreds of new spaces', Klavdiev writes, 'For example, inside of me', the playwright confesses. 'Inside many of my friends, and in some people that have never even seen you. Such is your mystique. lol' (Klavdiev, 2014).

Conclusion

In my analysis of the productions discussed in this book's previous chapters, I have sought to illuminate the innovative and generative nature of documentary theatre in twenty-first-century Russia. In the introduction, I argued that underground theatre in twenty-first-century Russia has developed as a significant venue for social change. I suggested that the form of *documentary* theatre specifically, as it has developed in the post-Soviet Russian cultural environment, offered an important and unique set of tools to theatre artists who have used them to address widespread cultural anxieties about the evidentiary status of documents, the dynamics of cultural memory, and the performance of justice in twenty-first-century Russia. In an effort to root my argument in concrete practical developments, I pointed to the fact that more and more theatres in Moscow and around the country had begun producing documentary work. I mentioned that the inclusion of verbatim playwriting in the curriculum for young actors and directors at the Moscow Art Theatre was indicative of a growing appreciation for and interest in the form, even among Moscow's more conservative theatre-makers. I included these points to argue in support of my premise that Russian documentary theatre has developed as an effective venue for political action. As my research on this topic has developed however, I have come to realize that an emphasis on the quantity of documentary theatre practice in twenty-first-century Russia is always secondary to analysis of the form's quality.

Conclusion 165

In view of the case studies included in *Witness onstage*, as well as a consideration of documentary theatre's shifting role in contemporary Russian culture, it is clear that the efficacy of theatre as a method of social action cannot be measured by how many venues produce documentary work or how many audience members are in attendance. In fact, an attempt to estimate the value of any creative movement based on sheer volume serves only to divert us farther away from the heart of the matter. As the collection of plays discussed in this book demonstrates, it is not the breadth of documentary theatre in twenty-first-century Russia that inspires the kind of hope to which Vyrypaev refers in his letter as quoted in the previous chapter. It is rather the depth of commitment in twenty-first-century Russian documentary theatre that has endowed the form with its unique ability to quicken and encourage the imaginations of what is, admittedly, a small percentage of the population. And it is precisely this depth of commitment, the inner workings of the form and the mechanics with which it facilitates communication between its participants as allies and as citizens, that this study has sought to interpret.

In her book *Utopia in Performance: Finding hope at the theatre*, Jill Dolan analyses how live performance can offer participants access to a renewed and reanimated relationship to civic society. Her work 'investigates the potential of different kinds of performance to inspire moments in which audiences feel themselves allied with each other, and with a broader, more capacious sense of a public, in which social discourse articulates the possible, rather than the insurmountable obstacles to human potential' (2005: 2). Dolan analyses her own experiences as an audience member in her attempt to unlock what she describes as those 'ineffable moments of insight, understanding, and love' (8) in which she participates as she shares with her reader the content, context, and location of each performance she includes in her study. In so doing, Dolan explores 'the potential for intersubjectivity not only between performer and spectators but among the audience as well' (10).

In my inquiry into the depth and significance of documentary theatre practice in twenty-first-century Russia, I have tried to decode similar types of ineffable moments and to understand how the content, context, and location of the plays included in this book stage a confluence of meaning for those in the theatre space at the time of performance. I have drawn on my own experiences as an audience member, a performer, and a researcher in order to describe the cultural framework within which Russia's documentary theatre repertoire has emerged and developed. I have situated the plays under discussion within a wider cultural context and provided insight into the specific codes, connotations, and communicative methods each of the plays employs.

Considered in relation to one another, the plays discussed in this book illustrate how Russian documentary theatre practice consistently addresses important contradictions embedded in the daily life of contemporary culture. This research shows how the plays in Russia's documentary theatre repertoire create communities within the theatre space. As Dolan describes, audiences and artists come together to build alliances with one another as persons who wish to think critically about their society. The plays themselves may not always share narratives of hope. *One Hour Eighteen Minutes*, for example, leaves an audience with very little to feel optimistic about, especially given the developments in Magnitsky's case since the production premiered in 2010, as discussed in Chapter 3. Nonetheless, the experience of negotiating collectively the testimonies included in the play gives its participants the opportunity to engage in a judicial process. The trial-like staging of the play implicates each person in the room and asks both artists and audiences to consider their own relationship to the events recounted onstage. In this way *One Hour Eighteen Minutes* encourages its participants to reengage with contemporary notions of justice and, potentially, gain access to a renewed investment in their broader community.

The experience of community involvement, of civic engagement, and of intersubjectivity within the theatre space endures beyond the temporal and spatial boundaries of a performance. It is true, as Dolan writes, that 'we can't measure the effectiveness of art as we can a piece of legislation, or a demonstration, or a political campaign for candidates or for issues' (2005: 20). However, as *Utopia in Performance* suggests, 'the experience of performance, and the intellectual, spiritual, and affective traces it leaves behind, can provide new frames of reference for how we see a better future extending out from our more ordinary lives. Seeing that vision, we can figure out how to achieve it outside the fantastical, magic space of performance' (2005: 20). In the first two decades of Russia's twenty-first century, the structures and methods of documentary theatre practice provided an evocative method with which to pursue precisely the goals that Dolan describes.

As stated in the introduction, this book set out not only to uncover what documentary theatre in twenty-first-century Russia has come to represent or indicate in the context of Austin's theory of speech-acts. Rather, I have approached my analysis of the plays and the broader Russian documentary theatre repertoire with an intent to discover and decode the mechanics of what exactly twenty-first-century Russian documentary theatre *does* or, in Austin's terms, performs. By investigating the connections between memory, justice, sincerity, and belief in Russian documentary theatre practice, I have illustrated how the form offers audiences and performers opportunities to make manifest a renewed investment in the civic sphere.

Documentary theatre in twenty-first-century Russia has given participants a source of hope for a better future, a glimpse into 'the possible', as Dolan writes, 'rather than the insurmountable obstacles' (2005: 1). As this book has argued, in order truly to invest in the experience of the present it is essential to sort through the complexities of one's personal and national pasts. Through their embodiment of narratives of the past, Russia's documentary theatre artists bring their stories into the here and now. Russia's twenty-first-century documentary theatre artists root their work in materials from real-life events and refrain from an attempt to suspend their audiences' disbelief. In this way, their work makes legible the fungibility of history and ideology in twentieth and twenty-first-century Russian history. Its barebones style stands in stark contrast to the highly produced and propagandistic qualities of state-sponsored media and political life in Russia, and the artists' commitment to social justice provides artists and audiences with access to a collective sense of civic engagement.

By occupying the space between an international study of documentary theatre practice, and a culturally specific investigation of how the form functions in its specifically Russian cultural context, this book interprets the mechanics of theatre as a venue for social change. It traces the history of the form and thereby reflects the way Russian documentary theatre has been informed by notions of speech, performance, and paradox in the late-Soviet years. It suggests that through their presentation of historical narratives, the artists of Russian documentary theatre provide audiences singular access to the past in the present. Additionally, *Witness onstage* argues the reciprocal speaking of and listening to documentary texts from the recent past implicates participants in an active process of witnessing and judging that invokes a temporary community of citizens charged with the implicit, and sometimes explicit, responsibility of articulating a new relationship to justice. Considered in relation to one another, the plays included in this study highlight how Russia's documentary theatre artists confront the contradictory status of documents in contemporary culture, particularly as they represent untrustworthy elements of official discourse in post-Soviet Russia. Lastly, the case studies at the centre of *Witness onstage* highlight how documentary theatre in twenty-first-century Russia has given artists and audiences a space for the creative embodiment of historical narratives in which the stories told are not merely remembered and thereby marked as absent, but are in fact revealed as acts of anamnesis.

In the introduction to this study, I considered three different definitions of this key term. In medicine, as I have previously described, anamnesis is the process through which a patient recounts a personal medical history, a live oral practice that is proven to result in a greater chance at an accurate diagnosis. In philosophy, anamnesis is a term that points to the existence of alternative bodies of knowledge, those that are exclusively accessed through the process of remembering. In the liturgy, anamnesis refers to an act of recollection that calls up a subject from the past so as to make that subject operable in the present. Each of these understandings of the word help us decode the efficacy of documentary theatre in the first two decades of Russia's twenty-first century. The staging of documents and personal narratives constitutes a communal recounting of events that helps participants gain a greater understanding of their cultural condition. The embodiment of historical narratives facilitates a process through which artists and audiences gain access to a new perspective on their history and its relevance in the present day. Through the reenactment of texts and events from the past, Russia's documentary theatre artists enact new cultural narratives in the present.

As I have argued elsewhere in this study, Russian documentary theatre is far from the only form of theatre or performance that can be understood through the concept of anamnesis. Indeed, the term could be applied productively to different modes of international theatre practice across history. However, as I have sought to illustrate, the form of documentary theatre as it was practiced in Russia, particularly between 2008 and 2012, is an especially evocative instance of anamnesis in performance. Detailed consideration of the creative movement, its development and expression, informs our comprehension of the structures of feeling that emerged in these years as we see how the form spoke directly to cultural anxieties of the era. It also brings into view the gradual development of an emotional regime throughout the Putin years that has placed freedom of expression increasingly under threat. In this way, *Witness onstage* provides perspective on the relationship between art and society in the twenty-first century and analyses the efficacy of theatre as a space for social change. Though, perhaps most importantly, close analysis of documentary theatre as it emerged in the first two decades of Russia's twenty-first century, has offered rare glimpses into what Gremina described earlier in this study as those 'magical moments of true art, which as is well known, comes and goes as it pleases' (Gremina 2004: 4).

BIBLIOGRAPHY

Adler, Nanci (1993), *Victims of Soviet Terror: The story of the Memorial movement*. Westport, CT: Praeger.
— (2005), 'The Future of the Soviet Past Remains Unpredictable: The resurrection of Stalinist symbols amidst the exhumation of mass graves', *Europe-Asia Studies*, 57/8 (December): 1093–119.
— (2012), *Keeping Faith with the Party: Communist believers return from the Gulag*. Bloomington: University of Indiana Press.
Afisha Plus (2014), 'Ministerstvo kul'tury uvolilo avtoritetnykh ekspertov po sovremennoi dramaturgii', *Afisha* (8 April), http://calendar.fontanka.ru/articles/1467/ (accessed 21 August 2018).
Agata B. (2012), 'Vtoroi akt. Vnuki', Online blogpost (26 December), http://agata-w.livejournal.com/80808.html (accessed 4 February 2017).
Aizman, Ania (2015), 'Documenting migrant labour in Moscow's Teatr.doc', *Maska*, 30/172–4 (July): 116–25.
Alyukhov, Maxim (2017), 'How Does Russian Propaganda Really Work?', *openDemocracy Russia* (8 May), https://www.opendemocracy.net/od-russia/maxim-alyukov/how-does-russian-tv-propaganda-really-work (accessed 19 June 2018).
Amnesty International (2016), 'Darya Poliudova: Facing two years' imprisonment for blogging' (10 May), https://www.amnesty.org.uk/blogs/womens-action-network/darya-poliudova-facing-two-years-imprisonment-blogging (accessed 24 August 2018).
Argumenty i fakti (1991), photo caption, No. 34 (August): 1.
Ash, Lucy (2015), 'Russia's most daring theatre company', *BBC News* (16 April), http://www.bbc.co.uk/news/magazine-32320896 (accessed 21 August 2018).
Assman, Aleida (2013), 'Europe's divided memory', in Uilleam Blacker, Alexander Etkind, and Julie Fedor (ed.) *Memory and Theory in Eastern Europe*. New York; Basingstoke: Palgrave Macmillan: 25–42.
Assman, Jan (1992), *Das kulturelle Gedächtnis: Schrift, Erinnerung und politische Identität in frühen Hochkulturen*. Munich: C.H. Beck.
Austin, J.L. (1975), *How to Do Things with Words*. Cambridge, MA: Harvard University Press.

Autant-Mathieu, Marie-Christine (2010), *Les nouvelles écritures russes*. Pézenas: Domens.
Badmatsyrenov, Zhargal with Mark Nikolaev and Erlan Seitkaznov (2014), 'Stand-up prikhodit v Ulan-Ude!', *Infopol.ru* (24 April), http://www.infpol.ru/kultura2/item/3163-stand-up-prikhodit-v-ulan-ude.html (accessed 17 January 2016).
Banasiukevich, Anna (2015) 'Prikliucheniia "doka" v Rossii', *Teatr*, 19 (April): 57–67.
— (2017), unpublished interview conducted by the author, 5 November, Moscow.
Bar-On, Dan (1989), *Legacy of Silence: Encounters with children of the Third Reich*. Cambridge, MA: Harvard University Press.
Bassin, Mark (1990), *Imperial Visions: Nationalist imagination and geographical expansion in the Russian far east, 1840–1865*. Cambridge: Cambridge University Press.
Bassin, Mark and Catriona Kelly (2012) (eds), *Soviet and Post-Soviet Identities*. Cambridge: Cambridge University Press.
Batalov, Talgat (2012), *Uzbek*, unpublished script.
Belenitskaia, Nina (2007), *Pavlik — moi Bog*, unpublished script.
— (2013), unpublished interview conducted by the author, 2 June, Moscow.
Belinskii, Vissarion Grigorievich (1948), 'Belinskii o drame i teatre', in B.A. Ostrovskii, M.B. Zagorskii, and A.M. Lavretsenkii (ed. and trans.) *O drame i teatre: v dvuh tomakh*. Moscow: Gosudarstvennoe izdatel'stvo isskustvo.
Belyi, Andrei (1978) *Petersburg*, ed. and trans. Robert A. Maguire and John E. Malmstad. Bloomington: Indiana University Press.
Berman, Nikolai (2012), 'Eto my, migranty', *Gazeta.ru* (15 May), http://www.gazeta.ru/culture/2012/05/15/a_4583853.shtml (12 June 2015).
Beumers, Birgit (2004), 'Pop Post-Sots, or the popularization of history in the musical Nord-Ost', *Slavic and East European Journal*, 48/3, Special Forum Issue: Innovation through Iteration: Russian Popular Culture Today (Autumn): 378–95.
Beumers, Birgit and Mark Lipovetsky (2008), 'Reality Performance: Documentary trends in post-Soviet Russian theatre', *Contemporary Theatre Review*, 18/3: 293–306.
— (2009), *Performing Violence: Literary and theatrical experiments in Russian New Drama*. Chicago: Chicago University Press.
— (2010) 'The Desire for the Real: Documentary trends in contemporary Russian culture', *Russian Review*, 69/4: 559–62.
Birksted-Breen, Noah (2016), *Alternative Voices in an Acquiescent Society: Translating the new wave of Russian playwrights (2000–2014)*. Unpublished Ph.D. dissertation, Queen Mary University of London.
Blakkisrud, Helge and Pål Kolstø (2016), *The New Russian Nationalism: Imperialism, ethnicity and authoritarianism 2000–15*. Edinburgh: Edinburgh University Press.
Blok, Aleksander (1986), 'On Theatre', in Michael Green (ed. and trans.), *Russian Symbolist Theatre: An anthology of plays and critical texts*. Ann Arbor, MI: Ardis.
Boeck, Elena (2010), 'Strength in Numbers or Unity in Diversity? Compilations of miracle-working virgin icons', in Jefferson J. A. Gatrall and Douglas Greenfield (eds) *Alter Icons: The Russian icon and modernity*. University Park: Pennsylvania State University Press.
Bondarenko, Ekaterina (2014), Facebook post (15 October), https://www.facebook.com/katya.abu/posts/763220143739853?pnref=story (accessed 21 August 2018).
Bondarenko, Ekaterina and Anastasiia Patlai (2013), unpublished interview conducted by the author, June 4, Moscow.
Boobbyer, Philip (2000), *The Stalin Era*. New York: Routledge.
Borodina, Polina (2017), unpublished interview conducted by the author, 4 November, Moscow.
Boym, Svetlana (2002a), *The Future of Nostalgia*. New York: Basic Books.
— (2002b), 'Stil' PR', *Neprikosnovennyi zapas*, 6: 78–82.
Briusov, Valerii (1902), 'Nenuzhnaia pravda', first published in *Mir iskusstva*, available online at http://dugward.ru/library/brusov/brusov_nenujnaya_pravda.html (accessed 21 August 2018).
Brodie, Ian (2008), 'Stand-up Comedy as a Genre of Intimacy', *Association Canadienne d'Ethnologie et de Folklore Érudit*, 30/2: 152–80.

Brooker, Peter (1994), 'Key Words in Brecht's Theory and Practice of Theatre', in Peter Thompson and Glendyr Sacks (ed.), *The Cambridge Companion to Brecht*. Cambridge: Cambridge University Press: 209-24.

Browder, William (2010), 'An Assessment of the Russian Judicial and Law Enforcement System: The torture and murder of Sergei Magnitsky', *Testimony to the Tom Lantos Human Rights Commission* (6 May), http://russian-untouchables.com/docs/D106-2010-05-06-Browder-Testimony-Lantos-Commission.pdf (accessed 27 July 2018).

Bulin, Dmitrii (2011), 'Populiarnost' Stalina v Rossii stremitel'no rastet', *BBC Russia* (27 April), http://www.bbc.co.uk/russian/society/2011/04/110427_stalin_vciom_support.shtml (accessed 21 August 2018).

Burliuk, David, Aleksei Kruchenykh, Vladimir Maiakovskii, and Velimir Khlebnikov (1912), 'Poshchechina obshchestvennomu vkusu', in *Poshchechina obshchestvennomu vkusu*. Moscow: Kuz'min: 3-4. English translation: 'A Slap in the Face to Public Taste', in Anne Lawton and Herbert Eagle (eds) (1998), *Russian Futurism through its manifestoes, 1912-1928*. Ithaca, NY: Cornell University Press: 51-2.

Cassiday, Julie (2000), *The Enemy on Trial: Early Soviet courts on stage and screen*. DeKalb: Northern Illinois University Press.

Chachko, Asia (2012), 'Interview with Talgat Batalov', *Bol'shoi gorod* (25 June), http://bg.ru/society/talgat_batalov_uzbeki_eto_opasnaya_naciya-11284/ (accessed 21 August 2018).

Clark, Katerina (1981), *The Soviet Novel: History as ritual*. Chicago: University of Chicago Press.

Colta (2014), 'Glava teatr.doc Elena Gremina: "Eto voina biurokratii protiv zhivoi zhizni"', online blogpost (October 23), http://openrussia.org/post/view/544/ (accessed 21 August 2018).

Connerton, Paul (1989), *How Societies Remember*. Cambridge: Cambridge University Press.

Dalton-Brown, Sally (2000), *Voices from the Void: The genres of Liudmila Petrushevskaia*. London and New York: Berghahn Books.

Davydova, Marina (2005), *Konets teatral'noi epokhi*. Moscow: Otdelnoe izdanie.

— (2018), *Kul'tura zero: Ocherki russkoi zhizni i evropeiskoi tseny*. Moscow: Novoe literaturnoe obozrenie.

Dawson, Gary Fisher (1999), *Documentary Theatre in the United States*. Westport, CT: Greenwood Press.

Denisova, Sasha (2011), 'Molchanie ili gumanism', in *Ekspert online* (May 26), http://expert.ru/russian_reporter/2011/20/molchanie-ili-gumanizm/ (accessed 23 April 2019).

Dix, Gregory (1945), *The Shape of the Liturgy*. London: Continuum.

Dobrenko, Evgeny (2007), *The Political Economy of Socialist Realism*. New Haven, CT: Yale University Press.

Dolan, Jill (2005), *Utopia in Performance: Finding hope at the theatre*. Ann Arbor: University of Michigan Press.

Dondurei, Daniil (2006), interviewed in advance of the 2006 New Drama Festival, *Teatral'naia moskva* (September), http://subscribe.ru/archive/culture.theatre.yan/200609/21175426.html (accessed 21 August 2018).

Dozhd (2015), 'Opera "Tangeizer" v postanovke Timofei Kuliabina' *Libretto* (29 March), http://tvrain.ru/articles/opera_tangejzer_v_postanovke_timofeja_kuljabina_libretto-384733/ (accessed 27 July 2018).

Druzhnikov, Iurii (1988), *Donoschik 001*. Moscow: Moskovskii rabochi. English translation: *Informer 001: The Myth of Pavlik Morozov* (1997). New Brunswick, NJ: Transaction Publishers.

Eisenstein, Sergei (1937), *Bezhin Lug*, available online at https://www.youtube.com/watch?v=uidYVgnbeb4 (accessed 27 July 2018).

Ekho moskvy (2013), 'Teatral'nyi arrest - est' li budushchee u politicheskogo teatra' (9 March), https://echo.msk.ru/programs/kulshok/1025184-echo/ (accessed 21 August 2018).

Etkind, Alexander (2009), 'Stories of the Undead in the Land of the Unburied: Magical historicism in contemporary Russian fiction', *Slavic Review*, 68: 631-58.

— (2013), *Warped Mourning: Stories of the undead in the land of the unburied*. Stanford, CT: Stanford University Press.

Farmer, Lindsay (2010), 'Trials', in Matthew Anderson, Catherine O. Frank, and Austin Sarat (ed.) *Law and the Humanities: An introduction*. Cambridge: Cambridge University Press: 455–76.
Favorini, Attilio (1995), *Voicings: Ten plays from the documentary theatre*. Hopewell, NJ: Ecco Press.
Fedorovskaia, Marina (2013), 'Teatr-Talgat Batalov', *InStyle* (November): 43.
Ferretti, Maria (2003), 'Memory Disorder', *Russian Politics and Law*, 41: 38–82.
Filewood, Alan (1987), *Collective Encounters: Documentary theatre in English Canada*. Toronto: University of Toronto Press.
Fitzpatrick, Sheila (1996), *Stalin's Peasants: Resistance and survival in the Russian village after collectivization*. Oxford: Oxford University Press.
Forsyth, Alison, and Chris Megson (eds) (2009), *Get Real: Documentary theatre past and present*. Basingstoke: Palgrave Macmillan.
Freedman, John (1997), *Moscow Performances: The new Russian theatre 1991–1996*. Amsterdam: Harwood.
— (1998) (ed. and trans), introduction to *Two Plays by Olga Mukhina*. Amsterdam: Harwood: xi–xxiii.
— (2010), 'Contemporary Russian Drama: The journey from stagnation to a Golden Age', *Theatre Journal*, 62/3 (October): 389–420.
— (2013), 'Chas vosemnadtsat'', kak potriasli mir', *Gogol*.tv, a filmed conversation with actor Anastasiia Patlai (20 March), http://gogol.tv/video/1070 (accessed 29 June 2018).
— (2014), 'Closing the Book on an Era in Russian Theatre History', *AATSEEL Newsletter*, 57/3 (October), available at https://johnfreedmanarchive.wordpress.com/2018/07/11/closing-the-book-on-an-era-in-russian-theater-history-2014/ (accessed 15 July 2018).
Freedom House (2009), 'Undermining Democracy: 21st century authoritarianism', *Freedom House; Radio Free Europe/Radio Liberty; Radio Free Asia* (June), https://freedomhouse.org/sites/default/files/russia.pdf (accessed 21 August 2018).
Freud, Sigmund (2009), *Mourning and Melancholia*, ed. Leticia Glocer Fiorini, Thierry Bokanowski, and Sergio Lewkowicz. London: Karnac.
Frost, Warwick and Jennifer Laing (2013), *Commemorative Events: Memory, identities, conflicts*. London: Routledge.
Gabowitsch, Mischa (2016), *Protest in Putin's Russia*. Cambridge: Polity Press.
Gapps, Stephen (2010), 'On Being a Mobile Monument', in Iain McCalman and Paul A. Pickering (ed.) *Historical Reenactment: From realism to the affective turn*. Basingstoke: Palgrave Macmillan: 50–62.
Gazeta.ru (2013), 'Avtobusy s "reklamoi" Stalina vnov' poiaviatsia na ulitsakh rossiiskikh gorodov v nachale fevralia', *Gazet.ru* (31 January), http://www.gazeta.ru/social/news/2013/01/31/n_2732201.shtml (accessed 21 August 2018).
— (2014) 'Department imushchestva ob'iasnil vyselenie Teatr.doc "nesoglasovannoi pereplanirovkoi"', *Gazeta.ru* (15 October), http://www.gazeta.ru/culture/news/2014/10/15/n_6565501.shtml (accessed 7 September 2015).
Genoux, Georg (2013), unpublished interview conducted by the author, 3 June, Moscow.
Getty, J. Arch (1999), 'Samokritika Rituals in the Stalinist Central Committee, 1933–38', *Russian Review*, 58/1 (January): 49–70.
Ginkas, Kama (2003), *Provoking Theatre: Kama Ginkas directs*, ed. and trans. John Freedman. Portland, ME: Smith & Krauss.
Gittoes, Julie (2008), *Anamnesis and the Eucharist*. Farnham: Ashgate.
Gogol.tv (2013), 'Moskovskii protsessie so tseny na ekran', a conversation with the producers (28 March), http://gogol.tv/video/1076 (accessed 21 August 2018).
Goldman, Wendy Z. (2007), *Terror and Democracy in the Age of Stalin: The social dynamics of repression*. Cambridge: Cambridge University Press.
Golub, Spencer (1984), *Evreinov: The theatre of paradox and transformation*. Ann Arbor, MI: UMI Research Press.
Gorbovskii, Aleksandr (1999), 'Bol'shaia entsikoplediia stuka', segment entitled 'A Generation of Pavliks' (Pokolenie Pavlikov), *Ogonek*, 36 (November).

Gorky media (2018), 'Vospitala tysiachi zritelei i tysiachi grazhdan', https://gorky.media/context/vospitala-tysyachi-zritelej-i-tysyachi-grazhdan/ (accessed 21 May 2018).
Goscilo, Helena (2013) (ed.), *Putin as Celebrity and Cultural Icon*. New York: Routledge.
Green, Michael (1986), *Russian Symbolist Theatre: An anthology of plays and critical texts*. Ann Arbor, MI: Ardis.
Gremina, Elena (ed.) (2004), *Dokumental'nyi Teatr: P'esy Teatr.doc*. Moscow: Tri kvadrata.
— (2010), *Chas vosemnadtsat'*, unpublished script.
— (2012), Unpublished transcripts from the Svidetel' na tsene symposium held at Teatr.doc on contemporary Russian documentary theatre.
— (2014a), Facebook post (15 October), https://www.facebook.com/elena.gremina/posts/10204053482651469 (accessed 21 August 2018).
— (2014b), Facebook post (30 December), https://www.facebook.com/elena.gremina/posts/10204565722177137 (accessed 21 August 2018).
— (2017), Unpublished interview conducted by the author, 4 November, Moscow.
Gromova, M.I. (2009), *Russkaia dramaturgiia kontsa XX–nachala XXI veka*. Moscow: Izdatel'stvo 'nauka'.
Gross, Kenneth (1992), *Dream of the Moving Statue*. Ithaca, NY: Cornell University Press.
Grotowski, Jerzy (1968), *Towards a Poor Theatre*, ed. Eugenio Barba. Holstebro: Odin teatrets forlag.
Groys, Boris (1992), *The Total Art of Stalinism: Avant-garde, aesthetic dictatorship, and beyond*. Princeton, NJ: Princeton University Press.
Halbwachs, Maurice (1992), *On Collective Memory*. Chicago: University of Chicago Press.
Hammond, Will and Dan Steward (2008) (ed.), *Verbatim Verbatim: Contemporary documentary theatre*. London: Oberon.
Hanukai, Maksim (2017), 'After the Riot: Teatr.doc and the performance of witness', *TDR*, 61/1 (Spring): 43–55.
Hopf, Ted (2002), *Social Construction of International Politics: Identities and foreign policies in Moscow 1955 and 1999*. Ithaca, NY: Cornell University Press.
Iampolskii, Mikhail (1995), 'In the Shadow of Monuments', in Nancy Condee (ed.) *Soviet Hieroglyphics: Visual culture in late twentieth-century Russia*. Bloomington: Indiana University Press: 93–112.
Ianovskii, Semen (1989), 'Rozhdenie Memoriala', *Ogonek*, 6 (February): 1.
Irmer, Thomas (2006), 'A Search for New Realities: Documentary theatre in Germany', *TDR*, 50/3 (Autumn):16–28.
Ivanov, Viacheslav (1986), 'The Need for a Dionysian Theatre', in Michael Green (trans. and ed.) *Russian Symbolist Theatre: An anthology of plays and critical texts*. Ann Arbor, MI: Ardis: 113–20.
Jakobson, Roman (1975), *Pushkin and His Sculptural Myth*. The Hague: Mouton.
Johnston, Rebecca Adeline (2013), *Culture in the Crucible: Pussy Riot and the politics of art in contemporary Russia*, unpublished MA thesis, University of Texas, http://repositories.lib.utexas.edu/bitstream/handle/2152/21294/JOHNSTON-THESIS-2013.pdf?sequence=1 (accessed 21 August 2018).
Jonson, Lena (2015), *Art and Protest in Putin's Russia*. New York and London: Routledge.
Kadri, Sadakat (2013), 'Sergei Magnitsky Trial: This is Putin's kind of justice', *Guardian* (12 July), http://www.guardian.co.uk/commentisfree/2013/jul/12/magnitsky-trial-putin-justice (accessed 18 August 2018).
Kahn, Jeffery (2013), 'Freedom of Expression in Post-Soviet Russia (Contribution to the Symposium Building BRICS: Human rights in today's emerging economic powers)', *UCLA Journal of International Law and Foreign Affairs*, 18 (15 February).
Kalinin, Il'ia (2010), 'Nostal'gisheskaia modernizatsia, ili: Rossia vpered!', *Neprikosnovennyi Zapas*, 6/74: 6–16.
Kaluzhskii, Mikhail (2010), *Gruz molchaniia*, unpublished script, 2010.
— (2012) 'Performing Memory: Current trends in Russian documentary theatre', unpublished presentation, University of Cambridge, 1 March.

— (2015), 'Novosibirsk's Cultural History of Loss', *openDemocracy Russia* (8 April), https://www.opendemocracy.net/od-russia/mikhail-kaluzhsky/novosibirsk%27s-cultural-history-of-loss (accessed 15 August 2018).

Kaluzhskii, Mikhail and Aleksandra Polivanova (2012), *Vtoroi akt. Vnuki*, unpublished script.

Karev, Igor and Aleksei Krizhevskii (2014), 'Evakuatsiia baz prokatnogo udostovereniia', *Gazet.ru* (31 December), http://www.gazeta.ru/culture/2014/12/31/a_6365497.shtml (accessed 18 August 2018).

Kelly, Catriona (2005), *Comrade Pavlik: The rise and fall of a Soviet boy hero*. London: Granta.

Khapaeva, Dina (2016), 'Triumphant Memory of the Perpetrators: Putin's politics of re-stalinization', *Communist and Post-Communist Studies*, 49/1 (March): 61–73.

Klavdiev, Iurii (2014), Facebook post (30 December), https://www.facebook.com/yurii.klavdiev/posts/10152690326670805?fref=nf (accessed 27 June 2019)

Klimeniouk, Nikolai (2017), 'Death by Crimea', *open Democracy Russia* (20 March), https://www.opendemocracy.net/od-russia/nikolai-klimeniouk/crimea-international-law-opposition (accessed 24 June 2018).

Kolstøs, Pål (2013), 'Society: Moscow: City of xenophobia', *Transitions Online* (30 July), http://www.tol.org/client/article/23876-moscow-city-of-xenophobia.html (accessed 4 May 2015).

Koval'skaia, Elena (2012), 'The New Drama: Plays for a non-existent theatre', unpublished conference presentation. *Literary Theatricality: Theatrical Text*, Princeton University, Princeton, NJ, 27 October.

— (2015), 'Dvizhenie "solidarnost": na otkrytie Teatr.doc', *Teatr*, 19: 16–25.

— (2018), 'Vy dolzhny pisat', blogpost on the website for the journal *Teatr* (19 May), http://oteatre.info/vy-dolzhny-pisat/ (accessed 21 May 2018).

Kroupnik, Maria (2014), Facebook post (15 October), https://www.facebook.com/Maria.Kroupnik/posts/10205141120026280 (accessed 21 August 2018).

Kurochkin, Maksym (2013), unpublished interview conducted by the author, 27 May, Krasnoiarsk.

Kurochkin, Maksym and Aleksandr Rodionov (2015), 'Kak my poliubili verbatim tekst', *Teatr*, 19 (April): 112–19.

Kuromiya, Hiroaki (1990), *Stalin's Industrial Revolution: Politics and workers, 1928–1932*. Cambridge: Cambridge University Press.

Kuzio, Taras (2016), 'Nationalism and Authoritariansim in Russia: Introduction to the special issue', *Communist and Post-Communist Studies*, 49/1 (March): 1–11.

Lahusen, Thomas and Peter H. Solomon (2008) (ed.), *What is Soviet Now? Identities, Legacies, Memories*. Berlin; London; Piscataway, NJ: Transaction Publishers.

Larina, Ksenia (2010), 'Kul'turnyi shok: Istoriia Sergeiia Magnitskogo na tsene teatra v spektakle "Chas vosemnadtsat"', *Echo Moskvy* (6 June), http://www.echo.msk.ru/programs/kulshok/684833-echo/#element-text (accessed 18 August 2018).

Ledeneva, Alena V. (2006), *How Russia Really Works: The informal practices that shaped post-Soviet business and politics*. Ithaca, NY: Cornell University Press.

Lemon, Alaina (1998), 'Your Eyes Are Green Like Dollars: Counterfeit cash, national substance, and currency apartheid in 1990s Russia', *Cultural Anthropology*, 13/1: 22–55.

Lenoe, Matthew Edward (2004), *Closer to the Masses: Stalinist culture, social revolution, and Soviet newspapers*. Cambridge, MA: Harvard University Press.

Lenta (2014a), 'Putin zapretil mat v SMI I proizvedeniiakh iskusstva' (5 May), https://lenta.ru/news/2014/05/05/mat/ (accessed 18 August 2017).

— (2014b), 'Dorogim chitateliam ot dorogoi redaktsii' (12 March), http://www.colta.ru/news/2412 (accessed 19 August 2018).

— (2018), 'Serebrennikov nazval prichinu ugolovnogo presledovaniia' (9 June), https://lenta.ru/news/2018/07/09/7studio/ (accessed 23 August 2018).

Levchenko, Aleksei (2009), 'Stalin vstaet iz-pod zemli', *Gazeta.ru* (26 August), http://www.gazet.ru/politics/2009/08/26_a_3240785.shtml (accessed 19 November 2013).

Levy, David (2003), *Scrolling Forward: Making sense of documents in the digital age*. New York: Arcade Publishing.

Limon, John (2000) *Stand-up Comedy in Theory, or, Abjection in America*. Durham, NC and London: Duke University Press.

Lipman, Masha and Michael McFaul (2001), '"Managed Democracy" in Russia: Putin and the Press', *Harvard International Journal of Press/Politics*, 6/3 (June):116–27.
Lipovetsky, Mark (1999), *Russian Postmodernist Fiction: Dialogue with chaos*. Armonk, NY: M.E. Sharpe.
— (2004), 'Post-Sots: Transformations of Socialist Realism in the popular culture of the recent period', *Slavic and East European Journal*, 48/3, Special Forum Issue: Innovation through Iteration: Russian Popular Culture Today (Autumn): 356–77.
Lisitsina, Anastasiia (2012), 'Veriu stanislavskogo peremestilos' v grazhdanskuiu plokost'', *Gazeta.ru* (24 July), http://www.gazeta.ru/culture/2012/07/24/a_4691369.shtml (accessed 24 August 2018).
Lisovskii, Vsevolod (2014), Facebook post (30 December), https://www.facebook.com/lisoev.vaha/posts/10203264897324274?fref=nf, https://www.facebook.com/lisoev.vaha/posts/10203268681378873>, and https://www.facebook.com/lisoev.vaha/posts/10203268814822209?fref=nf (accessed 21 August 2018).
— (2017), unpublished interview conducted by the author, 23 June, Kyiv.
Lunacharskii, A. (ed.) (1908), *Kniga o novom teatre: Sbornik statei*. St Petersburg: Izd. Shipovnik.
Mally, Lynn (2009), *Manufacturing Truth: The documentary moment in early Soviet culture*. DeKalb: Northern Illinois University Press.
Marsh, Cynthia (1999), 'Realism in Russian Theatre, 1850–1882', in Robert Leach and Victor Borovsky (ed.) *A History of Russian Theatre*. Cambridge: Cambridge University Press: 146–65.
Martin, Carol (2006), 'Bodies of Evidence', *TDR*, 50/3 (Autumn): 8–15.
— (ed.) (2010), 'Introduction: Dramaturgy of the Real', in *Dramaturgy of the Real World Onstage*. Basingstoke: Palgrave Macmillan: 1–14.
— (2013), *Theatre of the Real*. New York; Basingstoke: Palgrave Macmillan.
Matvienko, Kristina (2014), '"Novaia drama": pobeda bez triumfa', *Isskustvo kino*, 3 (March), http://www.kinoart.ru/archive/2014/03/novaya-drama-pobeda-bez-triumfa (accessed 29 August 2018).
McLaughlin, Robert L. (2004), 'Post-Postmodern Discontent: Contemporary fiction and the social world', *Symploke*, 12/1: 53–68.
Mediazona (2017), 'Politseiskie prishli v "Teatr.doc" na chtenie dnevnikov Ali Feruza, no pereputali pomesheniia' (25 October), https://zona.media/news/2017/10/25/dnevnik (accessed 21 July 2018).
Medvedev, Roy (1989), *Let History Judge: The origins and consequences of Stalinism*, trans. George Shriver. New York: Columbia University Press.
Megson, Chris (2009), 'Half the Picture: "A Certain Frisson" at the Tricycle Theatre', in Alison Forsyth and Chris Megson (ed.) *Get Real: Documentary theatre past and present*. Basingstoke: Palgrave Macmillan: 195–208.
Meirerkhol'd, Vsevolod (1969), 'The Fairground Booth', in Edward Braun (trans. and ed.) *Meyerhold on Theatre*. New York: Hill & Wang: 119–42.
Memorial (2012), 'Delo o sobytiiakh na Bolotnoi ploshadi 6 maia 2012 goda', https://memohrc.org/ru/special-projects/delo-o-sobytiyah-na-bolotnoy-ploshchadi-6-maya-2012-goda (accessed 24 August 2018).
— (n.d.), http://www.memo.ru/about/text0000.htm (accessed 16 August 2015).
Merridale, Catherine (2003), 'Redesigning History in Contemporary Russia', *Journal of Contemporary History*, 38/1 (January): 13–28.
Monastyrskii, Andrei (1999) (ed.), *Slovar' terminov moskovskoi konseptualnoi shkoly* (Moscow: 1999).
Nekhezin, Viktor (2014),'telekanal "Dozhd"' pod ugrozoi prekreshcheniia veshcheniia', *BBC Russia* (29 January), http://www.bbc.co.uk/russian/russia/2014/01/140129_tv_rain_conflict.shtml (accessed 21 August 2018).
Nora, Pierre (1996), *Realms of Memory: Rethinking the French past*. New York: Columbia University Press.
O'Conner, Jacqueline (2013), *Documentary Trial Plays in Contemporary American Theater*. Carbondale: South Illinois University Press.

Paget, Derek (1987), '"Verbatim Theatre": Oral history and documentary techniques', *New Theatre Quarterly*, 3/12: 317–36.
— (1990), *True Stories? Documentary drama on radio, screen and stage.* Manchester: Manchester University Press.
— (1998), *No Other Way to Tell It: Dramadoc/docudrama on television.* Manchester: Manchester University Press.
Palveleva, Lilya (2015), 'Ukrainian Filmmaker Remains Behind Bars Despite Growing Support', *Radio Free Europe/Radio Liberty* (9 January), http://www.rferl.org/content/ukraine-filmmaker-sentsov-jailed/25436572.html (accessed 21 August 2018).
Papazian, Elizabeth (2009), *Manufacturing Truth: The documentary moment in early Soviet culture.* DeKalb: Northern Illinois University Press.
Paperno, Irina (2001), 'Exhuming the Bodies of Soviet Terror', *Representations*, 75/1 (Summer): 89–118.
Patico, Jennifer (2002), 'Chocolates and Cognac: Gifts and the recognition of social worlds in post-Soviet Russia', *Ethnos Journal of Anthropology*, 67/3: 345–68.
Pervoe Kino (2008), 'Reportazh so s'emok', video report detailing Evgenii Grigoriev's panoramic cinema method of filmmaking (16 September), https://www.youtube.com/watch?v=JYFKel-tDmU#t=25 (accessed 21 August 2018).
Peterson, Ronald E. (1986), *The Russian Symbolists: An anthology of critical and theoretical writings.* Ann Arbor, MI: Ardis.
Planeta.ru (2014), Teatr.doc fundraising page, http://planeta.ru/campaigns/7976 (accessed 21 August 2018).
Pomerantsev, Peter (2015), *Nothing is True and Everything is Possible: Adventures in modern Russia.* London: Faber & Faber.
Pomerantsev, Vladimir (1953), 'Ob iskrennosti v literature', *Novii mir*, 12 (December), English translation at http://www.thedrawers.net/pomerantsev.htm (accessed 21 August 2018).
Ponomareva, Iulia (2013), 'Half of Russians Remain Positive about Stalin', *Russia Beyond the Headlines* (4 March), http://rbth.co.uk/society/2013/03/04/half_of_russians_remain_positive_about_stalin_23503.html (accessed 11 October 2014).
Post-show discussions following performances of *Gruz molchaniia* (2010–11), complete video archive.
Post-show discussions following performances of *Chas vosemnadtsat'* (2010–12), complete video archive.
Reddy, William (2010), *The Navigation of Feeling: A framework for the history of emotions.* Cambridge: Cambridge University Press.
Reeves, Madeleine (2013), 'Clean Fake: Authenticating documents and persons in migrant Moscow', *American Ethnologist: Journal of the American Ethnology Society*, 40/3: 508–24.
Reinelt, Janelle (2006), 'Towards a Poetics of Theatre of Public Events: In the case of Stephen Lawrence', *TDR*, 50/3 (Fall): 69–87.
— (2009), 'The Promise of Documentary', in Alison Forsyth and Chris Megson (ed.) *Get Real: Documentary theatre past and present.* Basingstoke: Palgrave Macmillan: 6–23.
Reuters (2012), 'Is it a bird, a plane? No, it's Putin, human crane' (6 September), https://www.reuters.com/article/us-russia-putin-cranes/is-it-a-bird-a-plane-no-its-putin-human-crane-idUSBRE8841AF20120906 (accessed 24 August 2018).
— (2015), 'Russian court jails blogger for five years for 'extremist' posts' (30 December), https://uk.reuters.com/article/uk-russia-blogger/russian-court-jails-blogger-for-five-years-for-extremist-posts-idUKKBN0UD16O20151230 (accessed 24 August 2018).
RFERL (2018), 'European Parliament Urges Russia to Release Sentsov, Other Ukrainain Political Prisoners' (14 June), https://www.rferl.org/a/european-parliament-urges-russia-to-release-sentsov-other-ukrainian-political-prisoners-/29290146.html (accessed 23 August 2018).
Ria novosti (2013), Zakon o zaprete propagandy gomosekualizma: aspekty i traktova', https://ria.ru/infografika/20130709/948546631.html (accessed 24 August 2018).
Roach, Joseph (1996), *Cities of the Dead: Circum-Atlantic performance.* New York: Columbia University Press.

Rogoża, Jadwiga (2014), 'Russian Nationalism: Between imperialism and xenophobia', *European View*, 13/1 (June): 79–87.
Rokem, Freddie (2000), *Performing History: Theatrical representations of the past in contemporary theatre*. Iowa City: University of Iowa Press.
Ross, Yana (2006), 'Russia's New Drama: From Togliatti to Moscow', *Theatre*, 36/1: 26–43.
Roudakova, Natalia (2017), *Losing Pravda: Ethics and the press in post-truth Russia*. Cambridge: Cambridge University Press.
Ruble, Blair A. (2015), 'Theatre and the Heart of a City: Moscow's Teatr.doc's confrontation with authority', *Wilson Center/Kennan Institute* (7 January), http://www.wilsoncenter.org/publication/theater-and-the-heart-city-moscow%E2%80%99s-teatrdoc%E2%80%99s-confrontation-authority (accessed 11 January 2015).
Rudnev, Pavel (2011), 'Ne khochet znat', *Chastnyi correspondent* (11 March), http://www.chaskor.ru/article/ne_hotet_znat_22554 (accessed 17 August 2018).
— (2012), *Replika*, 4/15, http://issu.com/replikamagazine/docs/replica_15 (accessed 4 April 2014).
— (2013), unpublished interview conducted by the author, 25 May, Krasnoiarsk.
— (2014) 'Let's talk about Faith: Political theatre in Russia in the year 2014', *Theaterbrief aus Moskau* (3 July), http://www.nachtkritik.de/index.php?option=com_content&view=article&id=9597%3Atheaterbrief-aus-russland-political-theater-in-russia-in-the-year-2014&catid=708%3Atheaterbriefe-aus-russland&Itemid=99 (accessed 22 August 2018).
— (2017), 'Theatre in Period of Archaization', in Andrei Erofeev and Lena Jonson (ed.) *Russia – Art, Resistance, and the Conservative–Authoritarian Zeitgeist*. New York: Routledge: 295–303.
— (2018), *Drama pamiati: Ocherki istorii rossiiskoi dramaturgii 1950–2010-e*. Moscow: Novoe literaturnoe obozrenie.
Russian Untouchables (2012), 'Magnitsky Murder and Cover-Up Report', http://russian-untouchables.com/eng/cover-up-presentation/ (accessed 21 August 2018).
Rutten, Ellen (2008), 'Strategic Sentiments: Pleas for a New Sincerity in post-Soviet literature', in *Dutch Contributions to the Fourteenth International Congress of Slavists. Ohrid, September 10–16, 2008*. Amsterdam; New York: Rodopi: 201–15.
— (2017), *Sincerity after Communism*. New Haven, CT: Yale University Press.
Sadykov, Murat (2013), 'Central Asia: Labor migrants caught in Russian politician's crosshairs', *Eurasia.net* (18 June), http://www.eurasianet.org/node/67135 (accessed 21 August 2018).
Saidova, G. Sh. (2013), 'Zhizn' evakuirovanniikh detei v Uzbekistane s gody Vtoroi mirovoi voiny', *Molodoi uchenyi*: 757–60.
Sakharov Center website (2014), http://www.sakharov-center.ru/news/2014/inagenty.html>, and http://www.sakharov-center.ru/news/2015/545.html (accessed 21 August 2018).
Schechner, Richard (2002), *Performance Studies: An introduction*. London; New York: Routledge.
Schneider, Rebecca (2011), *Performing Remains: Art and war in the times of theatrical reenactment*. New York: Routledge.
Schramm, Jan-Melissa (2010), 'Testimony, Witnessing', in Matthew Anderson, Catherine O. Frank, and Austin Sarat (ed.) *Law and the Humanities: An introduction*. Cambridge: Cambridge University Press: 478–95.
Schulze, Daniel (2017), *Authenticity in Contemporary Theatre and Performance: Make it real*. London: Bloomsbury.
Schwirtz, Michael (2012), 'In Russia, Charges Are Dropped in Jail Death', *New York Times* (April 9), http://www.nytimes.com/2012/04/09/world/europe/russia-drops-charges-against-doctor-in-jail-death.html (accessed 21 August 2018).
Senelick, Laurence (1996), 'Russia 1848–1916', in Claude Schumacher, Glynne W. Wickham, and John Northam (ed.) *Naturalism and Symbolism in European Theatre 1850–1918*. Cambridge: Cambridge University Press: 193–260.
Shchipaev, Stepan (1950), *Pavlik Morozov*. Moscow: Sovetskii Pisatel'.
Sherlock, Thomas (2016), 'Russian politics and the Soviet past: Reassessing Stalin and Stalinism under Vladimir Putin', *Communist and Post-Communist Studies*, 49/1 (March): 45–9.

Shubina, Maria (2012), 'Kto ia? Gde ia?', *Radio svoboda* (28 November), http://www.svoboda.org/content/article/24783999.html (accessed 21 August 2018).
Shumiatskii, Boris (1988), 'O filme Bezhin Lug', in Richard Taylor and Ian Christie (trans. and ed.) *Film Factory: Russian and Soviet Cinema in Documents 1896-1939*. London: Routledge: 378-9.
Sierz, Aleks (2001), *In-Yer-Face-Theatre*. London: Faber & Faber.
Smelianksii, Anatolii (1999), *The Russian Theatre After Stalin*. Cambridge: Cambridge University Press.
Snyder, Timothy (2010), *Bloodlands: Europe between Hitler and Stalin*. London: Basic Books.
Solntseva, Alena (2018), 'Pamiati rovesnikov. O Mishe Ugarove i Lene Greminoi', *Seans* (22 May), http://seance.ru/blog/portrait/ugarov-gremina-in-memoriam/ (accessed 21 August 2018).
Sologub, Fedor (1986), 'Theatre of One Will', in Michael Green (ed. and trans.) *Russian Symbolist Theatre: An anthology of plays and critical texts*. Ann Arbor, MI: Ardis.
Solov'ev, Vladimir (1990), *Sochineniia v dukh tomakh*. Moscow.
Solzhenitsyn, Aleksandr (2007), *The Gulag Archipelago: An experiment in literary investigation*, Vol. 1, trans. Thomas P. Whitley. New York: HarperCollins.
Stronski, Paul (2010), *Tashkent: Forging a City, 1930-1966*. Pittsburgh, PA: University of Pittsburgh Press.
Svidetel' na tsene (2012), unpublished transcripts from the symposium held at Teatr.doc on contemporary Russian documentary theatre.
Taylor, Diana (2003), *The Archive and the Repertoire: Performing cultural memory in the Americas*. Durham, NC: Duke University Press.
Teatr.doc (2010), unpublished 'briefing on the play' (instruktsiia k spektakliu), printed to accompany the production *Chas vosemnadtsat'*.
Tomlin, Liz (2013), *Acts and Apparitions: Discourses on the real in performance practice and theory, 1990-2010*. Manchester: Manchester University Press.
Triboi, Mihaela (2012), 'The Contemporary Russian Dramaturgy: Currents, personalities of the New Wave', *Cinematographic Art & Documentation*, 6/10: 55-9.
Trilling, Lionel (1974), *Sincerity and Authenticity*. London: Oxford University Press.
Trimmer, Nicole (2010), *Do You Feel it Too? The post-postmodern syndrome in American fiction at the turn of the millennium*. Amsterdam and New York: Rodopi.
Tsvetova, Natalia S. (2015), 'Concept of the World in the Prose of Zakhar Prilepin: On the problem of the creative personality evolution', *Journal of Siberian Federal University*, 3: 452-59.
Turner, Victor (1977), *The Ritual Process: Structure and anti-structure*. Ithaca, NY: Cornell University Press.
— (1982), *From Ritual to Theatre: The human seriousness of play*. New York: Performing Arts Journal Publication.
Vartanova, Elena (2004), 'The Russian Network Society', in Manuel Castells (ed.) *Network Society*. Cheltenham: Edward Elgar, 84-98.
Vasenina, Ekaterina (2012), '"Akyn-opera": teatr kompaktnogo prozhivaniia', *Novaya gazeta* (17 November), http://www.novayagazeta.ru/society/55474.html (accessed 21 August 2018).
Vedomosti (2014), 'Miniust priznal insostrannym agentom Obshchestvennuiu komissiiu po sokhraneniiu naslediia akademika Sakharova' (26 December), https://www.vedomosti.ru/politics/articles/2014/12/26/minyust-priznal-inostrannym-agentom-obschestvennuyu (accessed 22 August 2018).
Vislova, A.V. (2009), *Russkii teatr na slome epoch rubezh xx - xxi vekov*. Moscow: Universitetskaia Kniga.
Vyrypaev, Ivan (2014), '"Teatr.doc" nadezhda na zhizn"', *Colta.ru* (2 November), http://www.colta.ru/news/5216 (accessed 22 August 2018).
Weinberger, David (1996), 'What's a Document', *Wired*, 4:8: 112.
Weygandt, Susanna (2016), 'The Structure of Plasticity: Resistance and accommodation in Russian New Drama', *TDR*, 60:1 (Spring): 116-31.

Widdis, Emma (2004), 'Russia as Space', in Simon Franklin and Emma Widdis (ed.) *National Identity in Russian Culture: An introduction*. Cambridge; New York: Cambridge University Press: 30–50.
Willett, John (1978), *The Theatre of Erwin Piscator*. London: Eyre Methuen.
Williams, Raymond (1977), *Marxism and Literature*. Oxford and New York: Oxford University Press.
Williams, Raymond (1977), 'Structures of Feeling', in *Marxism and Literature*. Oxford and New York: Oxford University Press: 128–35.
Wilson, Andrew (2005), *Virtual Politics: Faking democracy in the post-Soviet world*. New Haven, CT: Yale University Press.
Wood, Elizabeth A. (2005), *Performing Justice: Agitation trials in early Soviet Russia*. Ithaca, NY: Cornell University Press.
— (2011), 'Performing Memory: Vladimir Putin and the celebration of World War II in Russia', *Soviet and Post Soviet Review*, 38: 172–200.
Yaroshevski, Dov B. (1990), 'Political Participation and Public Memory: The Memorial movement in the USSR, 1987–1989', *History and Memory*, 2/2 (Winter): 5–31.
Yurchak, Alexei (2006), *Everything Was Forever, Until It Was No More: The last Soviet generation*. Princeton, NJ: Princeton University Press.
— (2008), 'Post Post-Communist Sincerity: Pioneers, cosmonauts, and other Soviet heroes born today', in Thomas Lahusen and Peter H. Solomon (ed.) *What is Soviet Now?* Piscataway, NJ: Transaction Publishers: 257–76.
Zhdanov, A.A. (1934), 'Speech to the First All-Soviet Writers Congress in August 1934', published in *Pervyi vcesoiuznyi s'ezd sovetskikh pisatelei 1943: stenograficheskii otchet* (Moscow: Sovetskii pisatel', 1990): 2–5. Available in translation at http://www.marxists.org/subject/art/lit_crit/sovietwritercongress/zdhanov.htm (accessed 21 August 2018).
Zuin, Marco, Gianluca Rigatelli, Giovanni Zuliana, Giuseppe Faggian, and Loris Roncon (2016), 'The Secret of the Questions: Medical interview in 21st century', *European Journal of Internal Medicine*, 35 (November): 21–2.

INDEX

Akyn-opera 8, 9, 49–54
anamnesis 14, 15, 70, 95, 98–9, 113, 16–18
Austin, J.L. 13, 70, 129, 166
authenticity 3, 4, 7, 8, 35, 37, 40, 49, 83, 116, 120, 128–39
  see also sincerity; truth

Banasiukevich, Anna 11, 46
Batalov, Talgat 23, 24, 46, 119–40, 163
Belenitskaia, Nina 21, 23, 97–117
Beumers, Birgit 6, 8, 10, 27, 31, 37, 50 n. 3, 120, 149, 156
  see also Lipovetsky, Mark; *Performing Violence*
Blok, Aleksandr 36, 37
Blythe, Alecky 18, 33
Bogaev, Oleg 29, 30, 43
Boiakov, Eduard 27
Boym, Svetlana 12
Brecht, Bertolt 33, 39
bribery 87, 125–7
  see also corruption

Central Asia 8, 119–20, 123–4, 129, 130–1, 139

civic engagement 2, 10, 11, 15, 141–42, 149, 155, 166–7
  see also human rights; justice
commemoration 11, 13, 14, 51, 52, 53, 58–9, 60, 62, 67–9, 71, 73 n. 4, 97, 99, 104–5
  see also anamnesis; memory
corruption 23, 48, 75–7, 79, 81–3, 87–9, 95, 120, 127–8, 133, 137, 141, 143, 149, 154
  see also bribery
Crimea (annexation) 123, 145–6, 149

Davydova, Marina 10, 11, 159
Deavere Smith, Anna 18
Denisova, Sasha 9, 57
documents, status of 2, 5–7, 9, 22, 24, 132–3, 164, 167
Dodgson, Elyse 32
  see also Royal Court
Dolan, Jill 165–7
Dugdale, Sasha 32
Durnenkov, Mikhail and Viacheslav 27, 46, 50 n. 3

Etkind, Alexander 12, 60–2, 65–6
  see also memory

Index

Freedman, John 11, 27, 29, 147, 156
Futurists
   Neo-Futurists 16, 25 n. 1
   Russian Futurists 38

Gabowitsch, Mischa 143, 156, 157
   see also Protest in Putin's Russia
Genoux, Georg 17, 19, 22, 32, 47, 50 n. 3, 52, 54, 72, 121
   see also Joseph Beuys Theatre
Get Real: Documentary theatre past and present 4
Golden Mask Festival 27, 32, 121
Gremina, Elena 23, 27, 32, 33, 48, 50 n. 3, 77, 80, 87, 95, 142, 147, 150–1, 153–4, 156, 159, 160–1
Grishkovets, Evgenii 45, 120
Grotowski, Jerzy 79
Gulag 8, 22, 59, 60, 62

historical narratives 5, 12–13, 22–3, 25, 34, 52–3, 67–8, 79, 97, 99, 106, 109, 112–13, 167
   see also memory
human rights 48, 57, 59, 75, 76, 89, 131
   see also civic engagement; protest

immigration 8, 120–4, 128–33, 139
'In-Yer-Face-Theatre' 31
   see also Ravenhill, Mark

Joseph Beuys Theatre 16–17, 47, 53, 97, 117 n. 1, 121
justice 1, 2, 3, 22–5, 66, 74–80, 83–7, 91, 94–5, 97, 99, 102, 115–17, 140, 164, 166–7
   see also testimony; witness (witnessing)

Kane, Sarah 31
Klavdiev, Iurii 27, 50 n. 3, 163
Kovalskaia, Elena 11, 30, 33, 49 n. 1, 160–1

Lipovetsky, Mark 6, 8, 10, 27, 31, 37, 50 n. 3, 120, 135, 137
   see also Beumers, Birgit; *Performing Violence*
Lisovskii, Vsevolod 8, 45, 149, 150–1

Liubimovka New Playwriting Festival 27–9
Losing Pravda 6

Martin, Carol 3, 5, 86
Matvienko, Kristina 11, 156
Memorial 53, 58–61, 67–8, 71–2, 91, 144
memory 5, 11, 15, 23–5, 49, 58, 68, 70–2, 102, 113, 117
   cultural memory 12–14, 22, 51–3, 55, 57, 60–1, 66–7, 103, 119, 140, 164
   embodied memory 12, 22, 53, 68–9
   see also commemoration; historical narratives
Moscow Art Theatre 27–8, 34–8, 49, 100, 164
Mukhina, Olga 29–30, 43

national identity 31, 35, 119–23, 129–30, 134, 136, 139
New Russian Drama 1, 6, 10–11, 26–33, 37, 49 n. 1, 50 n. 2, 156
New Sincerity 121, 134–6

Paget, Derek 4
Performing Violence 8, 27, 32
   see also Beumers, Birgit; Lipovetsky, Mark
Petrushevskaia, Ludmilla 27, 42–3
post-show discussion 57, 61, 73 nn. 1–2, 90–1, 96 n. 6
practice research 16–19, 69–70
protest 7, 19, 20, 73 n. 4, 75, 93–4, 131, 142–3, 149, 153, 155–7
   see also civic engagement; human rights
Protest in Putin's Russia 93, 156
   see also Gabowitsch, Mischa
Pushkin, Aleksandr 38, 11, 121
Pussy Riot 93–4

Ravenhill, Mark 31, 147, 154
reenactment 3, 12, 15, 69, 71, 87–8, 104, 168
   see also Schneider, Rebecca
Roudakova, Natalia 6
Royal Court 1, 19, 22, 25 n. 2, 31–3

Rudnev, Pavel 10–11, 20–1, 69, 72, 90, 145, 162
Sakharov Center 3, 16, 22, 52–3, 57, 63, 71–2, 92–4, 97, 117 n. 1, 121, 144
Schechner, Richard 68, 130
Schneider, Rebecca 12, 69, 87, 104
  see also reenactment
September.doc 48
Serebrennikov, Kirill 145
Shatrov, Mikhail 43–4
sincerity 2, 22–3, 25, 37, 40–1, 43, 49, 83, 116, 119–21, 133–40, 166
  see also authenticity; New Sincerity; truth
Socialist Realism 39–40, 43, 49
Stalinism 12, 22, 41, 43, 59, 61, 66–7
Stanislavsky, Konstantin 28, 34–8
  see also Moscow Art Theatre
Stoppard, Tom 147
structures of feeling 24, 142, 158, 168
  see also Williams, Raymond
Symbolists 34, 36–8, 49, 50 n. 4, 112

Taylor, Diana 12–14, 68–9
testimony 2, 22–3, 37, 77, 79–84, 89, 128, 132–3, 139–40
  see also justice; sincerity; truth; witness (witnessing)
Transformer.doc 45
  see also Lisovskii, Vsevolod
trials
  mock trials 38, 84–6
  show trials 85, 92
  trial plays 77, 83, 85
  tribunal plays 31

truth 3–4, 6–8, 34–42, 54, 59–60, 67, 114, 116–17, 133, 135, 149
Turner, Victor 68, 130

Ubu and the Truth Commission 83
Ugarov, Mikhail 11, 23, 27, 32, 45, 48, 50 n. 3, 77, 95, 97, 116, 142, 154–5, 157, 159, 160–1
Ukraine 7, 32, 51, 60, 123, 145–6

Vampilov, Aleksandr 42
  post-Vampilov generation 41–4, 49
verbatim theatre 1–3, 18, 22–3, 26, 31–3, 42, 45–6, 75–7, 83, 95, 116, 130, 140–1, 158, 164
  see also Paget, Derek; witness theatre
Vorozhbyt, Natalia 19, 50 n. 3
Vyrypaev, Ivan 32, 147–9, 165

war 5, 51, 52, 54, 56, 81, 83, 109, 133, 137–8
  Chechnya 32, 48
  Donbas 7, 51, 123, 146, 154
Weil, Mark 121–2
Weiss, Peter 33, 44, 82–3
  see also trial plays
Williams, Raymond 142, 158
  see also Structures of Feeling
witness (witnessing) 13, 23, 54, 57, 59, 69, 71, 78–9, 88, 91–3, 102, 114, 155, 167
witness theatre 2, 3, 158

Yurchak, Alexei 12, 41–3, 134, 136

zero position 47–9, 157, 160

EU authorised representative for GPSR:
Easy Access System Europe, Mustamäe tee 50,
10621 Tallinn, Estonia
gpsr.requests@easproject.com

www.ingramcontent.com/pod-product-compliance
Lightning Source LLC
Chambersburg PA
CBHW070239240426
43673CB00044B/1849